Mouse Tracks

This inner sleeve from a Disneyland LP showcases the Magic Mirror Storyteller series. (© Disney Enterprises, Inc.)

Mouse Tracks

THE STORY OF WALT DISNEY RECORDS

Tim Hollis and Greg Ehrbar

UNIVERSITY PRESS OF MISSISSIPPI   JACKSON

www.upress.state.ms.us

The University Press of Mississippi
is a member of the Association of American
University Presses.

First Edition 2006

Library of Congress Cataloging-in-Publication
Data

Hollis, Tim.
  Mouse tracks : the story of Walt Disney Records/
Tim Hollis and Greg Ehrbar.— 1st ed.
      p. cm.
  Includes bibliographical references and index.
ISBN 1-57806-848-7 (cloth : alk. paper) — ISBN
1-57806-849-5 (pbk. : alk. paper) 1. Walt Disney
Records—History. 2. Sound recording industry—
United States. 3. Popular music—United States—
History and criticism. I. Ehrbar, Greg. II. Title.
  ML3792.H63 2006
  781.64'0973—dc22

                              2005024081

British Library Cataloging-in-Publication Data
available

To my mother and father, Carol and Harold Ehrbar,
who first brought Disney records into our home.

Greg Ehrbar

Contents

Foreword by Leonard Maltin   ix

Acknowledgments   xi

Introduction   3

1. Davy Crockett Blazes the Trail   5

2. The Mickey Mouse Club Opens the Door   13

3. The Stars Shine   27

4. Annette to the Rescue   43

5. The Buoyant Days   55

6. *Mary Poppins* Blows Off the Roof   72

7. In Which Pooh and Friends Come to Disney Records   87

8. *The Jungle Book* Goes for the Gold   100

9. The Road to Oz and the End of an Era   117

10. Scrooge McDuck Strikes Again   131

11. Mickey Mouse Goes Double Platinum   145

12. Mickey Makes a Big Splash   158

13. It's a Gold Record, Charlie Brown!   170

14. You Can Always Be Number One 181

Appendix: Grammy Nominations and Awards 189

Bibliography 193

Index 195

Foreword by Leonard Maltin

Walt Disney's life and career offer a seemingly inexhaustible source of material for fans, writers, collectors, and social scientists. As a lifelong Disneyphile, I am amazed at how much I continue to learn with each passing year as scholars dig into the many facets of this remarkable man's empire. It doesn't hurt that there is so much documentation of the studio's activities (both in its archives and in the clippings files of libraries everywhere) or that a number of participants are still alive to help fill in the blanks.

One of my first clear memories is singing a line from "The Ballad of Davy Crockett" at the age of four in what we then called nursery school. I think that qualifies me to bear witness to the enormous impact of Disney music in the 1950s and beyond. I wore out my share of Little Golden Records and Disney storybook albums, and I even remember singing "One Song" from *Snow White and the Seven Dwarfs* with my junior high school choir.

Yet I must confess that I know very little about the workings of the studio's music operations, and as soon as I started reading Greg Ehrbar and Tim Hollis's book, I found myself saying more than once, "I never knew that!"

The miracle of Walt Disney's career is that he constantly surrounded himself with creative and ambitious people—and then gave them the freedom to pursue their goals. It isn't accidental that Disney merchandise, Disney comic books, and Disney records were so popular; in every area of enterprise there were talented, inventive people who believed in their products and worked hard to achieve success.

This book finally gives credit where credit is due, to the businessmen, songwriters, arrangers, composers, and performers who built an operation that was the equal—in stature and popularity—of Walt's movie studio.

Mouse Tracks couldn't have been written on assignment by journeymen; it had to be a labor of love, and that is precisely what it is, the culmination of many years' loving and enthusiastic research by two people who share my lifelong fascination with all things Disney. I'm sure like-minded readers will respond the same way I did to the fruits of their labors.

Acknowledgments

The authors believe that the most rewarding experience of being associated with the fine people listed below can be summed up in a quote from philosopher Étienne De Grolier that was a personal favorite of *Mickey Mouse Club* leader Jimmie Dodd: "I expect to pass through life but once. If therefore, there be any kindness I can show, or any good thing I can do, to any fellow being, let me do it now and not defer or neglect it, as I shall not pass this way again."

We also thank David Smith and Robert Tieman of the Walt Disney Archives.

Greg thanks his wife, Suzanne, and his kids, Katie and Colin, for their patience throughout this project.

David Agnew	Steve Burns	Diana Craig	Danny Gould
Jay Aldrich	Dennis Burnside	Scott Craig	Desirée Goyette
Jim Andron	Lonnie Burr	Mike Curb	Marge Grabeau
Xavier Atencio	Corey Burton	Florence Daniel	Howard Green
Ellie Baer	Bettina Bush	Merrill Dean	Larry Groce
Charlotte Baker	Paul Camarata	Jay Deane	Vic Guder
Glenn Barker	Tutti Camarata	Roy E. Disney	Phil Guerini
Phil Baron	Al Capps	Beverly Edwards	Dawn Halloran
Dick Beals	Eddie Carroll	Sam Edwards	Jerry Hausner
Gypsy Belew	Philip Chapman	Brian Fahey	Roger Heath
Kimberley Birdseye	George Charouhas	Jim Fanning	Ron Hicklin
Lois Blaisch	Gennifer Choldenko	Stan Farber	Jim Hollifield
Larry Blakely	Ysanne Churchman	Bill Farmer	Douglas Houston
Lucille Bliss	Jim Clark	Jorge Finkielman	Charles Howerton
Tom Bocci	Lynn Cline	Shelby Flint	Alvin Hudson
Ed Bogas	Bill Cole	June Foray	Richard Huemer Jr.
Bruce Botnick	Gini Colvig	Jymme Frederickson	Brian Ingoldsby
Derek Boulton	Carol Connors	Eddie Frierson	Donnie Jarrell
Bob Brunner	Kevin Corcoran	Conor Garrett	Ann Jillian
Anita Bryant	Mary Costa	Mary Espinosa Goff	Glynis Johnson
Jimmy Bryant	Bill Cotter	Dan Goldmark	Grey Johnson
Fulton Burley	Jerome Courtland	Dale Gonyea	Betty Joyce

Jean Kanady

Carol Kaye

Jane Keefer

Ron Kidd

Maria Kleinman

Jim Korkis

Gary Krisel

Ted Kryczko

Sam Kwasman

Lois Lane

Diana Lee

Tim Lee

Gail Lopata Lennon

Pat Lentz

Robie Lester

Mel Leven

Carol Lombard

Betty Luboff

Deanna Sylte Lucas

Kent Madison

Guy Maeda

Jymn Magon

Gia Maione

Leonard Maltin

Doug Marsh

Stacia Martin

Bob McGrath

Dal McKennon

Michael McNiel

Eddy Medora

Gene Merlino

Chris Merritt

John Michaud III

Bob Mitchell

Bambi Moé

Francois Monferran

R. Michael Murray

Rose Mussi

Marcia Muth

Marni Nixon

Loulie Jean Norman

Ben Ohmart

Laura Olsher

Fess Parker

Pat Parris

Pat Patrick

George Patterson

Penny Peed

Les Perkins

Kim Petersen

Cheryl Philbert

Donnie Pitchford

Ray Pointer

Gary Powell

Mark Pyle

Thurl Ravenscroft

Pete Renaday

Deanda Sylte Roberts

Tammy Rock

Rita Rose

Pauline Rousseau

Susan Rubenstein

Will Ryan

Paul Salamunovich

David Scheibner

Rick Schulman

Joan Sylte Schween

Keith Scott

Tom Sharpe

Richard M. Sherman

Robert B. Sherman

Roberta Shore

Gary Shortall

Michael Silversher

Patty Silversher

Billy Simpson

Jim Snead

Fred Steiner

Shepard Stern

Sally Stevens

Gil Stratton

Jason Surrell

Sally Sweetland

Jim Tadevic

Rod Taylor

Bob Tebow

Randy Thornton

George Tipton

Sheila Tracy

Ginny Tyler

Randy Van Horne

Janet Waldo

Jackie Ward

Hames Ware

Elizabeth Weinhold

Paul Whitehead

J. Franklyn Whiteley

Jerry Whitman

Lisa Whitman

Nancy Wible

Kelly Wilson

Jack Wood

Aubrey Woods

Tom Worrall

Teri York

Alan Young

April Young

Mouse Tracks

Co-author Tim Hollis doing preliminary research for this book at age two.

Co-author Greg Ehrbar has made it a point to share the magic of Walt Disney Records with his children, Katie and Colin. (Photograph by Suzanne Ehrbar)

Introduction

Countless books have covered nearly every imaginable aspect of Walt Disney's life and his enterprises, from films and theme parks to toys and comics. Curiously, however, no volume has ever been entirely devoted to the history of Disney records.

Phonograph records were not some sort of rarified, obscure products of the Disney merchandising machine. They were part of the lives of millions and, in the days before home video, among the only ways audiences could bring home a Disney property and have it "speak." Mass-marketed through music shops, five-and-dime stores, supermarkets, direct mail, and any other business frequented by children and parents, Walt Disney Records remain the best-selling children's recordings in the world.

The story of Disney's in-house recording company is rich in successes and failures, great ideas and misfires. More than anything else, it is the story of hardworking, talented people.

The sole previous published documentation of these recordings to date is R. Michael Murray's fine work, *The Golden Age of Walt Disney Records, 1933–1988* (Dubuque, Iowa: Antique Trader, 1997). We gratefully acknowledge Murray's volume as a valuable resource, as it is the most extensive Disney discography ever compiled. Its seven-page "Short History of Recorded Disney Music" was the first of its kind in book form.

In the interest of length and focus, this book does not cover Disney recordings created by outside labels such as RCA and Decca, though a few are mentioned. It would take at least another volume to delve into that territory. This book covers why and how Walt and Roy Disney got into the record business as well as the vinyl discs (and occasional cassettes) that flowed most directly from their initial enterprise. The compact disc era, which could also fill a book as well, is encapsulated in chapter 14.

Our goal is to help heighten interest in these recordings and especially the artists who created them. It has been a privilege to get to know the great people involved with Disney records and to learn their wonderful stories. To one and all, we are grateful.

Every effort has been made to make this book as thorough as possible, but a history this rich always leaves room for more. As more Disney fans and historians discover and enjoy the world of Disney recordings, we are hoping this will not be the final book on the subject. Whether we write it or simply read it, we look forward to learning more.

And so, to quote the Disneyland Story Reader, "Let's begin now . . ."

1

Davy Crockett Blazes the Trail

By the middle of the twentieth century, Walt Disney was, by his own admission, a reigning monarch. When asked by his friend, novelist Ray Bradbury, whether he might consider running for mayor of Los Angeles, Disney answered, "Ray, why should I be mayor when I'm already king?" It was a stature difficult for even Disney's harshest critics to dispute. For almost three decades, when many people thought of fairy tales and cartoons, they thought first of Walt Disney. His retellings and new mythologies were the product of arguably the century's greatest single corporate assemblage of artistic talent.

From meager beginnings, Walt Disney became America's homegrown Santa Claus, forever finding new ways to tell old stories and bringing out new technological wizardry at seemingly every turn. Thanks in no small part to the resourceful financial acumen of his older brother, Roy, Walt literally built an entertainment empire on a mouse, as he was often quoted. Many theories have attempted to explain Disney's astounding success: one is that he hired and inspired some of the best artists of the day; another is that he was never satisfied with conquering just one particular form of entertainment.

Walt Disney forever focused on the next horizon, moving in an amazingly short time from modest black-and-white Mickey and Minnie shorts to more ambitious Silly Sym-

phonies and adding color, special effects, and other such innovations along the way. At the same time, the Disney merchandising machine steadily gained momentum, producing toys, clothes, books, and merchandise of every kind. Aware that short cartoons offered little growth potential, Walt gambled everything to produce the first American feature-length animated feature, *Snow White and the Seven Dwarfs* (1937). *Snow White* was as much a success in stores as it was in theaters. By the late 1940s, when Disney's stable of cartoon characters seemed, in many minds, more flesh and blood than pen and ink, Disney's multi-million-dollar merchandising industry generated a more consistent flow of cash for the company than the hit-or-miss movie business. The name *Walt Disney* became a bona fide brand and a cultural symbol of immense media presence and influence. The volume of merchandise was such that no individual, Walt included, could feasibly comprehend and experience all of it, from every comic book to every recording based on Disney characters and stories. Walt was aware of and often personally approved the various ancillary products bearing his name, but it is unlikely that he had either the time or the inclination to read, watch, listen to, or play with every licensed product.

While Walt's dreams ignited all these enterprises, they blossomed and flourished under the guidance of his brother and company cofounder, Roy O. Disney. Roy handled diverse business interests, including insurance, operations, and the growing merchandise division. "Walt was less interested in [merchandising]," recalled Roy Edward Disney, son of Roy O. Disney and director emeritus of the Walt Disney Company. "Walt's viewpoint was, 'I'll do what I do, and you can sell whatever you like behind it.' I doubt that he saw much outside of that." The studio produced the cartoons and feature films inhouse, but all the lunchboxes, games, dolls, candies, toys, apparel, books, and other products were licensed and manufactured by outside companies. For the first twenty years or so of the company's existence, these products included phonograph records.

○

Music had been a key part of Disney projects since Mickey first squeaked and played improvised musical instruments in *Steamboat Willie* (1928). Songs in the cartoons were usually either public-domain pieces or original compositions, which had the potential to add revenue in the form of sheet music and records. Walt and Roy Disney did not consider themselves well versed in music publishing or record production, and they consequently relied on music publishers to handle this side of the business. Veteran music negotiator Saul Bourne, who had helped "God Bless America" composer/lyricist Irving Berlin make a success of his music company, realized the potential of Disney music the moment he and his wife, Bonnie, saw *Three Little Pigs* (1933). As soon as he heard the film's catchy theme song, "Who's Afraid of the Big Bad Wolf?" he wasted no time in contacting Roy Disney to secure the rights for Irving Berlin Music. It was a lucrative association for both parties that produced, among other things, recordings of "Big Bad Wolf" on the Victor label by the Don Bestor Orchestra and on Bluebird Records by the Bill Scotti Orchestra. Disney's first hit song became a popular Depression-era anthem, symbolizing Americans' brave fight against the wolf at the door.

Disney next began licensing recording rights to various record companies. Those labels, in turn, had the option of using their own talent or, if the budget allowed, hiring Disney artists to perform on the discs and create packaging art. "Mickey Mouse and Minnie's in Town" was the B side of a seven-inch, 78-rpm picture disc produced by Victor in 1934. The song and its companion, "In a Silly Symphony," were written and sung by Frank Luther (1905–80). Known as the Bing Crosby of the sand pile set, Luther had careers as an evangelist, professional tenor, author, composer of hundreds of songs, and host of various children's radio and television programs. His recordings remained on sale through the 1970s.

No one had ever placed the actual soundtrack recordings from any film on disc until Disney and RCA released 78-rpm records with selections from *Three Little Pigs, The Grasshopper and the Ants, The Pied Piper, Lullaby Land, Mickey's Grand Opera, Three Little Wolves, The Orphans Benefit,* and *Who Killed Cock Robin?* They appeared first in 1936 on RCA's HMV label in England, and a year later made their debut in the United States. These are considered to be the first original true soundtrack recordings. Hollywood musicals were cranking out hit tunes by the dozens during the 1930s, but direct-from-soundtrack records were not the norm. From Edison's time until World War II, it was more technically feasible to re-create songs from the films and shows in a separate studio, either with or without original cast members. Instead of replicating the style of the original work, the arrangements were often reinterpreted for dancing and radio play. Victor's 1938 three-disc set of songs from Disney's *Snow White and the Seven Dwarfs* (1937) became the first soundtrack album from a feature film, followed by the soundtracks of *Pinocchio* (1940) and *Dumbo* (1941).

○

Roy Disney had been reluctant to relinquish the music rights to *Snow White and the Seven Dwarfs* to an outside firm. However, in the end, the film desperately needed funding for completion, and Saul Bourne's lively sales pitch had made it hard to disagree. A few years later, Berlin and Bourne separated their companies. Bourne Music Company retained ownership of the scores from early cartoons in addition to *Snow White*, *Dumbo*, and *Pinocchio* (which included the Disney signature song "When You Wish upon a Star"). In spite of numerous renegotiation attempts by Roy and his successors at the Walt Disney Company, the Bournes steadfastly retain their ownership of these valuable scores to this day.

Disney continued to share the profits with music publishers and record companies through the first half of the 1940s. After *Bambi* was released in 1942, the domestic and international economic consequences of World War II brought slow times to the studio. No feature-length animated films were released for eight years. The Disney features of this period were either live-action films with animated sequences, such as *Song of the South* (1946), or themed packages of short cartoons, as was *Make Mine Music* (1946). The latter genre yielded a substantial number of potential hit parade songs, performed by popular recording stars such as Dinah Shore, the Andrews Sisters, Andy Russell, Nelson Eddy, Roy Rogers, Dennis Day, and Benny Goodman. The songs were produced for records by each artist's contracted record label.

○

Hopes were high for *Cinderella*, Disney's "comeback" to animated features in 1950. To assure merchandising success as well as a box office hit, in 1949 Roy convinced a reluctant Walt to screen the rough working print of *Cinderella* for key licensees, including Jack Burgess of RCA, one of the "big three" popular record labels, and Bob Bernstein and Arthur Shimkin of Golden Records, whose six-inch children's yellow 78s were selling in the multimillions for Simon and Schuster Publishing. Also attending this historic meeting was an up-and-coming Disney merchandising executive, Jimmy Johnson, who little knew how much Disney records would affect his future life.

James Alexander Johnson Jr. had risen through the Disney ranks. Fresh out of col-

Jimmy Johnson, as head of the Walt Disney Music Company, was the guiding force behind the first twenty years of Disneyland Records. (Courtesy of Grey Johnson)

lege with a major in journalism, he was hired as an assistant in publicity in September 1938. *Snow White and the Seven Dwarfs* had just become a sensation, and he was there when *Pinocchio* and *Fantasia* were the next big projects. In his unpublished 1975 manuscript "Inside the Whimsy Works," Johnson recounted the first studio screening of *The Sorcerer's Apprentice*. "It was the most thrilling moment of my life," he wrote.

"When the film finished, everyone stood and cheered and applauded until all hands were red."

Publicity had a management change and Johnson faced termination, but he had been bitten by the Disney bug and searched for any job that would enable him to stay with the company. He was accepted into the traffic department, delivering items around the studio, including to the story department, where he hoped to find a permanent home. Instead, he was transferred into what was known as the Mole Hole, a basement of the Animation Building where accounting assigned him to balance figures. He was subsequently drafted into the army, and after the war, he returned to Disney as assistant to the company secretary, who handled everything from insurance policies to worldwide merchandising issues.

When Roy split Disney Publications apart from merchandising in 1950, Johnson had gained sufficient experience to head the new publishing department. He also was asked to handle business affairs for the new Walt Disney Music Company, which Fred Raphael had established in late 1949 to handle what was hoped to be a parade of hit songs from *Cinderella*. "All the chips were riding on *Cinderella*," Johnson recalled. "Books, records, and toys appeared in the marketplace in time for Christmas 1949, and began selling extremely well immediately. The film was released in February 1950 and was a box office and critical smash. The release of the merchandise in advance of the film undoubtedly had great effect on the box office, and this pattern has been followed by the Disney organization ever since."

In Hollywood, RCA produced a *Cinderella* multidisc album with a storybook that followed the records word for word. Original voice cast members Ilene Woods, Eleanor Audley, Lucille Bliss, and Jimmy Macdonald reenacted the film story. The album sold 750,000 copies and hit Number 1 on the *Billboard* magazine pop charts, a rare accomplishment for a children's album. In New York, Little Golden Records also recorded versions of the *Cinderella* songs featuring its stable of singers, including Anne Lloyd, Daniel Ocko, and the Sandpipers. The recordings were directed by Mitch Miller, before his phenomenal success at Columbia Records and his TV sing-along fame. These records also sold millions at a retail price of twenty-five cents each.

Disney records were becoming big business. They were still not produced in-house, but Raphael supervised studio control of selection, performance, and recording of Disney songs. Raphael also decided to make the Walt Disney Music Company a hit parade competitor. Several big hits with no connection to Disney productions resulted, including Frankie Laine's "Mule Train," Patti Page's "Would I Love You (Love You, Love You)," and Jo Stafford's "Shrimp Boats."

○

As with *Cinderella*, music and records were important to the success of Disney's 1951 animated feature release, *Alice in Wonderland*. The film evolved through several major changes in story, music, design, and direction. Top songwriters were hired to write dozens of songs, but the team of Bob Hilliard and Sammy Fain wrote most of the tunes that were finally selected. Fain personally presented the *Alice* songs to studio staff when they were trying to decide whether to produce *Cinderella* or the Lewis Carroll fantasy first. Had *Alice* been released before *Cinderella*, the Disney studio might have met a very different fate. *Alice* was a financial disappointment in its first release. It stayed out of theatrical release for twenty-three years but has since found a modern audience appreciative of its brash, surreal style. The *Alice* score, however, took on a life of its own. "I'm Late," "Very Good Advice," "All in the Golden Afternoon," and "The Unbirthday Song" became Disney evergreens. Such stars as Rosemary Clooney and Doris Day recorded many versions. The next feature, *Peter Pan* (1953), was a box office hit. Books, music, and records adapted from Disney's take on the Sir James Barrie play were hot sellers.

At the same time, Raphael was becoming increasingly enamored with the popular music end of his business. It seemed to Walt and Roy that Raphael was forgetting the real purpose of the Walt Disney Music Company, spending heavily on acquiring popular songs, moving his office from Disney's Burbank lot to Hollywood, enlarging his staff, and even opening a New York office. Despite his best efforts, Raphael produced twenty failing songs for every one hit and the music company was losing money. When Raphael called Roy to say he would start his own music company unless he received a 25 percent interest in Disney's, Roy wished him success in his new venture.

Roy got off the phone with Raphael and told Jimmy Johnson, "You've been working with [Fred] and know as much about music publishing as anyone else around here. You run the company!" "Since nobody else knew anything," Johnson wrote, "my knowledge was just a fraction above zilch." What Johnson did have in abundance was business savvy. When *Bambi* was about to be reissued overseas in 1952, Johnson confronted performing-rights organization Broadcast Music Incorporated (BMI) about what he felt was a shoddy publishing job in conjunction with the film's original release ten years earlier. BMI offered to give the *Bambi* music rights back to Disney if the company started a BMI music publishing firm of its own. Johnson

Jimmy Johnson with Roy O. Disney's wife, Edna. Jimmy could be telling Edna how her husband made him president of the Walt Disney Music Company. (Courtesy of Grey Johnson)

established Wonderland Music Company for BMI material. The American Society of Composers, Artists, and Publishers (ASCAP) would continue to handle rights for Walt Disney Music Company songs, with the composers' union affiliations determining which entity would control a particular song. Johnson ended the music company's pop music dalliances and shaved his staff down to three. In 1954, the music company made a profit for the first time.

o

As the 1950s unfolded, things were moving fast for Walt Disney Productions. Walt was squeezing his Disneyland dream park out of orange groves around Anaheim, California. Roy was scrambling to obtain funding for this risky venture through various corporate partners. They needed to make Disneyland a household name, and television came along just in time.

Unlike other Hollywood producers, who

feared or underestimated television, Walt saw it as a tool to promote his films and park. The fledgling ABC-TV network made a substantial investment in Disneyland and in return struck a deal with Disney to air a weekly anthology series. Also called *Disneyland*, it premiered in October 1954, with Walt as host. During the planning for this series, Jimmy Johnson learned of a meeting about *Disneyland* TV episodes featuring folk hero Davy Crockett. Johnson decided to crash the meeting but was caught by Walt, who wanted to know what Johnson was doing there. Johnson suggested Crockett's possible book tie-ins. "Okay, sit in," Walt said. Johnson was glad he did, because he witnessed a seminal moment in Disney music history. As he recalled it, Walt eyed the storyboard proposals for the TV miniseries with concern. "We are going to try to tell about thirty-five years of a man's life in three one-hour television shows," he said. "That's a long time." Studio music man George Bruns entered as Walt continued. "We need a little song to tie it all together," he said. "It should have a lot of verses to tell the history, and a short chorus like 'Davy Crockett, Davy Crockett, best frontier man of them all. . . .' Something like that."

Bruns and Crockett screenwriter Tom Blackburn subsequently wrote "The Ballad of Davy Crockett," a perfect link for the story sequences. Because the song seemed to have the makings of a hit, it presented Johnson's first chance to get Disney more directly into the record business. He had approached Capitol Records for distribution of the Crockett theme song, but they wanted to do so under their own label. Roy had bigger plans. "We don't need Capitol for anything but distribution," Roy told Johnson. "We should own the record company ourselves. I really think we should get into the business with these *Davy Crockett* records."

Roy did not think they were yet ready to take on every aspect of the record business, though he encouraged Johnson to make different kinds of deals for Crockett than the company had done with its earlier songs. Previously, outside recording companies produced their own master recordings. "With *Davy Crockett*," wrote Johnson, "I decided we would produce the masters ourselves and then lease them to a record company. Accordingly, we cut the Crockett song with Fess Parker. We also made three story-telling records with the original cast, matching the television episodes."

Fess Parker, who had no idea what a superstar he was about to become, walked excitedly to his first recording session in the small studio near the theater on the Disney lot. "It was in August, prior to the film shoot," Parker recalled. "I was called in immediately after I got the role. They didn't even know how to spell my name yet. I saw it somewhere spelled F-e-z!" The first recording of "The Ballad of Davy Crockett" featured Parker on guitar and George Bruns on bass as well as local musician Gino Quinn, who sang a verse on some versions. (The group is listed on some labels as The Frontiersmen.) The Disney executives had little anticipation that anything special was happening and certainly did not expect the phenomenon that followed. "They didn't have any conviction that TV, or any of this, was going to be as big as it was," Parker commented.

Using Disney masters, the resulting 45-rpm record was pressed privately by Capitol, with Wonderland Music Company on the label. It was considered at best a mere promotional disc, to let the public know about Davy Crockett's impending arrival on the television screen.

Sources differ about exactly what happened next. According to Parker, his promo

Fess Parker: Rigoletto in Buckskin

Perhaps the only person more surprised than Fess Parker about his recording success was his father, Fess Sr. "I wasn't very good at guitar and a terrible singer," Parker said with a chuckle. "My dad used to send me out of the house when I would sing!" But the native of Fort Worth, Texas, found himself doing many things he'd never dreamed of doing after Walt Disney chose him to play Davy Crockett for the *Disneyland* TV show. "When I went on my first interview, I brought my guitar," Parker said. "Walt noticed it and said, 'Why don't you play something?' I played a song called 'Lonely.' That's about trains. I realized later that trains were Walt's hobby. Maybe that's part of the reason they hired me. Suddenly I was looked at as a singer! The studio bought me a Martin guitar and sent me on road tours to forty-two U.S. cities and thirteen countries."

Millions know Parker from his Davy Crockett miniseries and his six years as NBC's Daniel Boone. But he also played Gale Storm's boyfriend on *My Little Margie* and performed on the *Ed Sullivan Show*, the *Soupy Sales Show*, and *American Bandstand*. Always up for a musical challenge, Parker donned a tux and belted out a Broadway-style "Hallelujah" for a *Mickey Mouse Club* "Guest Star Day" segment. "I didn't know what I was doing," he laughed. "But it was for the kids, and I guess it was okay by them." Parker's biggest departure was an appearance on the *George Gobel Show* during which he sang an operatic aria—on the same network that would present him as Daniel Boone a few years later.

Veteran song-and-dance man Buddy Ebsen, who costarred as Crockett's sidekick, Georgie Russel, partnered with Parker on stage, too. "Buddy and I sang with the Los Angeles Symphony and the Roger Wagner Chorale," Parker recalled. "It was hard on me, I'll tell you." There was an audience of twenty-five thousand people and absolutely no rehearsal. One of Parker's songs was "Farewell to the Mountains," adapted from a poem written by the real-life Davy Crockett.

For the new Disneyland Records label, Parker's version of "Green Grow the Lilacs" (aka "I'm Lonely My Darlin'"), from *Westward Ho! the Wagons,* sold half a million copies. With tongue in cheek, Parker sent his father an autographed "Ballad of Davy Crockett" inscribed "To my favorite music lover." Parker also brought western composer/performer Stan Jones to the studio. "I sang [Jones's] 'Wringle Wrangle' for Walt as a possible song for *Westward Ho!*" he said. "Walt said, 'Yeah, let's use it.'"

Ebsen and Parker launched a company, Musicland Publishing, and Parker subsequently founded his own label, Cascade Records. "It was in the late 1950s," said Parker. "I hired an A&R [artists and repertoire] partner, recorded two albums myself, and brought in some of the best musicians from Capitol." Cascade featured such performers as actor Dennis Weaver, then playing Chester on TV's *Gunsmoke*, and cartoon voice actors Paul Frees and Robie Lester. "Distribution was something I hadn't figured on," he said about Cascade's demise. "My business manager said to either get out of the record business or get myself another business manager!"

Now in his eighties, Parker enjoys running his California vineyards. At his twenty-one-room inn, he and wife, Marcella, host Thursday-night sing-alongs known as Marcella's Living Room. "I have a go at a tune or two," he said. "I still love music."

record was already getting some radio airplay and was especially popular in Boston before any other versions came out. He has long felt that the official commercial release of his rendition was deliberately held back. "Jimmy Johnson was going to start Disney's record company, so they didn't let me come out of the chute," he said. By Johnson's account, the release of Parker's record was held up by the inertia of Columbia Records. Columbia was very interested in leasing the Disney masters, but the internal gears of the CBS record giant took too long to grind. Archie Bleyer of the independent Cadence label also wanted to lease the Disney/Parker masters. Parker's version was not available to him, so he got permission to record a cover version of the song with Broadway and future daytime soap opera star Bill Hayes. Within two weeks, Hayes's "Ballad of Davy Crockett" was released and sold a million and a half copies. Fess Parker's version was released three weeks afterward. While not as spectacular a hit, it did inch its way to just below one million sold. The Crockett song also sold lots of sheet music for Wonderland Music Company, inspiring cover versions by Tennessee Ernie Ford, Fred Waring, and many others. (Waring's is the only version to include every verse.) Even Fess Parker revisited the tune for RCA Victor after becoming TV's *Daniel Boone* in the 1960s.

Roy was so impressed with the hit status of "The Ballad of Davy Crockett" that he decided to take Disney records to the next level.

2

The Mickey Mouse Club
Opens the Door

Disney's television agreement with ABC had included a deal for a daily children's program. So, when the Disney staff first conceived the idea of a daily *Mickey Mouse Club* television show, they more or less modeled it after established hits such as *Howdy Doody* and the *Pinky Lee Show*. The "regulars" would be adults performing for a studio audience of children. That wasn't unique enough for Walt Disney. Six months before the show's premiere, he sent out a memo declaring that children would be the main performers. The kids would be known as the Mouseketeers, and they had to be "real kids," not "little Shirley Temples."

This was unheard of in 1955. Disney sent his talent scouts to Los Angeles neighborhoods and schoolyards to seek children with that "certain spark," although the eventual lineup also included kids with some professional experience. Twenty-four youngsters were chosen for the first season's programming, including Nancy Abbate, Sharon Baird, Billie Jean Beanblossom, Bobby Burgess, Lonnie Burr, Tommy Cole, Johnny Crawford, Dennis Day (no relation to the famed tenor of the *Jack Benny Program*), Dickie Dodd, Mary Espinosa, Annette Funicello, Darlene Gillespie, Judy Harriet, John Lee Johann, Bonni Lou Kern, Paul Petersen, Mickey Rooney Jr.,

Tim Rooney, Mary Sartori, Bronson Scott, Michael Smith, Ronnie Steiner, Mark Sutherland, Doreen Tracey, and Don Underhill. The two youngest, known as the "Meesketeers," Karen Pendleton and Cubby O'Brien were often teamed for TV routines and records. Jimmie Dodd and Disney animation story gag man Roy Williams, who had been with the studio since 1929, were the adult leaders, along with versatile Portland, Oregon, children's radio personality Bob Amsberry.

But even long before "M-i-c-k-e-y" was being spelled out on home TV sets, merchandising was in full swing, with 78- and 45-rpm phonograph records figured into the plan. Eight different "Official Mickey Mouse Club Records" were developed to hit store shelves the same week the show premiered. The master discs were pressed by Golden Records and distributed by Am-Par Records, an arm of ABC's fledgling ABC-Paramount label. They also appeared as yellow plastic Golden Records, a rare combination of Disney-produced material with Golden's in-house "Sandpipers" versions.

These first Mickey Mouse Club Records bore little sonic resemblance to their video counterparts. An uncredited choir believed to be under Mitch Miller and/or Arthur Norman's direction performed most of the songs.

Jimmy Johnson and staff saw to it that the Mickey Mouse Club records were on store shelves the same week the TV show premiered in October 1955. (© Disney Enterprises, Inc.)

Jimmie Dodd:
The Heart of a Hero

Jimmie Dodd with Norris Goff as Abner of "Lum and Abner" in *So This Is Washington* (1943).

Rare indeed is the person in show business about whom no one has anything negative to say. One such rarity is Jimmie Dodd, the red-haired adult leader of the *Mickey Mouse Club*. His friends and co-workers are unanimous in their praise for him.

Dodd was born in Cincinnati in 1910. His early show business career consisted of amateur guitar playing on radio until 1940, when he strummed his way to Hollywood and married dancer Ruth Carrell. His movie work was erratic at best, involving films of wildly varying prestige. They include *Flying Tigers* (1942) with John Wayne; *Private Snuffy Smith* (1942), based on the Billy DeBeck comic strip; *My Favorite Blonde* (1942) with Bob Hope; *So This Is Washington* (1943) with radio comedians Lum and Abner; and *Buck Privates Come Home* (1947) with Abbott and Costello. Ironically, he was also featured in a Republic Pictures movie series called *Three Mesquiteers* (1942–43) with Bob Steele and Tom Tyler. Dodd's novelty songs were occasionally heard in the films.

Dodd and his wife were a devoutly Christian couple. They believed that faith helped them through rougher moments and attributed to God's grace the miraculous turn Jimmie's career would soon take. In 1954, Dodd was hired to write "The Pencil Song" for a proposed *Disneyland* television episode. As soon as Jimmy Johnson heard the demo recording, he offered Dodd a job in the studio music department.

The *Mickey Mouse Club* was being prepared early the next year and its producers were taken with Dodd's sincere warmth. Walt Disney approved Dodd's appointment as the lead Mouseketeer, and he made it his ministry to entertain and inspire children without patronizing them. He wrote and recorded more *Mickey Mouse Club* songs than anyone else, including the classic opening march. He was also able to convey his faith through daily "Mousekethoughts," also known as "Doddisms." These short messages were in effect little homilies, preparing American youth to seek high ground as they moved into what would be a volatile period in history.

Viewers did not know that Dodd suffered from a defective heart valve, which had exempted him from the military years earlier. As early as 1951, doctors had given up on him, suggesting that he donate his body to science. Nevertheless, Dodd lived for years after the *Mickey Mouse Club* ceased production, and his life still centered around it. Though his health was delicate and his appearance was gaunt, he appeared in new segments for the 1962 syndication of the program and made numerous personal appearances worldwide.

In 1964, the Dodds moved to Honolulu to do a local children's TV show. Jimmie's weakened heart could take no more, however, and he died on November 10 at the age of fifty-four.

The "Mickey Mouse March" and several other songs featured the MelloMen, at the time comprised of Bob Stevens (lead tenor), Max Smith (tenor), Bill Lee (baritone), and Thurl Ravenscroft (bass). The quartet would go on to perform on many subsequent Disney records, with Lee and Ravenscroft in prominent roles. Jimmie Dodd's wife, Ruth Carrell, joined him for two of his songs, "The Pussy Cat Polka" and "Cooking with Minnie Mouse."

o

Because the *Mickey Mouse Club* show was still being cast while the records were being made, few of the actual Mouseketeers appeared on the first recordings. One of them was Lonnie Burr, who recalled how his chance encounter with the recording session changed his young career: "There was a huge 'cattle call' for children to audition as Mouseketeers, but I was already established in show business, so I went to read for the character of Marty Markham in the serial *Spin and Marty*." he explained. "I read for the

The MelloMen were among the most versatile performers in the Disneyland Records repertory company, able to handle anything from serious patriotic music to comical character voices. (Courtesy of Tim Lee)

role at Capitol Records, where I also met Jimmie Dodd, who was cutting Mickey Mouse Club Records. A kid had dropped out at the last minute, so he asked me to fill in." Burr continued, "Jimmie, Roy Williams and [producer] Hal Adelquist were asking me, 'Do you sing and dance?' I had already worked with Sharon Baird. She had already been hired as a Mouseketeer and was at the session with Jimmie." Although Burr recalled few specifics about the making of those records, "they led to my being hired for the show."

Mickey Mouse himself occasionally appeared on the records. Mickey's voice was provided by Walt Disney in soundtrack snippets from *The Orphans Benefit* and by studio sound effects whiz Jimmy Macdonald in such

songs as "Happy Mouse," co-written by Walt's nurse, Hazel George. Walt Disney's myriad duties had moved him to name Macdonald as the official voice of Mickey in 1946, although Walt returned to the role for Mickey's daily TV introductions. The relative merits of Macdonald's interpretation of Mickey have enlivened many a Disney fan debate, and he continued to play the part through the 1970s.

The *Mickey Mouse Club* provided veteran performer Cliff Edwards a TV and recording comeback of sorts after his turns as the voice of Jiminy Cricket in *Pinocchio* (1940) and *Fun and Fancy Free* (1947). Several 1955 Mickey Mouse Club recordings featured Jiminy singing Dodd compositions including "Stop,

Archer and Gile: Folk Singers from the Far Corners

Several generations of record listeners enjoyed the vocal harmonies of Archer and Gile on some of the earliest Disneyland Records but probably knew very little about these two women.

Frances Archer was born in Corpus Christi, Texas; Beverly Gile was born in Los Angeles. Archer's mother was an amateur singer, while Gile's mother was a piano teacher in Beverly Hills. Little else is known about the two women prior to 1951, when the pair met and began performing together as members of the Beverly Hills Women's Club. As a later press release explained, "Even their shared liking of folk songs and the similarity of their artistic aims would not have been enough of a basis for much collaboration had their voices not complemented each other. A little vocal experimentation, however, soon showed them that they had voices which could be used either to blend together or to contrast each other, and the partnership was formed." Archer had the high soprano voice, while Gile had the deeper contralto. Gile was also the instrumentalist, accompanying their folk songs with guitar and woodblock.

After Walt Disney caught their act at a Palm Springs party sometime in 1955, Archer and Gile were booked to appear on the *Mickey Mouse Club*, and their television appearances led to their creation of *A Child's Garden of Verses*, the first recording to appear on the Disneyland Records label. In the early days, while the Disney label was still getting established, Golden Records simultaneously released some of Archer and Gile's *Mickey Mouse Club*–related songs. Their Disney work occupied their time off and on over the next five years, during which period they also made a number of highly successful personal appearance tours, along with appearances on such prestigious television series as *Today*, the *Tonight Show*, and *Omnibus*.

This sort of work apparently began to taper off during the early 1960s as a new breed of more political folk singers began to emerge. Archer and Gile were soon eclipsed, and at some point both women moved to Santa Fe, New Mexico. They carried on their separate lives in adjoining homes and Archer became an active member of the Christian Science church. Although they no longer sang together, they retained their interest in music. Their mutual friend Marcia Muth recalls how a group of enthusiasts would occasionally get together to attend local opera performances. "We would think the show was fine," she remembered, "until afterward over dinner, when Frances and Beverly would pick apart the whole performance and criticize the singers' technique until it sounded like the opera was totally worthless!"

Archer was known primarily as a voice teacher in Santa Fe, and the city now has a legion of her ex-students. One of them recalled, "Once when I had a bad cold and called in sick to

FRANCES   BEVERLY

ARCHER AND GILE

INTERNATIONAL SONGS AND BALLADS

JUST RELEASED!
"A COMMUNITY CONCERT WITH ARCHER AND GILE"
Disneyland Records - WDL 3023

Frances Archer and Beverly Gile were the first recording artists on Disney's new record label.

cancel my lesson, she said, 'All the more reason for you to exercise your throat muscles. You have a piano: I'll come to your house for your lesson.'" The same student also said, "Fran was always professionally dressed, which was something of a rarity back then here in Santa Fe." For her part, Beverly Gile remained involved in the local theater and arts scene, teaching voice at the College of Santa Fe and appearing frequently in local musical productions, where she retained her distinctive deep, husky delivery. She supplemented her income by becoming a professional photographer as well.

Frances Archer died in 1981, leaving no known survivors. Beverly Gile continued her work in Santa Fe until the late 1980s, when she moved her photography business back to her native Southern California. She was living in Hemet when she died on January 12, 2000.

Look, and Listen," "E-n-c-y-c-l-o-p-e-d-i-a," and his club signature song, "I'm No Fool."

○

An important link between the Official Mickey Mouse Club Records and the future Disneyland label was the debut of a folk duo discovered by Walt Disney. After hearing Frances Archer and Beverly Gile perform at a party in Palm Springs, Walt raved to Jimmy Johnson about their singing and style. "Of course, it was Saturday night," Walt admitted. "They might not sound so good on a Monday morning, but take a listen." Impressed, Johnson arranged for the guitar-strumming contralto Gile and soprano Archer to audition for *Mickey Mouse Club* producer Bill Walsh. The studio bought the rights to "Sho Jo Ji," a Japanese folk tune, and Archer and Gile sang the song on the program and recorded it for the Mickey Mouse Club label. (Eartha Kitt also cut her own popular version). Archer and Gile also appeared on the *Mickey Mouse Club* performing selections from Robert Louis Stevenson's *A Child's Garden of Verses*, which Gwyn Conger, ex-wife of novelist John Steinbeck, had set to music. The songs were an inspiration to Johnson. "Even though we were not officially in the record business at that time, we made a ten-inch LP of the Stevenson songs, backed with some other folk songs," he wrote. "This was the first LP to bear the Disneyland label, and later it was transferred to twelve-inch."

The *Mickey Mouse Club* provided truck-loads of sales for the Walt Disney Music Company, Golden Records, and ABC. However, after the first year, Golden and Am-Par handed the production reins back to Disney. (The network eventually sold out its interest in Disneyland as well, making the Walt Disney Company's 1996 purchase of ABC rather ironic.)

The success of the records based on Davy Crockett and the *Mickey Mouse Club* could not be denied. Roy Disney was fully convinced that the Disney company should enter the record business. "We knew it was chancy," Jimmy Johnson wrote. "We also knew that the reputations of the independent record distributors we would be using were pretty bad. So we decided to by-pass them." He continued, "We had a good experience with Charlie Hansen in the distribution of Disney printed music. Roy reasoned that printed music and records were sold in the same places, so he suggested to Charlie that he distribute our records for us nationally."

Roy's suggestion led to the involvement of one of the most influential figures in the distinctive Disneyland Records sound. In January 1956, Hansen met with Johnson about distributing Disneyland Records and brought along the multitalented Salvador "Tutti" Camarata. A New Jersey native, Camarata had been musical almost since birth. A violinist as a boy, he changed to trumpet at age eighteen when he entered the famed Juilliard School of Music. He had performed and arranged music for great bands of the 1940s, from Red Norvo and Charlie Barnet to Paul Whiteman and Jimmy Dorsey. For Dorsey, Camarata created several extremely popular Bob Eberle/Helen O'Connell duets in which the music shifted from ballad to fox trot in midplay. This type of arrangement, heard in such Dorsey hits as "Amapola," "Green Eyes," and "Yours," would later be revived in the Disneyland LP version of *Alice in Wonderland* (1956), in which "'Twas Brillig" suddenly shifts from Scottish jig to swing.

After serving in the Army Air Corps during World War II, Camarata cofounded and became head of London Records, a U.S. subsidiary of British Decca. He formed the Kingsway Symphony Orchestra and began a long association with outstanding British

Former big band arranger and composer Tutti Camarata was the person most responsible for the distinctive sound of Disneyland Records. (Courtesy of Richard M. Sherman)

Disneyland Records' original WDL LP's were meant to take their place alongside other movie soundtrack albums of the day. Not until later would they be considered primarily children's records. (© Disney Enterprises, Inc.)

COMING SOON again to your local theaters, CINDERELLA...to be reissued in 1957. Included here are all the hit songs from this best-loved fairy tale, such as, Bibbidi-Bobbidi-Boo, A Dream Is A Wish Your Heart Makes, So This Is Love, and The Work Song.

CINDERELLA WDL-4007 $4.98

BAMBI WDL-4010 $4.98

MUSIC

from the Original
Motion Picture Sound Tracks
Hours of Music for the Whole Family to Enjoy
Your favorites...Order Today!

PINOCCHIO WDL-4002 $4.98

DUMBO...the captivating music from the original sound track of the enchanting cartoon story of the little elephant with ears so big he could fly! Favorite songs include, Casey, Jr., When I See An Elephant Fly, Baby Mine, Look Out For Mr. Stork, and others.

DUMBO WDL-4013 $4.98

SONG OF THE SOUTH WDL-4001 $4.98

SNOW WHITE WDL-4005 $4.98

ORDER BLANK

TO: BUENA VISTA DISTRIBUTING COMPANY
1654 Cordova Street, Los Angeles 7, California

Please send me the following: ☐ Check ☐ Money Order

☐ WDL-4001
Song of the South

☐ WDL-4007
Cinderella

☐ WDL-4002
Pinocchio

☐ WDL-4010
Bambi

☐ WDL-4005
Snow White

☐ WDL-4013
Dumbo

The above prices include Federal Excise Tax. In California, please add 4% Sales Tax.

NAME

ADDRESS

CITY_____ ZONE_____ STATE_____

musicians, vocalists, and studio facilities. This network subsequently served Camarata well in his Disney career, as did his friendship with such legendary talents as Louis Armstrong, Bing Crosby, and Mary Martin.

As Disneyland Records' first artists and repertoire (A&R) director, Camarata's initial assignment was to create the soundtrack album debut of the 1946 live-action/animated feature *Song of the South*, which was about to be rereleased. When the film was screened for him at the studio, he caused a bit of a stir: "He shocked the Disney crew by watching the film with his eyes closed," Johnson remembered. "Tutti was listening for selections in the background score that might be melodious enough to be included in the LP."

Working with the Disney sound technicians and using original music tracks minus dialogue and sound effects, Camarata put together what became the first "official" album in the Disneyland Records line, catalog number WDL-4001, released in the spring of 1956. Its format was unique among soundtrack albums of the period. By the late 1950s, most soundtrack LPs consisted primarily of songs or background scores alone; the two elements rarely intertwined. The *Song of the South* LP combined songs and background music in a sequence that best suited the home listening experience. Perhaps because of his experience in classical music, Camarata approached soundtracks as musical suites, standing on their own as complete performances. *Pinocchio* was scheduled for theatrical reissue in fall 1956, so its album was created in the same format. Also produced during that time were similar albums for *Snow White and the Seven Dwarfs*, *Bambi*, *Cinderella*, and *Dumbo*.

✽

As Camarata was completing these initial recordings, Johnson and his sales staff made a curious decision: they would not market the discs as children's records. "We felt that the LPs would find their place alongside other Hollywood soundtracks and Broadway cast albums," he wrote. "We used rather sophisticated, adult art on the covers. We priced the albums at a suggested retail price of $4.98," a premium price for an LP in 1956.

The label's first soundtrack album from a Disney live-action film was *Westward Ho! the Wagons*, starring Fess Parker and several Mouseketeers at the height of their popularity. According to Johnson, in-studio buzz for the film was not at first particularly great—even Walt was not terribly excited. But Johnson seized the opportunity, convincing Walt to enhance the film with a song. Stan Jones, a former National Park Service ranger who had begun a new career as a songwriter with his 1949 hit, "Ghost Riders in the Sky," composed "Wringle Wrangle." Jones had already provided Disney success with his "Triple R Song" in the *Mickey Mouse Club* serial *Spin and Marty*. The campfire tune used multiple verses to sustain the plot and provide exposition. It was among the first tunes recorded for the Official Mickey Mouse Club Records released in October 1955. (Jones continued to contribute material to the company's music division until his death in December 1963.)

Famed matte artist Peter Ellenshaw painted the album art for the Disneyland *Westward Ho* LP, which featured a version of "Wringle Wrangle" designed for radio play. Parker even sang the song on the *Mickey Mouse Club*. "Wringle Wrangle" went on to be a great financial success, recorded by many singers, including Merv Griffin and, ironically, the chart-topping Davy Crockett balladeer Bill Hayes.

✽

Appropriately, Walt Disney's voice was the first one heard on the first nonsoundtrack record produced and distributed entirely by the in-house record company bearing his name. Titled *Walt Disney Takes You to Disneyland*, it is a gatefold album that opens up to reveal a collection of Disneyland park photos, with a map on the back cover. The disc is split into five sections of instrumental music and sound effects that correspond to the five sections of the park: Main Street, written by studio composer Oliver Wallace; Tomorrowland and Frontierland by George Bruns; and Fantasyland and Adventureland by Camarata. Some sections were completely original, while others interpolated familiar Disney songs. "I asked Walt if he would do introductory narration for each of the lands and he agreed to do so," Johnson wrote. "I believe this is the only instance of Walt's voice being used on a phonograph record." The only exceptions to this claim would be the occasional use of old cartoon soundtracks featuring Walt as Mickey and various promotional discs not sold to the general public.

This LP, which on its label carries an alternate title, *A Musical Tour of Disneyland*, was also released on 45-rpm records, one for each "land." Walt's narration was later augmented by new material featuring Cliff Edwards as Jiminy Cricket in a reissue aimed at the children's market, retitled *A Day at Disneyland* and packaged with an illustrated book.

○

Seven-inch 45-rpm discs were a mainstay of the Disney record company from the beginning, though Jimmy Johnson was among those most personally opposed to them. 45s had emerged out of corporate rivalry. Twelve-inch 33⅓-rpm long-play records had been developed in 1948 by CBS, which wanted the entire music industry to embrace the new technology. Rather than cooperating, RCA President General David Sarnoff ordered the promotion of the 45s his New Jersey labs had created. To heighten demand, special 45-rpm record players were sold below cost, including a Disney-licensed model. NBC, RCA's radio network, used big-name stars to hawk 45-rpm records on its entertainment shows. On an episode of the *Phil Harris and Alice Faye Show*, for example, guest Edward G. Robinson spoke of the benefits of 45s, including how easy it was to store them in a pants pocket.

"I was a foe of the 45 right from the start," Johnson later wrote. "The damage which RCA did to the record industry in general by their push on the 45, which caused double inventories and countless other ills, [was] still being felt 35 years later." (The whole mess would have a parallel in the 1970s, with the competing Beta and VHS home video recorder formats.) Johnson conceded, however, that "the 45 was ideal for kids." Despite Johnson's misgivings, Disneyland 45s were sold alongside others produced by children's labels such as Peter Pan, Cricket, and Golden. Disneyland Records were also released on ten-inch 78-rpm discs in the 1950s and six-inch discs in the 1960s, long after the major labels had abandoned the speed. As late as 1965, children could still be found playing 78s on phonographs with quick-wearing steel needles.

○

The first Disneyland album entirely featuring music from a Disney film that was not from the original soundtrack was *Alice in Wonderland* (1956). In 1951, Decca had been contracted to produce an *Alice* soundtrack at 78 and 45 rpm. When the film did not perform well, Decca declined, and the album was never made. (Disney art did make its way onto the cover of a Decca recording of *Alice* starring Ginger Rogers, but the recording had no relation to the Disney film. Rogers played Alice with a supporting cast and songs by early Disney record pioneer Frank Luther.)

Cliff Edwards: Wishing upon a Star

Cliff Edwards made dozens of Disney record appearances in character as Jiminy Cricket and occasionally as himself. (Courtesy of Will Ryan)

Cliff Edwards's fame reached such heights as the voice of Jiminy Cricket that it is amazing to discover that this role constituted just the final step in a long and distinguished career.

Edwards was born in Hannibal, Missouri, and began singing as a teenager. In stark contrast with his wholesome Disney image, his original venues were the bars of St. Louis, where he performed "for whatever coins the tipsy patrons would toss to him," as one biographer put it. Edwards accompanied himself on the ukulele, inspiring the nickname "Ukulele Ike," which he would use at random for the rest of his life.

During the 1920s, Edwards was a musical star of immense popularity and scope. His signature tune was the jazz hit "Ja Da," and he also sang such Jazz Age gems as "Sleepy Time Gal" and "Toot Toot Tootsie." Edwards became the first artist to perform "Singin' in the Rain" on the movie screen in MGM's *Hollywood Revue of 1929*. His film career flourished through the 1930s, including a small offscreen role in *Gone with the Wind*, where he played a hallucinating Confederate solider under the care of Scarlett and Melanie.

When Edwards was cast in *Pinocchio* (1940), both his name and voice were well known to audiences. His flawless performance as Jiminy revitalized his career for a time, and during 1941 and 1942 he provided comic relief in the Charles Starrett series of Western movies for Columbia Studios and then in a Tim Holt series at RKO Radio Pictures. Edwards appeared as himself, aka Ukulele Ike, on a "Guest Star Day" segment of the *Mickey Mouse Club*. Jiminy Cricket became one of the first characters from a Disney animated feature to appear extensively apart from his original function. Jiminy was a *Mickey Mouse Club* fixture in such educational segments as "I'm No Fool" and "You Are a Human Animal." The character also appeared on many Mickey Mouse Club and Disneyland Records between 1955 and 1967, with one solo album by Edwards again as Ukulele Ike.

As Jiminy Cricket, Edwards sang, "When you wish upon a star, your dreams come true."

His personal life, unfortunately, was not filled with such happy endings. He had financial difficulties beginning when his first marriage ended in divorce. As Charles Starrett told Western movie chronicler David Rothel, "Cliff's wife married her lawyer, and they really fleeced poor Cliff. He finally had to declare bankruptcy." A second marriage ended much the same way. By the 1960s, failed marriages and income tax problems left Edwards surviving mostly on his Disney record residuals. Failing health soon ate up that income. Jimmy Johnson recalled that the last time Edwards's housekeeper brought Edwards to the studio, the once robust man was disoriented and did not seem to recognize anyone.

Edwards was living on welfare at the Virgil Convalescent Hospital when he died on July 17, 1971, at age seventy-six. His death wasn't made public for several days because hospital officials didn't think it was newsworthy. They didn't know he had ever been famous.

For Disneyland Records to produce an *Alice* soundtrack LP, the company would have to take on substantial performance fees, making the budget unfeasible by 1956. Another difficulty was that in the *Alice* soundtrack, most of the songs were performed in a fragmentary manner, usually with no defined beginning or end. Some lasted for less than thirty seconds. The solution was to produce an entirely new recording of the *Alice* score, a type of album sometimes referred to as a "studio cast" or "second cast" album. Second cast versions were handy when a film soundtrack, TV performance, or theme park attraction lacked contractual provisions for recordings. Second casts also added to the product line, even when a soundtrack was available. For example, *Sleeping Beauty*'s film release in 1959 was complemented not only by a soundtrack LP but by a reported fourteen separate Disney record releases. Second cast albums usually sold at lower prices than soundtracks, but again, *Alice in Wonderland* was an exception. Camarata pulled out all the stops for his version, using a concert-sized orchestra and full chorus. In what many Disney audiophiles regard as her finest work, Mouseketeer Darlene Gillespie sang Alice's three solos with compelling depth. This version of *Alice* sold consistently even though the film remained out of theatrical release between 1956 and 1974 and received only a few early broadcasts on the *Disneyland* TV show. The album's success occurred largely independently of its source material.

○

In its first year, Disneyland Records' few forays out of the Disney film and theme park realm were the Archer and Gile material and an attempted comeback album for Cliff Edwards called *Ukulele Ike Sings Again*. By the mid-1950s, most audiences had forgotten Edwards's phenomenal impact on early popular music, and Walt Disney reportedly suggested this album as a reminder, with fresh renditions of 1920s hits such as "June Night," which had sold 3,200,000 records; "I Cried for You," which had sold 1,720,000 copies; "Sleepy Time Gal," which had sold just over a million; and "Singin' in the Rain," which Edwards had introduced in the movie *Hollywood Revue of 1929*, long before Gene Kelly made his splash in 1952. Walt also supposedly envisioned this LP as an extra source of income for Edwards, who had fallen on hard financial times at this late stage of his career.

Edwards reprised his Jiminy Cricket role in Disneyland Records' first holiday recording, and its only Yuletide selection for 1956, *The Night before Christmas*. Side A of the single featured Jiminy reciting the classic Clement C. Moore poem with no alterations to the original, except for the introduction, where he set the scene by explaining that "we crickets are so small, we can get into people's houses. We slip under doors, and get warm by their fireplaces. Well, one time I was standing on a hearthstone and, '—twas the night before Christmas . . .'"

Side B gave Edwards a chance to sing the 1940s ditty "Kris Kringle." The light crooning voice that made him so popular in the 1920s remained very much in evidence, and his spoken rendition of the second chorus was done in true Jiminy Cricket style. For some reason, two nearly identical versions of "Kris Kringle" have appeared at random on various LP, 45, and CD reissues over the years. One version adds a bell during the musical bridge, and each ends with a slightly different "Merry Christmas!" from Jiminy.

○

For the most part, Disneyland Records ended 1956 on a positive note, with a fresh catalog of products and even a hit song in "Wringle Wrangle." One of the few negatives was the termination of the record distribution deal with sheet music publisher Charles Hansen. "Our early experiment . . . just didn't work," Johnson commented, "and I decided that we had better go in a more traditional way." The separation apparently was amicable, as Hansen continued to distribute Disney sheet music for many years. As far as the record division was concerned, the hiring of former Capitol Records executive Al Latauska seemed to promise growth for the new business. "We made a bundle of money and got stars in our eyes about the record business," recalled Johnson. "When our board of directors met in February 1957, a general air of euphoria prevailed. Roy Disney felt that his judgment that we should go into the record business was a very sound one."

3

The Stars Shine

Roy Disney was so pleased with the new Disneyland Records division that he took it beyond the motion picture and television realm. "The amount of new music coming out of our Disney films is really not sufficient to support a major record catalog," he told Jimmy Johnson. "I think we should reach out for non-Disney artists and really go big time." Johnson and Camarata began approaching outside performers and applied Roy's "non-Disney" directive to help launch recording careers for the company's in-house talents.

In addition to her *Alice in Wonderland* work and numerous *Mickey Mouse Club* songs, Darlene Gillespie performed more album solos than any *Mickey Mouse Club* star other than Jimmie Dodd. She was the first Mouseketeer to headline her own LP, *Darlene of the Teens*. This pop collection, notable for her moving rendition of Elvis Presley's "Love Me Tender," was later issued as *Top Tunes of the 50's*. Though true stardom eluded her, many of Gillespie's recordings sold for decades, a testimony to her remarkable singing voice. In 1957, Fess Parker added two more distinctions to his career: narrating and starring in the first Disneyland story LP to feature soundtrack dialogue, *Old Yeller*, and recording *Yarns and Songs*, his first solo album for the label.

An unofficial Disneyland Records stock company began forming in 1957. Leading the list of talented Hollywood singers and actors who appeared frequently were singers Bill Lee and Thurl Ravenscroft. Along with their fellow MelloMen, they headlined an album of barbershop quartet favorites, *Meet Me Down on Main Street*. (The title song, composed by Oliver Wallace, had also been heard with different lyrics in the 1949 short cartoon *Crazy over Daisy*.) Sterling Holloway also joined the group of frequent Disney artists with an album combining narrated versions of *Peter and the Wolf* (from *Make Mine Music*) and *The Sorcerer's Apprentice* (from *Fantasia*). Already a favorite voice actor for Disney animated films, Holloway performed equally well in ensemble casts or as solo narrator.

O

Camarata placed his stylistic stamp on a number of other Official Mickey Mouse Club albums, extended-play records (EPs) and singles. There was a marked difference between his treatment of the material and the more kiddie-oriented versions heard on the first Mickey Mouse Club recordings. In contrast to the smaller-scale musical productions on early club records, a richer, more fully orchestrated sound could now be enjoyed on such LPs as *A Walt Disney Song Fest*, *Holidays with the Mouseketeers*, and *Songs from "Annette" and Other Walt Disney Serials*, a title that indicated how the public's embrace of Annette Funicello had eclipsed Darlene

Darlene Gillespie:
The Girl Most Likely

When Darlene Gillespie was selected as one of the original twenty-four Mouseketeers, the smart money around the Disney studio was on the talented youngster to become the breakout star. Her life instead took several unexpected turns.

Born in 1941 to a show-business-savvy family, Darlene was more mature than the other would-be Mouseketeers when she first auditioned for the *Mickey Mouse Club*. "I went down there with a group of other girls and did this little dance number," she said in 1975. "And then they said to us, because I guess they were looking for rounded talents, 'Can any of you sing?' And I was very innocent about it and said, 'Sure.' And I sang 'The Ballad of Davy Crockett.' I honest to God didn't do it like someone would say, 'What a sharp kid. She sang the favorite number.' I sang it, honestly, because I really liked it. And I guess they liked it too."

Much effort went into showcasing the multitalented fifteen-year-old, including starring her in the *Mickey Mouse Club* Western serial *Corky and White Shadow*, with Buddy Ebsen and Lloyd Corrigan. Darlene had a touching, natural singing voice that could put many adult singers to shame. Her tour de force 1956 recording of *Alice in Wonderland* sold through the 1980s in the United States and even longer in Japan.

But stardom was elusive. Annette Funicello suddenly started to get more fan mail than any other cast member. While most of Annette's costars adjusted to this shift in attention, rumors of a rift between the Gillespie and Funicello families spread around the lot. When production of the show ended, only Funicello had her contract renewed. Gillespie eventually changed careers, becoming a highly respected nurse specializing in heart surgery, though the *Mickey Mouse Club* continued to dog at her heels as badly as Pluto.

Gillespie clearly had mixed emotions about her Disney career. "Who wants to admit they were a fifteen-year-old mouse?" she told *TV Guide* when the show resurfaced in 1975. Her attempt at a country-singing career hadn't taken off. In 1976 she said, "If having been a Mouseketeer is the only thing I have to be remembered for, I'd just as soon be forgotten." She did, however, appear with her former costars on a 1975 NBC *Tomorrow* talk show with Tom Snyder. In 1980 Gillespie performed in Mouseketeer reunion shows, but in the 1990s she again refrained from participation. Bitter about her experience with Disney, she sued unsuccessfully for royalty payments on long-discontinued recordings for which she had been paid a standard flat rate.

After a long string of personal and legal difficulties, Gillespie vanished from public view in early 2002, and her former cast mates lost track of her. A performer with a stirring voice that entertained countless listeners for decades, Gillespie apparently never took comfort in her outstanding contribution to children's records.

Record stores could display this great banner promoting three new releases that tied in with the Disneyland park in one form or another. (© Disney Enterprises, Inc.)

and all the other Mouseketeers. The first cut on the album, "How Will I Know My Love?" was Annette's first single, released after she sang the song during a hayride sequence in the *Mickey Mouse Club*'s "Annette" serial. The studio was bombarded with requests for a recording of the song, and the resulting single sold 100,000 copies.

The last Official Mickey Mouse Club LP to feature material from the TV series was *We're the Mouseketeers*, released as the show was starting to wind down. It is an example of what Roy Disney termed "cross-pollination" and is now known as cross promotion or synergy. Many of the songs on this LP have little connection to the *Mickey Mouse Club* aside from some Mouseketeer performances. It includes all the songs from the Walt Disney "True-Life Fantasy" *Perri*, two from the multipart Disneyland TV adventure *The Saga of Andy Burnett*, and the theme from the ABC series *Zorro*.

○

Disneyland Records' "Storyteller" LP series began in 1957. Packaged with a full-

color illustrated book, these records would endure for decades. The first in the catalog was the revised version of Walt Disney's debut album, *A Day at Disneyland*, with a new Jiminy Cricket narration. A variety of recordings appeared in this format, but the bread-and-butter of the series was its adaptations of Disney film stories. The most prevalent Storyteller format involved a single narrator, who usually assumed a role from the film, telling the story and introducing the songs. Some albums, such as 1958's *Peter Pan*, included dialogue from the soundtrack. Later LPs completely redramatized the story using either members of the original cast or a second cast.

The first film-based Storyteller LP in the catalog was *Bambi*, with a script by Roy O. Disney's son, Roy E. Disney. "I was working on nature films with [producer/narrator] Winston Hibler when Jimmy got me to write the text for a Storyteller for *Bambi*," Roy recalled. "It sounded like fun, so I brought a record of the music home to listen to, suggested the order of the music, and wrote narrator's text

Sterling Holloway: The Cheshire Pooh

Most radio and animation actors affected a wide range of characterizations by altering and even disguising their real voices. Sterling Holloway portrayed such polar opposites as Winnie the Pooh and the Cheshire Cat simply through sheer attitude.

Holloway hailed from the small town of Cedartown, Georgia. He was the son of an entrepreneurial owner of a wholesale grocery house, a flour mill, and other businesses. At age fifteen, Holloway attended the American Academy of Dramatic Arts in New York. He quickly became a success in such popular 1920s revues as *Garrick's Gaieties*, the first big success of Rodgers and Hart, where he introduced the classic song "Manhattan."

His first attempt at Hollywood was less than notable. Holloway's look and sound were so offbeat that movie producers couldn't figure out what to do with him. But after director Frank Capra cast Holloway in a small role in his film *American Madness* (1932), the actor began to attract more attention. Walt Disney, in the planning stages of *Snow White and the Seven Dwarfs*, suggested Holloway as the model for Sleepy. Holloway's first voice for Disney was that of the stork in *Dumbo*. From that point onward, although he would continue his on-screen career primarily in low-budget B pictures, his voice became a staple of Disney animation to the point where some animators privately felt that Holloway's voice might have been overused.

By the time Disneyland Records came about, Holloway's stature gave him added clout with the label. His first contract with the Walt Disney Music Company, signed on September 17, 1957, ensured him star status on all of his recordings. Unlike many of his contemporaries, Holloway never performed uncredited.

In the early 1960s, Holloway was awarded his most beloved role in Disney's screen adaptation of A. A. Milne's *Pooh* stories. At around the same time, however, heart trouble began to plague Holloway. His condition affected his performances, particularly noticeably on records of the mid-1960s. By 1969, doctors discovered that medication was causing most of Holloway's vocal problems, and much of his old spirit returned.

Holloway's health took another downturn during the 1970s. His farewell Disneyland disc was 1976's *Winnie the Pooh for President*. Actors Hal Smith and Tony Pope were among the later Poohs, and Jim Cummings is the official voice today.

Sterling Holloway's remaining years were quiet and uneventful. Never married, he had an adopted son and a passion for fine art, amassing an extensive and valuable collection. He died on November 22, 1992, at the age of eighty-seven.

Dallas McKennon: Forever Young

Dallas "Dal" McKennon is one of the few actors whose Disney work spanned the record division, theme parks division, animation division, and live-action film.

McKennon first found fame in Portland, Oregon, as *Mr. Funny Buttons* on local children's radio. Film star Jimmy Stewart came to the area in 1952 to shoot location footage for his feature *Bend of the River*. At age thirty-two, McKennon managed to look much older in his cameo role as a toothless old gold miner. Stewart encouraged McKennon to move to Hollywood and helped him secure his first agent.

The tall, lanky McKennon was physically ideal for on-camera character roles, with a wide vocal range for animation. In his first Disney project, *Lady and the Tramp* (1955), he played four roles, including Toughy, the dog pound mutt who asks Peg (voiced by Peggy Lee) to sing "He's a Tramp." He was also heard in features such as *Sleeping Beauty* (1959), *101 Dalmatians* (1961), *Mary Poppins* (1964), *The Jungle Book* (1967), and numerous shorts.

His Disneyland Records debut may have been as British butler Perkins and Asian chef George in the "Triple R Song" from *Spin and Marty* in 1955, but McKennon really arrived when he auditioned for the 1958 *Stories of Uncle Remus* Storyteller album. "As I was leaving the studio," McKennon said, "I remarked to Jimmy Johnson that I hoped I could do a voice for him on his records someday. He replied, 'No, I'm sorry, you can't do a voice for us.' I was disappointed, of course. But then he continued, 'You're going to do all of them!'" It was the beginning of a long association during which McKennon played such diverse characters on vinyl as Scrooge McDuck, the Scarecrow of Oz, and Bagheera in *The Jungle Book*. On-screen, McKennon could be seen in Disney's *Son of Flubber* (1963) and *The Misadventures of Merlin Jones* (1964). In 1965, he teamed with former Crockett Fess Parker for NBC's *Daniel Boone* series, as comic relief tavern keeper Cincinnatus.

McKennon gathered animation credits all over Hollywood, performing supporting roles for Walter Lantz and as the voice of Gumby for Art Clokey. Producer George Pal chose McKennon for many Puppetoons characters in MGM's *tom thumb* (1957). In the Twentieth-Century-Fox musical *Doctor Dolittle* (1967) starring Rex Harrison, McKennon and Disneyland Records contemporary Ginny Tyler provided most of the animal sounds. McKennon joined the team of voice actors at the now-defunct Filmation Associates, prolific producers of Saturday morning television in the late 1960s and early 1970s. Beginning in 1968 with the *Archie Show*, McKennon played Archie, Mr. Weatherbee, Hot Dog, and many other Riverdale citizens.

Disneyland and Walt Disney World visitors have heard him on Big Thunder Mountain Railroad, the Country Bear Jamboree, and many other attractions. In the American Adventure at Epcot, he is the voice of Ben Franklin, the first Audio-Animatronics character to walk up stairs.

Now in his late eighties, McKennon has the energy of someone a quarter his age. He can still do all the voices, from Ben Franklin and Brer Rabbit to a stop-motion clay boy and a freckle-faced teenager!

Beginning with his 1957 LP of Uncle Remus stories, for which he provided all the voices, Dal McKennon would be heard in dozens of roles on Disneyland Records for the next fourteen years. (Courtesy of Tammy Rock)

to go with it. I sent it to Jimmy, and he loved it. It was just a little spare-time job." Roy's script was originally performed by lead Mouseketeer Jimmie Dodd. Other Storytellers were narrated by Annette Funicello (*Snow White*), Darlene Gillespie (*Alice in Wonderland*), Dallas McKennon (*Uncle Remus*), Cliff Edwards as Jiminy Cricket (*Cinderella* and *Pinocchio*), and Edward Brophy as Timothy Mouse (*Dumbo*). For *Dumbo*, Brophy's voice had aged a little in the sixteen years since he had last played Timothy, but his delivery remained sharp and funny. Brophy died at age sixty-five in 1960, making this his farewell performance as Timothy.

Stories of Uncle Remus eschews the live-action *Song of the South* story and contains just the three animated segments. It features character actor Dallas McKennon speaking and Oscar-winner James Baskett (from the film soundtrack) singing in the title role. A multifaceted voice artist, McKennon appeared in a staggering number of roles over the next dozen years.

○

The first non-Disney-related superstar to sign on to the Disneyland label was Broadway legend Mary Martin. The tireless Texan was an A-list star in the mid-1950s, with the

Mary Martin was the first big-name star to make original recordings for the Disney label.

smash *South Pacific* only a few years behind her and her ongoing TV appearances in the title role of *Peter Pan*. Camarata was an old friend of Martin and no doubt had a major role in her recording for Disney. He arranged and conducted many of her early records for Decca as well as the renowned live TV special *Together with Music* costarring Noel Coward.

Martin's first Disney release was a sensitive, reverent 1957 narrative called *The Little Lame Lamb: A Christmas Story of St. Francis*, a two-disc 45-rpm set rereleased the following year as an LP. Backed by a highly emotive Camarata score, Martin tells the story of a boy named Tonio and how his encounter with Father Francis leads to the creation of a Christmas crèche and a small miracle.

Martin then apparently announced, "I would like to sing some Disney songs." Walt Disney's reaction was, "I can't think of anyone I'd rather hear sing them." The result was *Hi-Ho: Mary Sings and Mary Swings Walt Disney Favorites* (1958), which boasted some of the most exceptional performances ever recorded, matching Martin's formidable energy with Camarata's versatility. The title track pushes the humble dwarfs' march into a pulsing, frantic tempo, suddenly halts to a slither and picks up again, with Martin displaying an astonishing range of octaves. Camarata never repeats himself on the disc. Every tune has a different mood, sometimes in keeping with the original film's intent, sometimes going in a new direction. For the finale, "I'm Late" is transformed from a White Rabbit's lament into a mad dash by a contemporary woman who's overbooked but never overwhelmed ("Gotta race, gotta dash, get to the bank and draw some cash! I'm late! I'm late!"). Another unique aspect of *Hi-Ho* was that many of the songs featured their original lead-in verses. These verses rarely presented themselves outside sheet music form, and were not actually heard in the movies for which they were written.

Johnson termed attending the album's recording sessions a "privilege" and recalled that "Mary's performance was unforgettable as she stood in the little soloist's isolation booth singing her heart out and gesturing gracefully into empty space. Or so it seemed. And yet, as I watched her, I knew she was feeling that the audience—her audience—was there. Sometimes the maze of mechanical, electrical and electronic equipment which is necessary in the making of phonograph records causes this magic spark between the performer and audience to be lost. Not this time!"

Martin's *A Musical Love Story* LP (1958) contained two extended medleys of songs done in an intimate, sophisticated cabaret style. Walt's wife, Lillian, must have been especially taken with this album; years later, a cassette reissue was donated in her name as part of "An Evening with Mary Martin and Friends," to benefit the Palm Springs Desert Museum. The same year Martin recorded the Storyteller album for the highly anticipated animated feature *Sleeping Beauty*, which would not be released until 1959. It was the most lavish nonsoundtrack story record produced by Disney, with a full chorus and orchestra arranged by Camarata to follow Martin's narration. Some of the song selections from this album were also released on Mickey Mouse Club and Golden Records.

○

Show albums were topping the charts in the 1950s. Both the Broadway cast and film soundtrack versions of Rodgers and Hammerstein's *Carousel* were among the recordings showered in gold records. Record labels commonly released their own versions of the scores. Even though *Carousel* was not a Disney property, Disneyland Records followed the trend and produced a version of the score with the original Broadway star, Jan Clayton. Though she had sung the role earlier for Decca, the Disneyland version was her only stereophonic recording of the score. Clayton, then well known as Jeff's mom on TV's *Lassie*, was reviving the show at the Brussels World's Fair, and the first Disney issue of the record was designed as a tie-in. This recording of *Carousel*, under Camarata's direction with the Gloria Wood Choir, may be the only version of the score to treat the "My Little Girl" section of the famous "Soliloquy" as an individual song. The album notes explain this as a request by Clayton in honor of her teenaged daughter, who had died in an auto crash months earlier. She donated her album royalties to the San Fernando Valley Youth Foundation in her daughter's memory.

Little Gems from Big Shows was another Disneyland salute to Broadway musicals, but this LP took the unique turn of including lesser-known songs as well as hits. The jacket proclaimed that the album featured "Disney's new stars of television," and the recording was clearly intended to promote the careers of rapidly maturing Mouseketeers Darlene Gillespie, Karen Pendleton, and Cubby O'Brien as well as comic singer/actor Henry Calvin of the ABC prime-time hit *Zorro*, and Jerome Courtland, star of the *Disneyland* multipart series *The Saga of Andy Burnett*. Among other 1957 releases to follow the non-Disney direction were two albums of Stan

Jerome Courtland: Ladies in the Sky with Disney

Jerome Courtland was a popular young Hollywood leading man and nightclub singer when Walt Disney chose him as the next Davy Crockett.

The son of female vocalist Mary Courtland of the *Your Hit Parade* radio series, the classically trained Courtland had music in his blood. Renowned baritone Lawrence Tibbett encouraged Courtland to go into opera. Under contract to Columbia Pictures, he made twenty-five films before leaving the studio to star in films and TV specials in Italy and Germany. "Walt saw me in a movie called *The Barefoot Mailman* with Bob Cummings," Courtland recalled. "He screen-tested me for the six-part miniseries *The Saga of Andy Burnett*, which was like Davy Crockett. One of the songs I sang in the show was 'Ladies in the Sky.' Looking back on it now, it was kind of corny! But they made a record of it as part of the cross-pollinating of every studio project."

Courtland's singing was already well known when he recorded the Disneyland album *Little Gems from Big Shows*. He sang a playful duet with the up-and-coming Darlene Gillespie, a comical tune with fellow Broadway performer Henry Calvin, and joined them both for the "Be a Clown" finale. His tender version of "Come to Me, Bend to Me" from *Brigadoon* was reissued on three subsequent albums. Today's audio technology allows many singers, instruments, and enhancements to be recorded separately. In 1958, however, *Little Gems* was recorded all at once. "They had a recording studio on the Disney lot," Courtland explained. "They put the orchestra on stage. Everyone performed the songs together, all the way through. If you screwed up, you had to start over again."

Courtland's most enduring Disney performance was singing the theme for *Old Yeller*. The soundtrack version appeared on the 1957 story album. The next year, Courtland sang it especially for records, with Kevin "Moochie" Corcoran calling at a barking Yeller (Jimmy Macdonald) in the background.

Courtland's Disney career took him further than even Walt expected. After a TV talk show, a weekly adventure series, a Broadway show, a solo album, and numerous live appearances, he decided to make a permanent change. "I became interested in directing and producing early in my career," Courtland said. "In the 1960s, I thought it was a good time to break into that side of the business. Walt knew I was serious. He brought me into the production office, and I learned how to break down scripts, do budgets, and work with the directors."

Courtland became associate producer on several Disney projects. Columbia hired him back to work on TV series pilots, one of which literally took off: from 1967 to 1970, he produced the beloved series *The Flying Nun*, starring Sally Field. He took charge of all aspects of the show, including the construction of a full-scale Convent San Tanco on the Columbia lot.

Besides paralleling the Disney tradition of tie-in toys, records, books, and other merchandise, *The Flying Nun* provided early acting work for actress Farrah Fawcett and director Henry Jaglom and still flies on in reruns throughout the world.

Courtland returned to the Disney studio to produce a string of hits including *Pete's Dragon*, *Escape to Witch Mountain*, and *The Apple Dumpling Gang*. For Columbia, he directed such hit series as *The Love Boat*, *The Partridge Family*, and *Falcon Crest*.

In 1994, after teaching producing and directing at UCLA, Courtland and his wife semi-retired to Chicago, where he joined the faculty of Columbia College, the world's largest film school. "The students looked all my old work up on the Net," he said. "It impresses them that I've produced films like *Pete's Dragon*. They'll say, 'That's was my favorite film,' or 'That was the first movie I ever saw!' It's a kick to contribute to these kids as filmmakers.

Jones's Western songs, *Creakin' Leather* and *This Was the West*.

Perhaps the most acclaimed album to result from these non-Disney projects was *Tutti's Trumpets*, a collection of standard and original compositions that explored the depth and range of the trumpet. Camarata assembled some of Hollywood's most highly regarded studio musicians for the project, including Conrad Gozzo, Pete Candoli, Shorty Sherock, Mannie Klein, Joe Triscari, and Uan Rasey, at one of the first stereo sessions ever at the famed Capitol tower building. "The air was electric on that recording date," Johnson recalled. "Something new musically was being done, and the musicians were happy to be a part of it. . . . At the end of Goz's playing of 'Trumpeter's Prayer,' the entire orchestra burst into applause. It was a thrilling and never-to-be forgotten moment." "Trumpeter's Prayer" and several other cuts received an enormous amount of radio play and became regional Top 10 hits. Before his death, Conrad Gozzo told Johnson that the only significant amount of fan mail he ever received concerned "Trumpeter's Prayer." The album was never a huge national hit, but musicians (especially those in Southern California) and jazz enthusiasts still regard *Tutti's Trumpets* as a premier popular jazz achievement. It was reissued many times on the Disneyland, Time, and Bainbridge Records labels. The album was never released in its entirety until 1970, when a unique version of "Stardust" was added to the Buena Vista reissue. For technical reasons Johnson did not make clear, the song had been omitted from the original release. In this arrangement the sound changes from mono to stereo, the audio equivalent of the moment in *The Wizard of Oz* when the film changes from sepia tone to Technicolor.

This Disneyland Records ad from the March 2, 1957, issue of *Billboard* demonstrates the company's attempts to appeal to the adult record-buying public even more than the kids. (© Disney Enterprises, Inc.)

Even if *Tutti's Trumpets* was not the million-seller everyone had hoped for, it did inspire several other LPs of the same type. A sequel of sorts was 1958's *All the King's Saxes*, led by former Benny Goodman saxophone legend Hymie Shertzer and several of his colleagues in renditions of classic swing tunes.

Those who think of Disneyland Records only as a "kiddie record" label would be startled to discover some of the albums released during this period. They include *Parisian Life* (highlights from Offenbach operettas), *Dancing in Peacock Alley* (Bernie Leighton on piano), *Melodies for Midnight* (Johnny La

Padula on accordion), and Camarata's four-volume "Seasons" set, which consisted of four instrumental LPs—*Autumn*, *Winter*, *Spring*, and *Summer*.

○

In addition to his grasp of numerous musical styles, Camarata had a fine ear for sound quality. Dissatisfied with recording facilities on the Disney Studio lot, he set about finding better acoustics in the Los Angeles area. Camarata didn't care whether the facility was originally intended for music recording. During his London Records days, he had produced albums in an English church with outstanding results. Hollywood movie sound stages were unacceptable because they were designed primarily to keep outside sound out; interior acoustic quality was not an issue. Camarata's quest for sound perfection eventually took him to an American Legion Hall on Hollywood's Highland Avenue. After clapping his hands to check the acoustics, he told Johnson, "We've got to try this place!" It was a dream situation for Disney. Not only was the hall perfect for recording, the company did not have to pay rent. The board members of the nonprofit Legion post, startled as they were, merely asked for a contribution to their post fund.

The first album recorded there was the highly innovative *Folk Songs from the Far Corners*. Delighted with the singing style of Frances Archer and Beverly Gile, Camarata dispensed with their established guitar-and-vocal folk song format and instead set the women's voices against three musical backgrounds: brass only, violins only, and full orchestra. Jimmy Johnson vividly remembered the first Legion Hall session: "We set a date, moved a ton of not-so-portable recording equipment into the second-floor offices, had miles of cable snaking throughout the building, and went to work. The results were sensational, the sound being absolutely fantastic, and Archer and Gile plus orchestral backing were something else again."

As a recording facility, the Legion Hall was hailed a great success—too great, in fact. Word spread among session musicians so fast that the American Legion couldn't handle the barrage of requests from other record companies. In desperation, they said no to everyone, with two exceptions: Camarata's versions of *Bambi* and *Cinderella* for Disneyland Records, and a performance of every Beethoven symphony conducted by Bruno Walter for Columbia Records.

O

Fantasia (1940) represented one of Walt Disney's boldest experiments, combining animated imagery with great classical music by Bach, Beethoven, Tchaikovsky, Dukas, Stravinsky, Ponchielli, and Mussorgsky. It was a natural for a record album, and Jimmy Johnson was eager to proceed, especially since he was a fan of the film's masterful conductor, Leopold Stokowski.

Johnson had first met Stokowski in 1938, when Johnson was running errands for the conductor, musical historian Deems Taylor, and Walt Disney. "I didn't meet Stokowski again until 1956 after we had decided to start the Disneyland Record company," Johnson wrote. "We wanted to release a three-LP set of the soundtrack of *Fantasia*, and to do this we needed Stokowski's permission." In Johnson's recollection, "'Stoki' thought the idea of a soundtrack set on *Fantasia* was a good one. I offered him the usual royalty of five percent of the retail price of the records and he accepted." Continued Johnson, "By this time, Stokowski had long since left the Philadelphia Orchestra, but he asked, 'What about a royalty for the orchestra?' I explained that we had a document signed at the time of the recording by all the members of the orchestra giving us all rights to their performances, including the right to make phonograph records. Stoki wasn't satisfied with that. 'I won't sign the deal,' he said, 'until you go to Philadelphia and make some kind of a royalty deal with the Orchestra Association.'" Johnson negotiated an additional 2.5 percent royalty for the association, and the album set was first released in 1957.

Johnson recalled that at the time, stereophonic sound was relatively new in households, and the album consequently caused quite a stir. "The fact that the sound followed the action on the screen created a ping-pong effect between the two stereo speakers,

Walt Disney's Christmas Concert marked the debut of Ludwig Mousensky and the All-Mouse Choir, a year before "The Chipmunk Song." (© Disney Enterprises, Inc.)

which proved to people that they really had stereo on their record player." The album was a steady best seller and was released in sixteen countries.

O

Walt Disney himself came up with the idea for the big 1957 Christmas record release. "You see," Walt told Johnson the previous summer, "there's this bunch of mice who live in the basement of a recording studio. They sing, they play instruments, and when everyone goes home at night they make records. We can use the sped-up voice technique we used for the mice in *Cinderella*." Johnson and Camarata set to work on *Walt Disney's Christmas Concert*, an extended-play 45-rpm release starring "Ludwig Mousensky and the All-Mouse Orchestra."

Jimmy Macdonald provided many (if not all) of the voices, drawing from his experience as Jaq and Gus in *Cinderella*. The EP com-

bines familiar holiday music with short comic introductions featuring the some-times-unruly musicians and Ludwig (whose accent drops in and out). Achieving the proper sound required some recording studio technical know-how. Camarata explained how this effect was obtained: "The established tempo at which the orchestra was recorded was at one-third the 15 IPS [inches of tape running through the recording machine per second]. The orchestration was pitched one-third lower than the original key, so that it would return to the original key when played at 15 IPS." He continued, "Most of the voices were overdubbed at the 7½ IPS speed, in the orchestra key, while others were done in natural falsetto by Gloria Wood. The choice of the key and the tempo at which we recorded was determined by breaking down the 15 IPS speed into increments of three." The album included an illustrated story

Thurl Ravenscroft: He's Grrrreat!

The bass singer with the deeper-than-deep voice actually had several separate careers going at the same time as part of a group, as a soloist, and as a character voice.

Thurl Ravenscroft was born in Norfolk, Nebraska. Although he originally planned to enter the art field, his marvelous singing voice soon led him in other directions, and in 1937 Ravenscroft and three other singers formed the Sportsmen Quartet. Ravenscroft sang bass with the Sportsmen during their early appearances on radio's *Jack Benny Program*, but when he enlisted in the military in 1942, another singer filled his spot in the quartet for the duration.

Returning to Hollywood after all the shooting was over, Ravenscroft found that the Sportsmen were doing just fine without him, so he formed a new quartet known as the MelloMen. In this capacity, Ravenscroft first began accumulating his numerous Disney credits. After singing in *Alice in Wonderland* (1951) and *Lady and the Tramp* (1955), the MelloMen were enlisted for the first Mickey Mouse Club records, and after Disneyland Records was formed, the group performed on many of the label's LPs.

Ravenscroft was first heard solo in some of the Mickey Mouse Club recordings (most notably "The British Grenadier"), but he really came into his own as a narrator in the late 1950s. His warm tones could convey a startling range of attitudes: straightforward, as in *Songs of the National Parks* (1958); whimsical, as in *All about Dragons* (1966); or humorous, in various *Winnie the Pooh* LPs of the 1960s (on which his performances as Eeyore were arguably funnier than the film voices). His bass reached a chilling level in the more somber LPs *Pirates of the Caribbean* (1967) and *The Haunted Mansion* (1969). In the Haunted Mansion theme park attraction, he is seen and heard as one of the singing graveyard busts.

Disney was not the only studio to recognize Ravenscroft's talents. In 1952 he became the official voice of Kellogg's Tony the Tiger, shouting "They're Grrrreat!" in Frosted Flakes commercials for the next fifty years plus. He sang on numerous popular recordings, including the Rosemary Clooney version of "This Old House" and "Where Will the Dimple Be?" He appeared on Johnny Mann's syndicated TV series, *Stand Up and Cheer*. Perhaps his most enduring television performance is the disdainful "You're a Mean One, Mr. Grinch" in Chuck Jones's 1966 animated special, Dr. Seuss's *How the Grinch Stole Christmas*.

Ravenscroft's Disneyland Records work became less frequent after the early 1970s, but his career forged on. He recorded a solo album for Light Records in which he performed famous gospel songs and related the stories behind them. After battling throat cancer in the 1990s, Ravenscroft held on to his marvelous vocal instrument, singing at Robert Schuller's famed Crystal Cathedral in Garden Grove, California, while continuing to record "Grrrreat" new Tony the Tiger dialogue. He died on May 22, 2005, at age ninety-one.

booklet by Disney story artist Bill Peet. It featured a backstory that claimed, "The engineers at Disneyland Records kept picking up faint musical strains on their ultra-sensitive equipment, and finally tracked the noises to the All-Mouse Orchestra, which was performing under a staircase in the basement."

Walt was disappointed in the finished product, saying, "I've never known a musician with a sense of humor." The public did not flock to buy the recording, and Johnson later reasoned that one reason for its tepid reception was that the recording never identified the performers as mice. Without looking at the record cover, it's hard to figure out just by listening to the album what the characters are supposed to be doing. Two other missing factors were catchy original songs and engaging character personalities, both of which were honed to perfection the following year by actor/composer Ross Bagdasarian, alias David Seville. "The Chipmunk Song (Christmas Don't Be Late)," on Liberty Records, won three Grammy Awards and was the fastest-selling record hit of the era. Walt never stopped ribbing Johnson about this misfire.

This holiday disappointment was only one

of many for Jimmy Johnson that year. After having started the year with a flourish, Disneyland Records was losing money by the fall of 1957. Al Latauska was trying to handle all the manufacturing and distribution, and his efforts were not garnering him favor with Roy Disney. As Johnson recalled a breaking point between Latauska and Disney, "Al and I were having lunch with [Roy]. We were talking about the deluxe *Fantasia* three-LP set. 'Never have listened to it,' Al volunteered. 'I don't listen to them, I just sell them.'" Johnson went on, "Roy hit the ceiling. 'You sound like every third-rate film salesman I've ever met in my life. You've got to have enthusiasm for your product and believe in it, or you're no good!'" Latauska left the company shortly thereafter, and Johnson assumed his duties. With his new responsibilities as national sales and production manager, Johnson traveled the country to learn more about the record business, and what he learned shocked him. Latauska had had a very overpriced, disorganized way of handling things. The mess had to be cleared up or Disneyland Records might be no more.

This direct mail advertising flyer from the early sixties offered Disneyland "Magic Mirror" Storyteller albums at a special price. The artwork is believed to be by the late George Peed, who worked on *Pinocchio*, *Fantasia*, and other films before his World War II service. As a freelance artist in New York, he created hundreds of Peter Pan record covers; designed *The Mighty Hercules* TV cartoon characters; and for Disney merchandise, he illustrated the recently reissued Disneyland Monorail Game and Babes in Toyland Game. He is the brother of Disney artist/children's author Bill Peet. (© Disney Enterprises, Inc.)

4

Annette to the Rescue

Disneyland Records was losing serious money by the end of 1957, but it wasn't for lack of trying.

As production costs climbed, a way for music producers to avoid domestic musicians' fees was to record in Europe. Thus, Germany's Symphonie Orchester Graunke performed for its first Disneyland Records release, Ferde Grofe's *Grand Canyon Suite*. It served as the soundtrack for Walt Disney's live-action nature short, *Grand Canyon*, which would accompany the yet-to-be-released *Sleeping Beauty* (also with a music score recorded in Berlin). Many albums of this kind would follow.

O

On the American side of the Atlantic, readers of the December 1958 *Family Circle* magazine were treated to a spectacular twelve-page illustrated poem, "A Christmas Adventure in Disneyland," which was designed to tie into Disney records. The verse was written by animation legend Dick Huemer, a top story artist who had migrated to Disney from the Fleischer studio. Among his many other credits, he had teamed with Joe Grant on *Dumbo* (1941). By the time Huemer created "A Christmas Adventure," he was a writer in Disney's comic strip department with two Disney children's record adaptations to his credit, *Snow White and the Seven*

Longtime Disney animator and gag man Dick Huemer wrote the original script for *A Christmas Adventure in Disneyland.* (Courtesy of Richard Huemer Jr.)

Dwarfs for Decca and *Adventures in Music: Melody* for RCA.

Huemer's verse for *Family Circle* follows two children who are magically transported to Disneyland on Christmas Eve. Maniacally chauffeured by Mr. Toad, they visit the unique Christmas trees in the various park lands. The story turns out to be a dream, but the children wake to find a note from their dad on their Christmas tree: they are going to spend Christmas day at Disneyland.

Though the complete musical Storyteller album of this poem would not be available until the following year, a 45-rpm EP called *Christmas Trees of Disneyland* was promoted at the end of the *Family Circle* magazine feature. The four original songs by Huemer and Tutti Camarata include "Storybook Land

Christmas Tree," describing lights made of sprites, "all personal friends of Tinker Bell"; the Adventureland "Jungle Tree," in which the animal kingdom gathers in peace around a tropical tree; and the Tomorrowland "Futuristic Tree," which resembles a rocket ship with "fingers pointing at the moon."

The most inventive and bizarre song comes from Fantasyland, where the witch in Snow White's dark ride (Gloria Wood) cackles "Jingle Bones" with her cronies in a twisted Christmas celebration (a precursor of sorts to Tim Burton's dark 1993 stop-motion feature for Walt Disney Pictures, *The Nightmare before Christmas*). These four songs, like the Jiminy Cricket holiday songs and All-Mouse Orchestra selections preceding them, were repeatedly repurposed in subsequent Disneyland Records Christmas compilations.

Also making its debut in 1958 was the song "From All of Us to All of You," first heard in a perennial *Disneyland* TV holiday collection of film clips. Penned by Paul Smith and Gil George (a pseudonym for Disney Studio nurse Hazel George), the Disneyland Records version of the song is performed by Cliff Edwards, with Jimmy Macdonald as Mickey Mouse and a particularly imbecilic-sounding Goofy.

Disney's first holiday LP, *Mickey Mouse's Christmas Surprises*, combined selections from all of these previous sources. It was issued on the Mickey Mouse Club label, although no Mouseketeers or club songs are included (not even "The Hap-Hap-Happy Snowman" from *The New Adventures of Spin and Marty*). The cover art depicted Santa Mickey in a sleigh pulled by Bambi.

Disneyland Records even touched on the sacred music market with *Jimmie Dodd Sings His Favorite Hymns*. Backed by organist Paul Pease and a children's choir directed by Ken Wilson, the album contains well-known hymns as well as original Dodd compositions such as "Do What the Good Book Says." "For me, this album represents the fulfillment of a long-cherished personal desire," Dodd wrote in the liner notes. "I am deeply grateful for having been privileged to see it become a reality."

○

One of the last albums in the Disneyland WDL series was *Songs of the Shaggy Dog* (1959), consisting of upbeat tunes including "Shaggy Dog Shag" and "C'est Chiffon" (a parody of the then-popular "C'est Si Bon"). They were linked by commentary from the Shaggy Dog himself, given a lovably gruff characterization by the legendary voice actor Paul Frees in his Disneyland Records debut. One of the film's stars, Roberta Shore, was featured as was Fred MacMurray on the saxophone. A booklet inside the album shows Shaggy signing his "recording contract" with Jimmy Johnson.

These fine recordings were not enough, however, to pull Disneyland Records out of its downward spiral between 1958 and early 1959. The little organization was struggling to survive in a music world that was changing so fast that even the major labels were treading water. These events couldn't have come at a worse fiscal time for Roy and Walt Disney. The studio was experiencing losses in grosses. Theme park and TV and movie projects were eating away at the budgets, and animation was becoming ever more expensive and time-consuming. "Walt was angry at the money we were losing in the record business," wrote Johnson. "He reasoned that he could make better use of the money in motion pictures and television. He suggested to Roy that we should take our losses and get out of the record business."

Walt had a remarkable instinct for knowing when a project needed to be trimmed or

Gloria Wood: Her Voice Was Every-where. Even Elvis's Truck

Whenever Americans enjoyed television, radio, and records from the 1940s to the 1970s, they usually heard Gloria Wood.

She was born in Medford, Massachusetts, into a musical family. She and her sister, Donna, joined cousin Virginia to enter show business in 1935 as the Glor-Vir-Don Girls. Gloria Wood made her first records with the Clyde Lucas Band and then moved to other bands before joining the Don Juans vocal group, which also included her brother, Chandler, and a young actor/singer named Art Carney (years before he played Ed Norton on *The Honeymooners*). They toured with the Horace Heidt band.

Donna was featured soloist until her health began to fail, Chandler went into drive-in movie theater management, but Gloria kept singing on numerous radio shows with such stars as Alan Young, Eddie Cantor, and Red Skelton. In 1946, she joined Kay Kyser's Kollege of Musical Knowledge band. Her solos included "On a Slow Boat to China," "Managua, Nicaragua," and the Academy Award–nominated "Woody Woodpecker Song." Wood recalled performing the song on Oscar night. "I was very loose and relaxed in that uptight atmosphere and danced up such a storm, I got the biggest ovation of the night. If they had voted that night, I would have won!"

Big band singing eventually took a back seat to commercial jingles and TV theme songs. Wood's four-octave range saw her through decades of constant work, from "Rice-a-Roni, the San Francisco treat," to *Dobie Gillis*, *Batman*, and *77 Sunset Strip*.

As a member of Jud Conlon's Rhythmaires, Wood sang regularly on Bing Crosby's radio program and for movies, including Disney's *Alice in Wonderland* and *Peter Pan*, for which Conlon served as vocal arranger. For Disney's record label, Wood led a choir for *Carousel* and

The Happy Wanderer in Europe albums. She can also be heard on *Little Gems from Big Shows*, *Songs from "Annette" and Other Walt Disney Serials*, *Holidays with the Mouseketeers*, and *Tinpanorama*. She did all the speaking roles for *A Christmas Adventure in Disneyland* (1958). Wood sang backup for Annette Funicello in a group sometimes called the Afterbeats and sang the initial vocal track for each song as a tone and pitch guide for Funicello. Wood performed her Disney single, "Ching, Ching," on Dick Clark's *American Bandstand*. Hayley Mills, for whom Wood sang guide tracks, also recorded the tune.

In 1953, a racy Capitol single, "Hey, Bellboy," combined jazz trumpeter Pete Candoli and Wood, who imitated musical instruments, scat sang, and cooed, "Hey, bellboy." The record became an underground sensation; disc jockeys and beatniks loved it. "They banned it in Boston," Wood recalled, "and here I was, a hometown gal." A young Elvis Presley heard the song while driving a truck in Memphis. He played the record so much he bought nine copies. Years later, Gloria sang in *Blue Hawaii* and *King Creole*. The latter film was to include a Presley/Wood duet that was cut from the final version, but the two became friends, with Presley throwing a party for Wood at which they exchanged teddy bears.

Wood sang offscreen vocals for numerous Hollywood stars, including Vera-Ellen in *White Christmas* (1952), and filled in challenging notes for Marilyn Monroe in *River of No Return* (1954) and Lucille Ball in *Mame* (1974).

By the mid-1970s, as a new generation was enjoying the reissue of *A Christmas Adventure in Disneyland*, diabetes slowed Wood's career. She spent her final years with her family and husband of thirty-five years, singing occasionally until her death in 1998 at age seventy-five. She left a volume of work few performers could match. "Sure, I was the girl behind the scenes," she said. "But I made a lot of money, used my talents, and had a wonderful life. I had many thrills because, as you know, my voice was everywhere."

cut completely. Animated scenes that were labors of love for Disney artists were cut to improve overall film flow. Entire films in development or even in production could be shelved or permanently halted if Walt sensed they were going nowhere. Now the plucky little record company bearing his name faced the same fate. In 1959, Jimmy Johnson needed to make some big marketing changes fast.

One of the first moves was to halt promoting Disneyland Records as adult products. Stores often placed the discs in children's record bins anyway, so a revamped line of Disneyland children's records was designed to be sold in supermarkets, toy stores, and five-and-dime shops. Some albums were shortened and aimed squarely at kids with new artwork by animation background artist Al Dempster, among others. The $4.98 retail prices were reduced to $1.98. Back cover LP advertising boasted of "Disney's Big Home Entertainment Value." The letters *DQ* preceded the catalog numbers on these albums, standing for "Disney quality" at affordable prices. This marketing strategy remains Disney's most successful and unmatched. "DQ" versions of *Pinocchio*, *Bambi*, and *Dumbo* sold well enough to remain in 1959 packaging for the following two decades. Also beginning that year, there were two kinds of Disneyland Storytellers: book and record sets retailing for $3.98 and single albums without books for $1.98. Reinforcing their new status as quasi-toys, some of the LPs of this period had wipe-off coloring book–type art on the back covers, giving kids something to do while listening to the album.

Darby O'Gill and the Little People (1959) was the first Storyteller LP without a book. Adapted from the live-action film, the LP was dramatized with a studio cast featuring Arthur Shields and J. Pat O'Malley. It also included a short soundtrack snippet of a young Sean Connery singing "Pretty Irish Girl" with costar Janet Munro.

Some remaining "adult" non-Disney titles received a reprieve thanks to a second in-house Disney record label created in the spring of 1959. Buena Vista Records was named after the street in Burbank where the Disney Studio still sits. Years earlier, Roy had dubbed his film distribution company Buena Vista because the name was more generic and might come in handy when the Disney name needed to be omitted from complex or contentious business situations. Roy also originally planned for the studio to release non-Disney films under the Buena Vista banner, but only a few came about, including 1959's *The Big Fisherman*, starring Howard Keel.

Buena Vista Records would remain family-friendly, but most discs would not be Disney-branded, with many aimed at more mainstream tastes. To help introduce the Buena Vista brand, the company released a highly eclectic sampler album of selections, *A Musical Kaleidoscope: A New Vista in Entertainment*, that combined teen pop, lush instrumentals, show tunes, big band jazz, country/western, and even accordion music.

The first true Buena Vista album, released in June 1959, was a studio cast version of the Bing Crosby film *Say One for Me*, featuring Roberta Shore, Tony Paris (who months earlier had crooned on the live *Date Nite at Disneyland* LP) and frequent Disney movie and TV narrator Rex Allen (who eschewed his traditional cowboy style for a smooth, Crosby-esque sound). The score of *Say One for Me* was a curious meeting of old school music with the emerging teen pop sound. It was the shape of things to come, as the teen and pre-teen market took hold of the music industry.

This timing was perfect for Buena Vista's major recording star, Annette Funicello, whose self-titled first album was released on the Disneyland label in 1958. The only person with misgivings about her singing career was Funicello herself. In her autobiography, *A Dream Is a Wish Your Heart Makes*, she wrote about the day Walt Disney told her about her impending recording contract:

> "But Mr. Disney," I replied politely, my voice surely betraying a hint of panic, "I don't sing. You *know* I don't sing."
> "Well, the public out there likes your voice a lot," he said, "and I want you to do more."

Disney introduced her to Camarata, who, she recalled, "took me into the recording studio and led me step by step through the entire process. I was extremely nervous, yet he put

Roberta Shore: A Sweet, Old-Fashioned Girl

Many a *Mickey Mouse Club* fan recalls singer/actress Roberta Shore as snobby Laura Abernathy in the *Annette* serial. She had the unthinkable task of acting mean to America's Sweetheart. In reality the two were good friends, both making their movie debuts in *The Shaggy Dog* (1959). "Annette and I did a lot of touring together when she had her records," Shore said. "She was a sweetheart."

While Funicello was relatively new to show business, Shore had been a TV veteran since age ten. Born Roberta Jymme Schourop in San Gabriel, California, she changed her last name to Shore during her tenure on the *Tex Williams Show*, broadcast live weekly from Knott's Berry Farm, but continued using Jymme as her first name. A year later she became a regular on a popular children's program, the *Pinky Lee Show*. "Every day I would sing songs," she recalled. "Then when he went to a circus format I was the ringleader. Pinky's show was Number 1, but the *Mickey Mouse Club* knocked him off the air."

Deemed too tall to be a Mouseketeer, Shore nevertheless made numerous *Mickey Mouse Club* appearances. She debuted on Talent Roundup Day, singing the Teresa Brewer hit "Old Fashioned Girl." Shore idolized Brewer, re-creating her distinctive squeak, a vocal effect Shore would repeat on subsequent Disney records. She was soon appearing alongside the Mouseketeers at Disneyland (including the 1955 grand opening), performing voices for animation, and even filling in "scream sounds" for Annette. Shore's inclusion in studio promotional material led to another name change. "When the studio would send out information without a picture, 'Jymme Shore' ended up referred to as a he," she explained. "Walt Disney actually was the one who suggested I use the name Roberta."

For the fledgling Disney record labels, Shore sang on the *Songs of the Shaggy Dog* LP; the first Buena Vista LP, *Say One for Me*; and several singles. For another label, music coach Sy Miller asked her to be the first to record a new song he had co-written, "Let There Be Peace on Earth."

Though Disney was her favorite studio, Shore made her way to the soundstages of *Maverick*, *Wagon Train*, and *Father Knows Best* and played the part of Ricky Nelson's girlfriend on *The Adventures of Ozzie and Harriet*. Her three-year stint as Betsy Garth on *The Virginian* included a Decca LP record with costar Randy Boone. She laughed about an appearance she made with Nancy Davis and Ronald Reagan on *Fireside Theater*. "I was supposed to slap him across his face. He said, 'Slap me as hard as you can,' so I did, and it loosened his bridge! That's my claim to fame with Reagan!"

An adept yodeler, Shore was invited by Disney Imagineers to yodel for a project they were working on. "I remember seeing plans, but it was all still under construction. Years later, I bought the sound track album of *It's a Small World* for my kids. When the Switzerland part came on, I realized it was *me* yodeling!"

Shore retired from performing after *The Virginian*. Raised in the Mormon faith, her values were strictly family-based. Now a Salt Lake City, Utah, resident, she is a manufacturer's representative for furniture, a business she learned from her late husband. "I'm just basically a mom," she said. "I still sing in church and at home. But I can't yodel, and the squeak went away years ago." She keeps in touch with her former cast mates and looks back fondly. "Hopefully my kids and grandkids will be able to watch shows like the *Mickey Mouse Club* and get a kick out of them. Annette and those other kids were all great."

me at ease with his gentle direction and good humor. It was a wonderful experience until I heard the playback of my voice. . . . This is a *disaster*, I thought to myself." Camarata did not use such harsh terms, but he did realize some assistance was needed. In his words, "After recording Annette's voice on a single track, I knew we had to do something to 'fatten up' her voice, as it was quite thin and hardly registered on the console meter," he related. "Echo alone did not seem to make enough of a difference and after many experiments, I decided that we needed an overlay of a *second* Annette voice." Camarata continued,

I then asked Annette if she could sing over her first track. She not only agreed but incredibly sang in perfect sync with the first track! This gave me the opportunity to leave her first voice sans echo and to add much echo to the second, thus preserving the presence and surrounding her with a big, round sound.

In the course of these experiments, our sound engineer, Charles de la Fuente, became totally exasperated and walked out. But a young second engineer named Doug Nelson (who later became chief engineer for NBC) asked me, "Mr. Camarata, is this what you want?" He then switched on the high-end [equalizer] and boom! the "Annette Sound" came to life.

"As long as I had those echo chambers behind me," Funicello later told the Disney Channel, "I felt very confident."

❍

The rise of Funicello's career awarded the Disney studio another highly precious

Annette Funicello:
The One You Can't Forget

No one was more surprised to become a household name than Annette Funicello. Her middle-class family had moved from Utica, New York, to California, where the shy young girl was enrolled in a local dance school. Walt Disney was in the audience during one of her recitals, and Annette became the last Mouseketeer selected. She had an inexplicable something that appealed to the home audience. Huge piles of fan mail propelled Funicello from the back row to front and center.

Annette was the first nonfictitious entity that the Disney Studios extensively marketed and merchandised. There were paper dolls, mystery novels, and other Funicello items, but her records had the most important impact on the company fortune. With Jimmy Johnson's business acumen and Tutti Camarata's musical vision, Funicello recorded a parade of best-selling Disneyland and Buena Vista records, including some LPs that played off her first name. "We started a series of albums. The first was *Hawaiianette* and the second one was *Italiannette*, and then we came out with *Dance Annette*," she recalled in an interview, "And somebody said, 'Why don't you do a *BassAnnette*, or a *KitchAnnette*? You know, we got kinda crazy with the whole thing! But it was fun and they worked. Some good songs came out of those albums, too."

In addition to vinyl, she starred in precursors to today's music videos. Coin-operated devices installed in music stores and soda shops played short films with hit songs. One film, "Rock and Roll Waltz," featured an appearance by Funicello's parents, Joe and Virginia.

The Sherman brothers came to Walt Disney's attention because they had written numerous Annette Funicello hits, including "Tall Paul" and "Pineapple Princess." This led them to *Mary Poppins*, a blockbuster of such magnitude it helped to finance the construction of the Walt Disney World resort. It may be a stretch, but to paraphrase a famous Walt quote, "It was all started by Annette."

Funicello never had any illusions about her capabilities as a singer. She commented, "After each song kind of made the charts, made some noise, I thought, How much longer can this go on? *I don't sing!*" This modest, unassuming attitude furthered her appeal. After her big-screen debut in *The Shaggy Dog*, she did three more Disney features before moving on to another iconic pop-culture entity, the beach party genre for American-International Pictures. Never abandoning her Disney roots, she sought Walt's approval on scripts and even her on-screen swimwear. While most were encouraged to refer to the studio chief as Walt, she always called him Mr. Disney.

"Annette was wonderful," recalled Tutti Camarata. "But she was very nervous when we started making her records. You can really hear her voice develop from album to album as

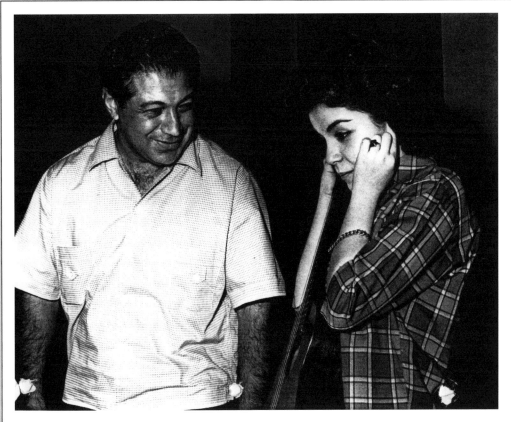

Annette Funicello credits Tutti Camarata as the force that shaped her successful recording career. (Courtesy of Paul Camarata)

she gained confidence." By the time her last Disney-produced album, *Something Borrowed, Something Blue* was released in 1964, Funicello was trilling with a vibrato.

Funicello semiretired from show business in the late 1960s to devote her time to children and family. She made occasional appearances on TV shows, including the *Mouse Factory* (1972) and the *New Mickey Mouse Club* (1977). She developed a line of collectible teddy bears and even a cologne. But by the time she reunited with costar Frankie Avalon in *Back to the Beach* (1987), she was beginning to experience the first signs of what turned out to be multiple sclerosis. Despite her illness, Funicello has continued to make appearances, written an autobiography, and fought for a cure for the disease. In 1993, she established the Annette Funicello Fund for Neurological Disorders at the California Community Foundation. Her valiant efforts continue.

For more information on the fund, visit www.calfund.org/8/giving_funicello.php.

Richard M. Sherman and Robert B. Sherman began their legendary Disney music careers by composing songs for Annette Funicello. (Courtesy of Richard M. Sherman)

Opera star Mary Costa, the voice of Sleeping Beauty on the first Disneyland Record nominated for a Grammy. (Courtesy of Jim Hollifield)

treasure in the form of Richard M. Sherman and Robert B. Sherman, two songwriters hired to create her pop songs. The Shermans crafted tunes that perfectly captured Funicello's personality and musical range. The Shermans also suggested the voice overlay that created the "Annette sound," a technique that they had previously used with some other singers' work. "They had written a song, 'Tall Paul,' on which a record had been made by another former Mouseketeer, Judy Harriet," Johnson explained. "It got a lot of airplay but didn't sell too well. We felt it was the right material for Annette." When Funicello's first solo album was reissued under the Buena Vista Records banner, "Tall Paul" sold 700,000 copies and hit Number 7 on the pop charts.

Another of Funicello's composers was pop idol Paul Anka, who wrote his hit "Put Your Head on My Shoulder" for her while the two were romantically involved. The couple shared the cover photo on her second album, *Annette Sings Anka*. A tad edgier than Funicello's other efforts, this album of Anka songs included "It's Really Love," which became the instrumental "Johnny's Theme" for the *Tonight Show Starring Johnny Carson* in 1962.

The record company's outlook was further brightened when *Sleeping Beauty* garnered Disney's first Grammy nomination as best soundtrack album of 1959. Even though Columbia's *Porgy and Bess* LP took the award, Disneyland's nomination was a sign that the label was at last a viable contender in the recording industry.

Somewhat surprisingly, virtually no Disneyland Records up to this point had starred the studio's signature characters except for brief appearances on the early Official Mickey Mouse Club Records. That was remedied in 1960 with *Donald Duck and His Friends*, a sing-along album hosted by Cliff Edwards as Jiminy Cricket. This album is decidedly low-budget, with little or no musical accompaniment, but the cast of actors involved makes it truly special. It is one of the few early Disneyland recordings with Clarence "Ducky" Nash as Donald. Jimmy Macdonald returned as both Mickey Mouse and Goofy.

Two gifted artists made their Disneyland Records bow as the sped-up voices of Chip 'n' Dale. Chip was voiced by veteran radio and animation actor Dick Beals, famed as the voice of Speedy Alka-Seltzer in hundreds of television commercials. For Hollywood solo singer Robie Lester, playing Dale was the beginning of a highly prolific career with the label.

Perhaps the most significant character appearance on the album was that of Uncle Scrooge McDuck. As voiced by Dal McKennon, it was the first time anyone had ever heard a voice attributed to the lovable tightwad. Scrooge had originated in Disney comic books, which, like records, took up little of Walt Disney's time and attention. "I never had any comment from him at all," Scrooge creator Carl Barks said of Walt in 1994. "I did not even know if anybody at Disney was reading those stories; [however], in recent years they have been giving me credit for a lot of that stuff and treating me as if I had done a big favor to the studio in inventing all those characters." Quite naturally, Scrooge received a Scottish burr, first by Dal McKennon in *Donald Duck and His Friends*, later by Bill Thompson in Scrooge's big-screen debut in 1967's *Scrooge McDuck and Money*, and beginning in 1974 by *Mister Ed* star Alan Young, whose authentic Scottish accent gives vocal life to Scrooge in current productions.

The songs on *Donald Duck and His Friends* are interrupted briefly by Scrooge's little story. Scrooge builds a rocket ship to

Sy and Jill Miller wrote the inspirational "Let There Be Peace on Earth," which was recorded for Disneyland Records by actor Jordan Whitfield. (Courtesy of Robie Lester)

transport his immeasurable fortune to the moon to keep it safe from the Beagle Boys (also created by Barks). After the money blasts off, Jiminy Cricket reminds Scrooge that he is now broke. "Oh, no! I never thought o' that!" gasps Scrooge, who confidently adds, "I'll now have ta go ta work and earn my millions all over again!"

O

The Scrooge segment, retitled *Donald Duck and Uncle Scrooge's Money Rocket*, was one of the first twelve titles in the new Little Gem 45-rpm and 78-rpm singles series. Most Little Gems were edited selections from Disneyland LPs; indeed, five of the first twelve came from *Donald Duck and His Friends*. Other 1960 Little Gem releases lifted from LPs included "London Bridge" and "Here We Go Round the Mulberry Bush" from the Sterling Holloway *Mother Goose Rhymes* (although Holloway himself did not appear on these cuts). From *A Child's Garden of Verses* came Frances Archer and Beverly Gile's "Frog Went a-Courtin'" and "Fiddle Dee Dee."

The Little Gems' recorded content might have been available on LP, but the cover art was almost always created especially for each picture sleeve. "Clementine" features a painting of Donald and his nephews in the apparent glow of a campfire; "I've Been Workin' on the Railroad" depicts Mickey driving a miniature train. Disney characters often appeared on the sleeves but not on the records. "London Bridge" shows Donald Duck and Mother Goose playing the game with a little girl; "Rockabye Baby" features a peaceful scene of a sleeping Bambi and his mother; and "Frère Jacques" finds Mickey Mouse in full French painter's regalia in front of the Eiffel Tower painting a picture of a beret-clad Pluto. The records themselves feature a children's chorus and/or Archer and Gile.

These fast-selling Little Gems, the focused marketing of the DQ series, and the immeasurable appeal of Annette Funicello helped save Disney's record division from oblivion. Now with two up-and-coming labels, Camarata was able to continue his mix of classical, jazz, pop, and kiddie tunes, and Jimmy Johnson was able to keep the division's detractors at bay.

5

The Buoyant Days

Jimmy Johnson described the early 1960s as "buoyant days at Burbank." "The problems faded away as the Disney Studio entered one of its more creative periods," he wrote. "The fierce pressures of the fifties were relaxed and Walt and his people seemed to be enjoying their work much as they did in the early days at [the earlier Disney studio] Hyperion."

One of the studio's emerging stars was Hayley Mills, who had earned a special Academy Award for *Pollyanna* (1960), which was also released as a story album. For her next film, *The Parent Trap* (1961), Mills was marketed to her fans as a pop singer but was every bit as reluctant to assume that role as Annette Funicello had been. "I remember standing in the booth with her when we recorded 'Let's Get Together,'" Richard Sherman said of her *Parent Trap* session. "And she said "I really *cahn't* sing these you know, I'm not a singer.' I said, 'But everybody loves you. You're a talented, talented girl. Just be yourself and do it.' She said, 'Well all right.' She goes and sings, 'Nothing could be greatah, say hey alligatah!' and she was just uniquely special!"

The *Parent Trap* LP, combining studio versions of songs by Mills, Maureen O'Hara, Tommy Sands, and Funicello, with extra film themes arranged and performed by Camarata (including a new stereo version of his arrangement of the *Alice in Wonderland* title song), was nominated for the 1961 Best Soundtrack Album Grammy Award but lost to *West Side Story*.

Richard and Robert Sherman, now the studio staff songwriters, joined Johnson for lunches at the coveted "writers' table" in a studio executive dining area called the Coral Room. Throughout the 1960s, Johnson and company would enjoy dining with the likes of Fred MacMurray, Julie Andrews, Dick Van Dyke, Tommy Steele, Peter Ustinov, Dean Jones, and Karl Malden.

The studio's new, lighter mood helped inspire Johnson to add scriptwriting to his regular Disneyland Records duties. As he recalled, "I was buoyant, too, partially because the record company was now a profitable enterprise, but more because I was having so much creative fun with it. In the very early days of the company I used to pay writers to adapt the Disney films into storytelling records for kids. I began writing these scripts myself. I didn't get any extra money, or royalty participation for the job. But I had a whole lot of creative fun."

At the same time, the *Peter Pan*, *Alice in Wonderland*, *Snow White and the Seven Dwarfs*, *Bambi*, and *Cinderella* Storyteller records were revised, with new Disneyland Storyteller Ginny Tyler reinterpreting the original scripts. New album covers featured a "Magic Mirror," a die-cut oval in the front

Jimmy Johnson and his longtime assistant, Rose Mussi. (Courtesy of Grey Johnson)

Beginning in the early 1960s, Ginny Tyler became the Disneyland Storyteller on numerous LPs. (Courtesy of Ginny Tyler)

cover revealing a section of the first-page art. More Storyteller discs apparently were manufactured than covers were printed. Through the 1960s and 1970s, newly packaged versions of these titles contained either the original 1950s recording or a 1960s Tyler version, with no way to tell which one had been purchased until the needle dropped into the groove. Confusing listeners even more, a few records had different narrators on the A and B sides.

Tyler also narrated the Storyteller album version of *101 Dalmatians*, which was released to tie into the film's 1961 premiere. Even though the story was about a songwriter, the film had few songs, which may have influenced the decision to emphasize the story, instead of music, for records. Tyler tells the story from the viewpoint of puppy Rolly, with cast members Betty Lou Gerson and J. Pat O'Malley supporting her. The LP is distinctive for its brisk, classic radio-drama style, an expanded rendition of the Kanine Krunchies Kommercial by Teri York, and an alternate version of "Dalmatian Plantation" entirely different from the song used in the film.

○

All this new production necessitated more recording studio time. With his ever-increasing volume of projects and limited Los Angeles facilities to handle them, Tutti Camarata approached Walt about building such a studio on the lot. "Why would I want to own a [recording] studio?" Walt replied. "I'd rather be a client." Deciding to leave the security and camaraderie of a staff position was difficult, but Roy Disney helped convince Camarata to move on to his own business. "Roy told me I'd do much better on my own," Camarata recalled. "Looking back, I wouldn't have all that I have today if I hadn't listened to him."

Camarata opened Sunset Sound Recorders

Ginny Tyler: If I Could Talk to the Animals

For some, tale spinning is a family legacy. Such is the case with the original "Disneyland Storyteller," Ginny Tyler.

While Tyler was growing up in a Native American family near Seattle, her family passed along the storytelling craft as well as the imitation of birdcalls and other animal sounds. Tyler's uncanny ability to re-create these sounds first put her before a radio microphone in the 1940s. In 1951, Tyler joined KOMO-TV in Seattle with a daily children's show in which she was known as Mother Goose, but she was getting more and more off-screen work as a vocal performer. In 1957 Mother Goose flew south to Hollywood.

One of her first jobs was as Olive Oyl on Spike Jones's recording of "I'm Popeye the Sailor Man." More novelty records quickly followed, and in the early 1960s she was added to the Disneyland Records stock company of regular players. When the *Mickey Mouse Club* was reedited and packaged for syndication in 1962, Tyler appeared to Southern California audiences as the host of new segments, often taking viewers behind the scenes at Disneyland.

Tyler's record and cartoon work gradually moved from straight narration to character voices. For Disney, she played the two amorous female squirrels in *The Sword in the Stone*, even though one of the roles has been inadvertently credited to Martha Wentworth, who had recorded her dialogue before Tyler was called in to redo it. In the "Jolly Holiday" sequence in *Mary Poppins* (1964), Tyler sings as several barnyard animals. Tyler developed an especially vivid wicked witch, whose chilling cackle was heard often, including in the Snow White's Scary Adventures dark ride at both Disneyland and Walt Disney World.

For other studios, Tyler was Casper the Friendly Ghost in his 1963 TV cartoons, space damsel-in-distress Jan of *Space Ghost*, coquettish Flirtacia of *The Adventures of Gulliver*, and all the females in the first thirteen episodes of *Davey and Goliath*. Tyler's most ambitious film project was the voice of Polynesia the parrot, performing with Rex Harrison in *Doctor Dolittle* (1967). Along with frequent Disneyland Records co-star Dal McKennon, she provided most of the other animal sounds in the film. Her parrot squawks were also heard on episodes of Jack Benny's and Lucille Ball's TV shows. When not emoting for live or animated characters, Tyler kept busy with her own children's theater workshop, known as the Whimsey Works.

When Tyler's husband became ill, she retired from show business to care for him and subsequently returned to her native Seattle. While she has resisted offers to return to work in the Los Angeles area, she stays as busy as possible, occasionally finding time to record a voice or two for local productions.

The Disney days remain special to Ginny Tyler. She recalled to Pat Williams for his book *How to Be Like Walt*, "One day I was at Disneyland with Walt. I was going on and on about how perfect and beautiful the park was. As I was raving away to Walt how wonderful Disneyland was, he said, 'And that goes for my Disneyland Storyteller, too.' That was me. I have never felt prouder in my entire life."

on the corner of Sunset and Cherokee in Hollywood. At first, the new facility was almost exclusively devoted to Disney records. In effect, Camarata remained very much a key player in the creative end of Disney records, and Sunset Sound functioned almost as an extension of the Disney lot. Over the next decade, virtually every original Disneyland and Buena Vista recording was made at Sunset Sound. Disney film soundtracks were recorded, edited, and mixed there, and even master discs were cut at the small but growing facility.

○

At around this time, veteran Disney voice Sterling Holloway, under contract with the music division since 1957, did some of his best work for Disneyland Records. *Grasshopper and the Ants* is a prime example of Holloway's remarkable gift for characterization without vocal manipulation. The various personalities are defined by changes in tone, leaving no doubt as to Holloway's skill as an actor. The story is considerably elaborated from both its original source fable and the 1934 Silly Symphony short. Hop the grasshopper, besides living his indolent life and scoffing at the hardworking ants, is menaced by the appetite of Bubba the buzzard. Starving to death and about to freeze in the snow, Hop feebly calls out to a higher power for help, and instead of the expected *deus ex machina,* Holloway intones, "He looked up, and there in the sky—was Bubba." Only

Sterling Holloway narrated *Aesop's Fables* to an audience of youngsters who were offspring of Disneyland Records president Jimmy Johnson (Grey and Glenys) and studio producer/director Bill Walsh. (© Disney Enterprises, Inc.)

Sterling Holloway gave a marvelous comic performance on the 1961 LP *The Story of the Absent-Minded Professor.* (Courtesy of Will Ryan)

Teri York: A Bright and Sunny Forecast

Disneyland Records listeners know Teri York as the second cast soloist of *Babes in Toyland*, *Lady and the Tramp*, and *101 Dalmatians*, but her role as genial host of *Acting Out the ABC's* may provide the best audio glimpse into her performance as a TV weather forecaster, entertainment anchor, and commercial spokesperson. "I've had a very checkered career," York laughed.

Born in Fort Smith, Arkansas, York was such an impressive child singer that she was featured on Ella Allen's *Children's Hour* radio show broadcast on radio station KFPW from the Goldman Hotel. "Then we moved out to California when I was about ten or eleven years old," she recalled. "We had visited several times before, and I was a candidate for some of those children's spots in those early motion picture days."

During her last two years at Hollywood High School, class valedictorian York sang with a local band. "These men went on to great heights," York said of the band members. Most notable was pianist and trombone player John Williams, many years before *Star Wars* and other musical fame. York and company affectionately called him Curly because of his short, red hair.

After marrying and having children, York found herself doing club dates with Hollywood studio musicians and appearing on a TV show called *Polka Parade*. She also recorded countless demos to help songwriters pitch their work. "Two of the guys that I did a lot of demo records for were the Sherman brothers," she said. "They would submit these demos to Doris Day or other singers. When they became contract writers for Disney, they introduced me to Tutti Camarata. The next thing I knew I was being called in to do these recordings. The biggest highlight was doing 'He's a Tramp.'" Another standout was her vinyl version of the "Kanine Krunchies Kommercial," a spot-on spoof of radio ads of the period. "That was a fun thing to do," she said.

At the same time, York logged numerous on-screen TV appearances. Her stint as pitch-woman for Bond's Clothing led to her weather and entertainment roles on the highly rated KTTV News with iconic anchor George Putnam, whom Walter Winchell called the "Voice of Thunder."

York decided to put performing on the back burner and moved to Scarsdale, New York, for three years during the late 1960s before returning to Los Angeles. Her entrepreneurial flair took her into a variety of lucrative enterprises. York's Disney projects were her only commercially available records except for *Romance Returns*, an as-yet-unreleased two-CD set of romantic songs recorded in 1985 with renowned composer/conductor/pianist George Greeley. "George still wants me to sing," she smiled. "There's a time and a place, and we'll see when there's the time and the place!"

She has stayed involved with show business through her three children. Eldest daughter Kelly became an executive vice president at Norman Lear's Tandem Productions and is now with Warner Brothers. Son Gil is a photographer/designer married to the daughter of actor Ricardo Montalbán. Youngest daughter Tracy married *Hill Street Blues* star Ed Marinaro. "I have lovely people in my life," York said. "And the people I worked with are the crème de la crème. It was a privilege to be associated with them. We had a lot of fun!"

hearing the way Holloway could punch across such punch lines can convey their true elegance.

Best Stories of Aesop and *Animal Stories of Aesop* featured Holloway relating more fables to an audience of children, comprised mainly of Disney Studio employees' progeny, who were pictured with a toga-clad Holloway on the album cover. These children included Jimmy Johnson's son, Grey, and daughter, Glenys, plus others believed to be offspring of Disney producer Bill Walsh. Ginny Tyler, as a challenging little boy named Bobby, joins them on the recording.

Perhaps Holloway's comic masterpiece for the label was 1961's *The Story of the Absent-Minded Professor*, based on the Fred MacMurray film comedy. Rather than a straightforward retelling of the film, this LP assumes its own irreverent tone, heightened by Holloway's jaunty narration and a barrage of vocal effects by veteran actor Sam Edwards, running the gamut from snarls and sobs to chatters and screams. (Holloway had previously worked with Edwards when they voiced grown-up Flower the skunk and Thumper the rabbit, respectively, in *Bambi*, and the two men had become friends during military service in World War II.)

Holloway's Grammy-nominated title, *Mother Goose Nursery Rhymes*, again partnered the actor with a roomful of children.

The Vonnair Sisters sang on many LPs and singles between 1961 and 1963. Little else has been discovered about them.

One in particular was young Ann Jillian, on the Disney lot for her role as Bo-Peep in *Babes in Toyland*, Walt's first attempt at a live-action musical, intended as a modernization of the operetta with young singing stars.

"Some of Walt's production people plugged hard for a Warner Brothers recording artist," Johnson wrote. "Much propaganda was spread about the inability of our own Annette to handle the Victor Herbert tunes. Tutti and I had faith in Annette and couldn't stand the thought of the sound track album going to another label." The demo of Funicello singing "Just a Whisper Away" and "I Can't Do the Sum" helped convince Walt to give her the role. Singer/TV spokesperson Teri York provided solos to guide Funicello, and those

solos were then released on a second cast album of the score.

Production was problematic. As Johnson recalled, "The director kept telling Ray Bolger how to dance." The resulting film had its bright moments, but it more resembled a two-part Disney TV show than a theatrical film. No true *Babes in Toyland* soundtrack was ever released. Members of the original cast re-created the songs at Sunset Sound. The arrangements blended aspects of George Bruns's film versions with the Camarata touch. Similar orchestral tracks were created for the aforementioned "second cast" LP that included Bill Lee and Thurl Ravenscroft singing in place of Ray Bolger, with Ginny Tyler (Floretta) and Bob Grabeau subbing for Tommy Sands.

An interesting item that came out of all the merchandising for *Babes in Toyland* was a single on the Buena Vista label, "Goodbye to Toyland." Tutti Camarata composed the song by setting new lyrics about teenage romance ("You took my teddy bear / I cried and pulled your hair / We didn't know we'd fall in love") against a countermelody of Victor Herbert's "Toyland." All in all, it was an extremely complex arrangement that produced a catchy sound. The Vonnair Sisters were credited as vocalists on this single as well as on other Disney recordings from 1961 to 1963. According to sparse information that has surfaced, their real names were apparently Sonya, Sheila, and Renee Von Ever.

○

In the early 1960s, comedy albums reached a level of popularity comparable to that of music LPs. Bob Newhart, Bill Cosby, Vaughn Meader, and Allan Sherman were topping the charts. This could be what helped inspire Johnson and Camarata to produce an LP with an accent on humor, and an accent was responsible for much of the humor.

Paul Frees: The Voice Heard around the World

Unquestionably one of the giants of the cartoon voice industry, Paul Frees was in such demand and commanded such a salary that the always budget-conscious Disney recordings used him only sparingly. The infrequency of his record work merely serves to make the few examples of it stand out all the more.

Frees was born in Chicago and began his acting career after serving in the military during World War II. From all accounts, he seems to have entered the related fields of radio and cartoon voices at much the same time. In the late 1940s he became a regular on many of the popular radio series of the day (and even starred in one, the oft-forgotten *Green Llama*) while making his animation debut as the second half of Columbia Pictures' *Fox and Crow* series.

In the early 1950s he graduated to the classier cartoons of the MGM studio, where he made many appearances in the *Tom and Jerry* and *Barney Bear* series and worked alongside Disneyland Records regular Dal McKennon in a number of Walter Lantz cartoons. Frees also broke into records during this period, primarily on the delightfully daffy recordings of Spike Jones. Only Jones would have conceived of having Frees recite the lyrics to "My Old Flame" in a pseudo–Peter Lorre voice ("What was her name? I'll have to look through my collection of human heads!"). Appearing on Jones's radio show, Lorre remarked that Frees "sounds more like me than me!"

Obviously impressed with Frees's gift for mimicry, Jones kept him on call for future recordings such as the single "Popcorn Sack" and the LP *Spike Jones' Spooktacular*, on which Frees duplicated the delivery of not only Lorre but also Boris Karloff and Bela Lugosi, among others. Prominently featured was frequent Disney records performer Loulie Jean Norman as Vampira. For MGM Records, Frees headlined an album of pop songs as sung by movie legends, *Paul Frees and the Poster People*.

With all the studios that were using his talents, it would seem that Disney might have picked up on Frees's abilities sooner than it did. Although Frees auditioned as the White Rabbit and other characters for *Alice in Wonderland* (1951), he did not join the studio's cast of voice regulars until the end of the decade. His first Disney record work was in the LP *Songs of the Shaggy Dog* (1959); Frees also narrated the movie and made a rare on-screen appearance as a psychiatrist.

Most of Frees's animation work was with such revolutionary studios as Jay Ward's, where he was a mainstay of the *Rocky and Bullwinkle* series. The popularity of this new style of more sarcastic and hip animation was reflected in Disney's introduction of the manic Ludwig von Drake in September 1961. With Frees supplying the mad professor's Austrian accent, the von Drake episodes of the *Wonderful World of Color* TV series reached heights of satire and parody never previously attempted by Disney. This performance carried over into Frees's *Professor Ludwig Von Drake* album for Disneyland Records.

In addition to his limited but important work for Disney, many other roles kept Frees busy, including animated TV pitchmen Toucan Sam and the Pillsbury Doughboy and the UPA feature *Gay Purr-ee* (1962), in which he costarred with Judy Garland.

Frees worked for virtually every major cartoon company, including Rankin/Bass, for which he provided memorable voices for such holiday specials as *Santa Claus Is Comin' to Town* and *The Little Drummer Boy*. Scores of Disneyland and Walt Disney World guests hear him daily as the Ghost Host in the Haunted Mansion attraction.

In real life, Frees was reportedly as much a character as his animated counterparts. Considered something of an eccentric by his co-workers, he was a notoriously private man. In a rare 1980 Associated Press interview, Frees explained why he had deserted Southern California in favor of the San Francisco area. "If I were interested in the adulation of strangers, I would have remained in Hollywood and gone on camera," he said. "I avoided that because I value my privacy above all else."

Frees's final performance was as a dinosaur in the prologue to the animated George Pal tribute film *The Puppetoon Movie* (1987), in which he also made a cameo appearance as the voice of the Pillsbury Doughboy. By the time the film was released, Frees was already gone. He had died on November 2, 1986, at the age of sixty-six.

Professor Ludwig von Drake made his TV debut on the revamped Disney series, renamed *Walt Disney's Wonderful World of Color*, in September 1961, but that summer he starred in his own self-titled album. Side 1 is a comic dissertation about, by no small coincidence, the wonderful world of color, with original songs by the Sherman Brothers.

Side 2 is a set of sketches about the recording process that culminate in a "live" session with misbehaving musicians.

Paul Frees, as von Drake, veers from an already amusing script in various ad-libs and asides, including one message to the listener: "In case you're wondering why we made this record, forget it. It's here, you bought it, forget

Rica Moore:
To the Manor Born

Singer/composer Rica Moore lived the life of the fabled poor little rich girl. Her family's affluence flowed from Moore's grandfather, founder of a nationwide chain known as Thompson Cafeterias. Moore's mother was raised in a 125-room mansion built from the proceeds of these restaurants, and Moore was the youngest of four children. Her mother attempted to raise Rica and her siblings in the atmosphere considered appropriate for multimillionaires. Moore was sent to boarding school in Connecticut, where one of her classmates was future First Lady Jacqueline Bouvier.

About her exclusive upbringing, Moore said, "Grandfather built a lovely place for my mother when she got married. Our home was 'only' twenty-five rooms—of course, all the hot-and-cold running chauffeurs, gardeners, nurses, maids, and everything else. It was growing up with the gold spoon in the mouth but not having the heart and guts. It just didn't go down well with me at all."

Moore's mother was determined to make her youngest daughter a renowned musician. "Mother had great plans for me to become a concert pianist," Moore said. "I started lessons at age three. I was soloist with the Chicago Symphony Orchestra at the age of eleven. It was a very lonely life. I had to practice by myself. I performed by myself, being scared with all the people sitting there. I really didn't like it very much."

After high school graduation, Moore attended the American Academy of Dramatic Arts in New York, and in 1951 she signed a contract with Columbia Pictures in Hollywood. She appeared in *All Ashore* (1953) with Mickey Rooney and *The Iron Glove* (1954) with Robert Stack, but her movie career was superseded by her love of songwriting.

"In my spare time I wrote songs for my children," she said. "A friend of ours was a director at the Walt Disney Studios. He and his wife were over for dinner, and we got on the subject of children's songs, and he was saying that 'There are no good children's songs around now.' My husband piped up and said, 'Well, Rica's written some.' So after dinner it would only do that I sat down and sang and played a few. The next thing I knew, I was meeting Walt Disney and Tutti Camarata. That was a wonderful relationship that spanned eleven or twelve years."

Tiring of the competitive nature of show business, Moore stepped away as her children grew older. She began to breed and raise the cute little dogs known as papillons. Eventually, Moore and her beloved canines settled in Massachusetts, where she fought a valiant battle against breast cancer that later spread to her bones.

In a rare interview just a few years before her death, Moore said, "I feel I have had a good life. I never wanted for food or a home. I have had the advantage of meeting a lot of famous people, which has been fun. I am glad I am not in show business any more. It has changed, and I just wouldn't like it. I'm not the kind to try to hang on to my youth and read and re-read my yellowed press clippings." Moore died at age sixty-seven in 1996.

it!" (Some of Frees's more colorful ad-libs reportedly did not make it onto the album but have been preserved for private listening.)

Beyond von Drake's lampooned lectures, Disneyland also debuted a series of bona fide educational records about arithmetic, telling time, and other subjects. The first in this series was *Acting Out the ABC's*, a collection of instructional songs, rhymes, and games hosted by Teri York. Ginny Tyler returned as the impertinent Bobby, along with a group of children that included York's son and daughter, Gil and Kelly. "My son was such a cut up!" York recalled forty years later. "He just loved singing at the wrong time. He kept interrupting until they had to take him out of one of the sequences. He still remembers it today." Jimmy Johnson's son, Grey, sang and recited a number of selections, finishing the album with a memorable duet with Tyler in the "Animal Imitation Song." With Tyler so well versed in re-creating animal sounds, Grey Johnson remembered his performance as rather silly. "They told me to get up to the microphone and just repeat whatever animal sounds Ginny made. And she was such a professional at what she did that mine came out sounding pretty lame." Two mathematical primers soon followed, *Addition and Subtraction* and *Multiplication and Division*. Both are narrated by Cliff Edwards as Jiminy Cricket and were showcases for singer/composer Rica Moore, who received a Grammy nomination for *Addition and Subtraction*.

In *More Mother Goose*, Tyler teamed with Robie Lester for a unique performance of nursery rhymes with a wide variety of voices. The musical accompaniment for *More Mother Goose* was an eclectic departure from the traditional sound of earlier records. Though there was the occasional bright, traditional sound, more often the rhymes were backed by odd rhythmic patterns and jazz riffs associated with beatnik poetry of the period.

Similarly, Camarata chose top jazz musicians to play for *Best Loved Fairy Tales*. Moore narrated as the combo improvised, creating a somewhat daring sound for a children's

Billy Bletcher, who voiced Peg Leg Pete and the Big Bad Wolf, narrated *The Legend of Sleepy Hollow* and *Rip Van Winkle* for a 1963 LP.

Lucille Bliss narrated three stories on 1963's *Peter Cottontail and Other Funny Bunnies*. (Courtesy of Lucille Bliss)

disc. So different was the sound that disc jockeys played the stories on the air. Walt Disney heard one of the unusual stories on the radio and was so impressed, Camarata recalled, that he told the record staff, "We should have done something like that." They already had.

○

Nineteen sixty-two saw the reissue of the Disney favorite *Lady and the Tramp* (1955). Peggy Lee's participation in the original soundtrack had necessitated the release of its songs on a 1955 Decca Records disc that combined studio versions of Lee's solos with a few soundtrack excerpts. In 1962, Disneyland Records created a new version of the story and score to tie in with the film reissue.

The *Lady* Storyteller LP is a cousin to *101 Dalmatians*. Speaking voices include Ginny Tyler as Lady and Dal McKennon as Tramp, with baritone Billy Bletcher (best known as Peg Leg Pete and the Big Bad Wolf) as Trusty the bloodhound; singing voices are Teri York, Bob Grabeau, Robie Lester, and Marilyn Hooven. Lester's double-tracked harmony of the "Siamese Cat Song" became one of her most durable Disneyland performances, reused for years on numerous compilations and singles.

○

Peter Cottontail Plus Other Funny Bunnies and Their Friends, a collection of stories and songs, hit the stores in time for Easter 1963. Two of the stories, "Alice in Wonderland Meets the White Rabbit" and "Grandpa Bunny," are word-for-word readings of 1951 Disney-licensed Little Golden Books. Grosset and Dunlap originally published the third, "The Story of Thumper," in 1942, during the original merchandising campaign for *Bambi*; it too would be reissued as a Little Golden Book a few years after this recording appeared.

The stories have sparse music and no sound

Bob Grabeau: The Voice of Hollywood

The crooner of "Just a Whisper Away" and "Bella Notte" for Disneyland Records also happened to be one of the top demonstration artists in Hollywood, the first person to record such hits as "Love Is a Many Splendored Thing" and "The Shadow of Your Smile."

Grabeau began singing professionally at age fifteen, when he had his own radio show on KGO in San Francisco. After signing with Capitol Records, he toured the United States with the Jan Garber orchestra. His astonishing ability to mimic popular singers led to his demand as a demo singer and studio vocalist for major motion picture and TV music giants from Johnny Mercer to Henry Mancini. This talent almost caused a lawsuit when he imitated Nat King Cole singing "Nature Boy" for a film so accurately that Grabeau had to prove it wasn't Cole.

Grabeau especially excelled at re-creating the big band sound. Time-Life Records asked him to sing eight classic Glenn Miller songs on its best-selling *Swing Era* album set. Live big band revivals followed at concerts and dances throughout the western states. In the 1990s, Grabeau headlined the Glenn Miller Reunion Band Tour to packed houses in Australia and similar tours in California. By 1997 he was touring fifty-four U.S. cities with the Big Band Alumni Orchestra. A documentary film called *The Street of Dreams* was planned, featuring Grabeau as "the last of the big band singers" and numerous interviews with famous songwriters. After his third swing tour to Australia and New Zealand, however, Grabeau began showing signs of Alzheimer's disease and became unable to continue performing. He now resides in the Motion Picture and Television Hospital. The film was never completed.

"Bob was just the sweetest person," said Disneyland Records singing partner Teri York. "He was one of the best singers in the world."

effects, carried only by the energy and range of their narrator, Lucille Bliss. In Disney films, she was stepsister Anastasia in *Cinderella* and the supremely silly Kanine Krunchies jingle singer in *101 Dalmatians*; on television, she voiced the title character in the pioneering 1949 Jay Ward TV series *Crusader Rabbit* and much later played Smurfette in the 1980s Hanna-Barbera *Smurfs* series. For all practical purposes, Bliss's three stories sound much like "auditions" for what would emerge as Disneyland Records' series of See . . . Hear . . . Read Little LPs in 1965. The "Alice" text would eventually turn up again as part of the series, as would other Disney-licensed Little Golden Books.

The *Peter Cottontail* album is especially notable because it features the rarely heard alternate lyrics to "Peter Cottontail." Steve Nelson and Jack Rollins, who also wrote "Frosty the Snowman," wrote the familiar version that refers to Easter festivities as well as another, nonholiday version about Peter giving signals with his ears to warn the bunnies when the wolf approached. Choosing this version for the Disneyland album made it suitable for year-round play.

Another "themed" album using various recorded materials is *Chip 'n' Dale Chipmunk Fun*, tied together loosely by a railroad theme. Dick Beals continues as Chip, Robie Lester plays Dale and narrates two stories, and Clarence Nash is Donald Duck. Dal McKennon voices the vinyl debuts of Ranger J. Audubon Woodlore and one of the villainous Beagle Boys. Hardy favorites such as "I've Been Workin' on the Railroad" and "Casey Jones" are handled by the Jack Halloran Quartet, with Lester singing Mel Leven's "The Litterbug Song" from a 1961 Donald Duck cartoon.

Lester also narrated the title track of the *Little Toot* album, joined by Thurl Ravens-

Thurl Ravenscroft was heard singing such traditional sea chanteys as "Asleep in the Deep" on the *Little Toot* LP. (Courtesy of Tim Lee)

croft for a duet on the song. In addition to "Admiral" Ravenscroft's sea chanteys, which fill up side 2, the album contains two Chip 'n' Dale sailor songs that also appeared on the 1962 syndicated *Mickey Mouse Club*.

Though she most often narrated solo, a legendary cast joined Robie Lester for *Mickey and the Beanstalk*, which assembled most of the voice cast from the 1947 feature *Fun and Fancy Free*. Jimmy Macdonald is Mickey Mouse and the oafish Willie the Giant (played by Billy Gilbert in the film); Clarence Nash is Donald Duck; and for the first time on a Disneyland Record, Goofy is played by his original voice actor, Pinto Colvig. Colvig was no stranger to children's records, having made pop culture history as the original Bozo the Clown beginning in 1946, when the character was created for Capitol Records (many years before it was adapted for television).

○

Camarata continued to arrange, conduct, and produce Disneyland Records at his Sunset Sound facility, but 1963 also saw him take on his sole Disney feature film credit. *Summer Magic* was a modest family comedy starring Hayley Mills and Burl Ives. Not technically a musical, it featured several memorable Sherman Brothers tunes that Camarata arranged for the big screen. "He supervised the vocals and arranged the songs," Richard Sherman recalled, "but he didn't want to be closeted up in a room and writing to a moviola to score the picture." Camarata preferred the continuity of live orchestral music to the start-and-stop fragmentation of film scoring. "He just pulled away after arranging for Burl Ives and the others," Sherman continued. "It was [Camarata's] choice." Camarata's only other credited Disney film project is the Oscar-nominated Ludwig von Drake short *A Symposium on Popular Songs*, again featuring songs by the Sherman brothers.

He may have eschewed film scoring, but for the *Summer Magic* cast album for Buena Vista, Camarata outdid even himself. He arranged and conducted a sweeping, majestic studio version that sounds arguably more spectacular than the film soundtrack. One of the songs, "Ugly Bug Ball," was a chart-topper in England and some four decades later inspired a live stage show at Disney's California Adventure theme park. *Summer Magic* also turned up on the Disneyland label with a player piano performing the songs. Player pianos obviously occupied a soft spot in Jimmy Johnson's heart. When Disneyland opened in 1955, the Wonderland Music Store had also opened on Main Street, U.S.A., under his direction. The store sold Disney recordings from other labels until Disneyland Records (and later Buena Vista) came along, as well as sheet music and player piano rolls. The vintage player piano flanking the storefront attracted guests and Walt's warm compliments.

O

The first animated feature score Walt Disney assigned to the Sherman brothers was his Christmas 1963 release, *The Sword in the Stone*. The DQ LP of songs from that film is one of the shortest Disney albums, running just under fifteen minutes. The Storyteller album, however, is a much more grand affair. It is the first of the Disneyrama LPs: records packaged with a book of three-dimensional pop-up panoramas. The Disneyrama albums, which open up to four sections that can be joined in a circular display, also include *Dumbo, Pinocchio, Mother Goose Nursery Rhymes,* and *101 Dalmatians.*

The *Sword in the Stone* Storyteller took a slightly different approach than most other Disney story albums. Rather than using dialogue and music from the soundtrack (as on the *Peter Pan* Storyteller) or having a second cast reenact the story, the LP brought together virtually the film's entire original voice cast, re-recording their lines to suit an audio-only experience. The phonograph record performances of the major voice actors—Karl Swenson as Merlin, Martha Wentworth as Madam Mim, and Junius Matthews as Archimedes the owl—differ markedly from their film performances, no doubt because animated feature dialogue is usually done in completely separate sessions. The LP was done all at once, in the fashion of the old-time radio shows to which all of these veteran performers were well accustomed.

O

Throughout the early 1960s, Disneyland and Buena Vista Records continued to showcase new talent, such as versatile singer Billy Storm (the first African American to headline a Disney album), and introduce legends to young audiences, like the beloved Maurice Chevalier. Johnson and Camarata began at this time to reuse existing recordings in new compilations. Repackaging is a mainstay of

Cartoon voice artist Nancy Wible was heard in various roles on Disneyland Records' *The Prince and the Pauper* and *Hans Brinker.* (Courtesy of Nancy Wible)

A singing trio known as the Sylte Sisters (Deanna, Deanda, and Joan) was featured on 1963's *Teen Street* album. (Courtesy of Deanna Sylte Lucas)

all children's record labels. Music and stories are forever cobbled together under various themes with ever-changing cover designs.

Disneyland Records discovered that taking songs from early LPs and making such eclectic collections as *Western Songs for Children* and *A Rootin' Tootin' Hootenanny* could be a mother lode of additional profit. Mickey Mouse Club albums were reissued with non-Mouseketeer titles. *Holidays with the Mouseketeers* became *Happy Birthday and Songs for Every Holiday.* Thirty reissued *Mickey Mouse Club* songs were combined on a lengthy LP called *Fun with Music.* The strategy worked; *Fun with Music* and *Happy Birthday* sold for years longer than any other *Mickey Mouse Club* song albums.

Disneyland Records could now boast a children's catalog without total dependency on films and TV. The company had enough material to launch one of its greatest merchandising successes, marketing the record line by direct mail. This resulted in selling many more units than could ever be moved through retail outlets.

Even bigger success was literally in the wind.

6

Mary Poppins Blows Off the Roof

Nineteen sixty-four was a year of several breakout recordings, culminating with a big-screen soundtrack blockbuster. Early that year, Laura Olsher, who had performed her first Disneyland narrations for *The Little Engine Who Could* and *The Submarine Streetcar*, read the copy for a sound effects album that would become one of the company's biggest successes. She received the unexpected assignment at the tail end of a session for a completely different project. "I got a call from Jimmy Johnson one day, saying that Walt Disney wanted to meet with me." Olsher recalled, "So I had lunch with Walt Disney and he proposed a record teaching kids how to tell time, to be called *Learning to Tell Time Is Fun.*" Walt was clearly aware of the Grammy-nominated *Addition and Subtraction* recording by Rica Moore and Jiminy Cricket. Telling time requires viewing a clock, however, and Walt suggested that the record jacket be used for that purpose, with cardboard hands for the clock included. On the recording, Olsher referred to the numbers on the green and yellow halves of the clock face to make her points.

As the recording session for *Learning to Tell Time* ended at around 11:00 P.M. Johnson approached Olsher with an additional script. "I've been thinking about something," he said. "Wouldn't it be fun if we made a Halloween sound effects record?" "Sounds like

fun," Olsher agreed, "but not at this time of the night!" Johnson handed her the script and insisted, since everything was set up to record. A mere fifteen minutes later, Olsher had finished narrating the Disneyland record that would become the biggest sales success up to that point. Johnson had the idea of collecting sound effects from the studio library and editing them by theme, adding brief narrations for side 1. The resulting *Chilling, Thrilling Sounds of the Haunted House* LP was royalty-free, since Olsher received a flat fee and the sound effects already belonged to the studio. The LP sold millions for more than two decades, making clear profit.

A debate continues today as to whether this LP was intended as a tie-in with the Disneyland park's Haunted Mansion. The cover painting by frequent record cover artist Paul Wenzel was originally created as early

Laura Olsher provided the deep, foreboding voice narration for 1964's best-selling *Chilling, Thrilling Sounds of the Haunted House.* (Courtesy of Laura Olsher)

Laura Olsher: Chilling, Thrilling Sounds

Laura Olsher's role for Disneyland Records was that of narrator rather than a stock player. Set apart from her colleagues, she recorded several distinctive albums and one of the most successful children's records of all time, *Chilling, Thrilling Sounds of the Haunted House*.

Her background was in radio. During her days at Northwestern University in Evanston, Illinois (with classmates Patricia Neal, Charlton Heston, and Paul Lynde), Olsher began her acting career playing ingenue parts on the network radio programs that were still originating from the Windy City. (One of these shows was *The First Nighter*, starring Barbara Luddy, whose later Disney work included voicing Lady in *Lady and the Tramp*.)

After graduation in 1948, Olsher concentrated on her husband and children, moving to Southern California in 1958. Shortly after her relocation, Olsher happened to tune in a children's program on the local public radio station. "I had never heard anything so awful in my life," Olsher said. She promptly called the station to give them a piece of her mind. Instead of being offended or indifferent, the station invited her in to give them a true mother's views on their offerings, and before she knew it, Olsher was writing and producing five hours of children's radio programming per week. The novelty and prestige of noncommercial radio was sufficient to help Olsher cast her program with well-known actors from the industry. But on a fateful day when a Rudyard Kipling story was scheduled, none of the other actors were available. Olsher went on the air and performed all the roles herself, opening a whole new direction for her career.

Signing with the well-known voice talent agent Jack Wormser, Olsher was soon making the rounds of the cartoon studios. One of her best-remembered TV voices is Mrs. Cratchit in 1962's *Mister Magoo's Christmas Carol*, distinguished as the first animated holiday special ever aired on television. During Olsher's cartoon voice days, Disneyland Records also signed her to narrate and help write scripts, much as she had been doing in radio all along. She cemented her place in recording industry history by narrating the best-selling LP *Chilling, Thrilling Sounds of the Haunted House* (1964).

By the mid-1960s, Olsher became an acclaimed writer for the long-running daytime TV drama *Days of Our Lives*. She continues to write and teach and resides in Southern California.

The Wellingtons:
Just Sit Right Back and You'll Hear a Tale

The Wellingtons' story sounds like a fairy tale: they were performing at the famed Coconut Grove one night when Walt Disney spotted them and signed them to a contract.

There's more to the story. It starts in Champaign-Urbana, Illinois, in the 1950s, where George Patterson's mother organized nine-year-old best friends Dave Shaul, Todd Dawson, Jerry Sommerville, and her son as a quartet. Also blooming musicians, they were soon playing and singing at local parties, school variety shows, service clubs, and church functions. "In the eighth grade we discovered the Four Freshmen," said George Patterson. "We fell in love with their close harmonies. We went to hear them in concert. By the time we hit high school, we could sound like many of the pop groups and started trying to find our own sound. We made our spending money singing for dances and conventions."

Calling themselves the Continentals, they all attended the University of Illinois. During this period, Dawson and Sommerville left the group and were replaced by Rick Jarrard and Doris Miller. Miller subsequently left as well, and the remaining members added Kirby Johnson and decided to become serious as a male quartet. The group changed its name to the Lincolns, and with encouragement from Donna Conklin of the King Family, they eventually headed for Hollywood.

Ed Wade had replaced Shaul by the time the foursome were performing at an upscale party at famed conductor Alvino Rey's house, which led to their headlining at the Disneyland Hotel. Folk singer Terry Gilkyson, who later wrote "The Bare Necessities," heard them audition and introduced them to Dave Kapp, who recorded an album with them on his label. Their first recording session was "On Top of Old Smokey" with famed pianist Roger Williams. "It was a fantastic experience," Patterson said. "We were walking into United Recorders, and out walks Elvis and the Jordanaires."

With a Kapp LP under their belt, the group members were playing clubs, appearing locally on Sam Riddle's *Jukebox Saturday Night* TV show and nationally on the ABC series *Shindig*. Song and dance legend Donald O'Connor was taken with their version of the Irish folk song "The Minstrel Boy" and invited them to tour with him. His manager, however, thought the name Lincolns would not be popular in the South. Riddle initiated a name contest, but the group eventually came across the Duke of Wellington in the dictionary and took the name. Columnist Hedda Hopper wrote of their March 22, 1963, opening performance, "Donald O'Connor was magnificent. . . . Appearing with Donald were the Wellingtons, four handsome folk singers from the University of Illinois. Disney grabbed them to record for *Savage Sam* and *Miracle of the White Stallions*."

The four recorded *The Wonderful World of Color*, *Folk Heroes*, and *Annette on Campus* LPs for Disney. They did not actually work with Funicello until they recorded her "Merlin Jones" single. Many single versions of Disney songs followed, including "The Ballad of Davy Crockett," "A Whale of a Tale," and "Thomasina."

After Jarrard left the group and the O'Connor tours ended, the Wellingtons were asked to sing a theme song to a TV pilot that producer Sherwood Schwartz was pitching to CBS. The series was *Gilligan's Island*, and the song helped sell the show. The trio appeared on a memorable episode as a rock and roll band called the Mosquitoes, a thinly disguised parody of the Beatles and other mop-topped groups gaining prominence at the time.

Left to right: George Patterson, Kirby Johnson, and Ed Wade, better known as the Wellingtons

Ironically, the same type of pop group the clean-cut Wellingtons were spoofing actually supplanted their popularity by the mid-1960s. The Wellingtons were first to record "The Girl from Ipanema," but the label did not promote the song and it became a hit for Astrid Giberto.

After the group disbanded, Wade became a lawyer and Patterson became a family therapist. Kirby Johnson achieved fame as a noted arranger, but a lifelong struggle with asthma and stimulants caused his death in 2002. Wade and Patterson still see each other frequently. They have families now and lead very different lives from their show business days. They still enjoy recalling when they hobnobbed with the likes of Judy Garland, Sammy Davis Jr., Shari Lewis, and Stevie Wonder. Said Patterson, "It was a magical time."

concept art for the attraction. The LP was released in May 1964, shortly after the exterior of the Haunted Mansion was completed in Disneyland's New Orleans Square. However, it would be another five years before the Haunted Mansion opened to the public, and in the interim much tinkering and adjustment of the ride's contents occurred. If the *Chilling, Thrilling Sounds* record was intended to promote the new ride, it would have to stem from an earlier, much darker vision of the Haunted Mansion than the more comedy-oriented version that would eventually materialize.

Disney fans have enjoyed identifying the sources of some of the sound effects over the years. Many of them were originally created for humorous purposes, but out of their original context they become more terrifying. For example, a blood-curdling, drawn-out scream that modifies into a deep bass groan is actually a whimsical ghost yawning and stretching in the 1937 Mickey Mouse cartoon *Lonesome Ghosts*. A hissing, spitting catfight was previously heard in Pluto cartoons and the 1952 Donald Duck short *Trick or Treat*. Because of its more intense nature, this was the first Disneyland Record with a disclaimer: "This particular Disneyland record . . . is not intended for young, impressionable children from three to eight. It is intended for older children, teenagers and adults."

◯

Olsher provided a particularly emphatic narration for *Hansel and Gretel*, an album that combined story material with opera excerpts from an earlier release, *Great Operatic Composers*. Michael Donohue and Ann Jillian played the leads, with the remarkable Martha Wentworth as the Witch.

Born in 1889, Wentworth had made her name in radio drama by developing an old hag voice used often in such programs as *The*

Witch's Tale and the classic 1937 Christmas serial *The Cinnamon Bear*. She also put this voice to good use in animated cartoons, most notably in the 1941 Tom and Jerry entry *Fraidy Cat*. Avoiding being typecast as an old crone, Wentworth could also portray a rich dowager, appearing on-screen as such in several 1940s motion pictures.

Her Disney work dated back to her 1934 Mae West impersonation for the Silly Symphony *Who Killed Cock Robin?* In 1963 she voiced Mad Madam Mim for the film and record versions of *The Sword in the Stone*. She was seventy-five when she cackled for the *Hansel and Gretel* LP, doing so one final time for 1965's *The Scarecrow of Oz* before her death in March 1974.

◯

The 1964 New York World's Fair featured four extremely popular Disney attractions. Two of them made it to records: *Great Moments with Mr. Lincoln* and *It's a Small World*. *Lincoln* already had a narrative format, so the soundtrack could be put on disc intact. *Small World* required special care, which it received under the supervision of the creators of its maddeningly catchy song.

Richard M. Sherman and Robert B. Sherman came to Walt Disney's attention after they scored several hits for Annette Funicello in the late 1950s. The studio had lacked staff songwriters since Frank Churchill in the 1930s. But having writers on staff would make it more feasible to develop storylines around music, and Walt again sought that advantage, asking Johnson to seek both emerging and well-known songwriters. None of the recruits clicked until the Shermans came to Walt's office to pitch "The Strummin' Song" for Funicello's *The Horsemasters*, an episode of the Disney anthology TV series. On a busy Monday morning, the Shermans stood nervously in Walt's office for the first

The Sherman Brothers: Dynamic Duo

Extraordinary talent as well as involvement in Disneyland and Buena Vista Records enabled Richard M. Sherman and Robert B. Sherman to rise from pop songsmiths to the premier creators of original film musicals in the late twentieth century.

"The Sherman brothers came up through the record division, that's for darn sure," said Richard Sherman. "Without the record company—without Jimmy Johnson and Tutti Camarata—we wouldn't have ever gotten to Walt Disney. They could have just taken our one song ['Tall Paul'] and forgotten about us, as so many people do, and hired everybody else who was hot at the time to do songs for Annette. But they came back to us, which I think was the greatest break in the world."

Music had been in the Sherman family for generations. Their father was prolific composer Al Sherman, whose many popular tunes included "Pretending" for Bing Crosby and "There's a Harbor of Dreamboats (Anchored on Moonlight Bay)" for Frank Sinatra as well as "You Gotta Be a Football Hero." The elder Sherman challenged his sons to "write a song a kid would give up his lunch money to buy." It was a daunting task, interrupted by military service and stints with other collaborators, but the Sherman brothers reunited on such hits as "You're Sixteen" and "Tall Paul," which eventually took them to Disney.

As staff songwriters, the brothers were called on to create songs for Disney films and TV shows as well as theme park attractions and records. Their storytelling skills served them well, as their songs often drove the narrative. Their first film assignment outside Disney was *James Bond* producer Albert R. Broccoli's epic, *Chitty Chitty Bang Bang* (1968). The film has become a beloved family favorite, inspiring a hit stage version.

When Walt Disney died after production of *The Happiest Millionaire* (1967), the studio became less and less receptive to the Shermans' projects. The brothers worked on two more big-screen musicals for Disney before moving on: *The One and Only, Genuine, Original Family Band* (1968) and *Bedknobs and Broomsticks* (1971).

After scoring *Snoopy, Come Home* (1971) for Charles M. Schulz and *Charlotte's Web* (1972) for Hanna-Barbera, they tackled their first film screenplay with the highly successful *Tom Sawyer* (1973). Literate screenplays and scores followed for *Huckleberry Finn* (1974) and *The Slipper and the Rose* (1974). Also that year, their award-winning Broadway musical, *Over Here!* opened with the Andrews Sisters and a then-unknown John Travolta.

The Sherman brothers continued to create songs for various Disney projects, including several for the Epcot theme park and *The Tigger Movie* (2000). Their second Broadway show, *Busker Alley*, was curtailed by star Tommy Tune's leg injury, but hopes are high for its future. New audiences continue to embrace the Sherman brothers' work. *Mary Poppins* has conquered the musical stage, while new renditions of their songs and reissues of their soundtrack are popping up on CD.

Walt Disney was not one to lavish praise on his associates: his usual approval statement was, "That'll work." But near the end of his life, as he passed the Sherman brothers in a studio hallway, he uttered a rare compliment: "Keep up the good work, fellas."

Richard and Robert Sherman have certainly followed through.

time. Rather than discuss *The Horsemasters*, Walt enthusiastically described an entirely different film story that would become *The Parent Trap*. Jimmy Johnson, who had called the meeting, had to remind Walt about why the Shermans were there, and he subsequently approved "The Strummin' Song." Then Johnson suggested to Disney, "As long as the boys are here maybe you'd like to give them a crack at the songs for the Hayley Mills picture."

Walt liked the Shermans' *Parent Trap* songs and asked them if they had ever heard of *Mary Poppins*. He gave them some Poppins

The Sherman brothers hold a special ceremony to present commemorative plaques to Jimmy Johnson and Tutti Camarata in gratitude for their influence on Disney music. (Courtesy of Grey Johnson)

books and told them to look for musical possibilities. Two weeks later, they played "Supercalifragilisticexpialidocious" and "Feed the Birds" for Disney. When he and Johnson were alone, Walt said, "I like these boys. I think I can work well with them. I'd like to put them on the payroll, but they want too much money for staff songwriters. Your music company is going to benefit from all these great song copyrights they are sure to produce, so I think you should bear half their salaries." They were paid this way for their first year.

Walt asked the Shermans to write a round-style theme for "It's a Small World" after the original music concept for the attraction, various anthems from the countries, did not did blend together well. The resulting song worked perfectly. Since the attraction itself was more of a tour than a traditional story-line, the Shermans adapted the LP narration from promotional material by Marty Sklar of WED Enterprises (now called Walt Disney Imagineering, the department that creates Disney park attractions). Disney writer/producer Winston Hibler narrated in the style he had used for so many "True-Life Adventure" films. *It's a Small World* became the first full-length Storyteller LP based on a Disney theme park attraction.

Camarata produced a second *It's a Small World* LP consisting of eighteen folk songs from around the world performed by the Disneyland Boys' Choir. The choir actually originated not at Disneyland but at the St. Charles Borromeo Catholic Church in North Hollywood, under the direction of Paul Salamunovich, who half a century later continues in that capacity. Salamunovich recalled herding his choirboys to Sunset Sound to record the songs in 1965, while the infamous Watts riots were taking place—the real world apparently having a long way to go before achieving the utopian *Small World* global harmony.

According to Salamunovich, the recordings had to be approved by Walt Disney before the LP could be released. "I called Walt's secretary in the morning to see if he had approved the record," said Salamunovich. "She said he was still listening to it. I called at lunch, and she said the same thing. I called that afternoon—he was still listening, she said. Finally, right at the end of the day I got word that he had approved the album to be released!"

Mary Blair, who had been responsible for

Two of the most prolific Disneyland Records artists, Robie Lester and Bill Lee, were also prominent Hollywood vocalists. (Courtesy of Robie Lester)

Pinto Colvig provided the voice of Goofy beginning in 1932, but his Disneyland Records work was concentrated between 1963 and 1965. (Courtesy of Jerry Hausner)

the design of the *Small World* attraction (as well as numerous classic Disney animated films), painted the album cover art, her only signed art for Disneyland/Buena Vista Records.

O

Existing material was repackaged for another 1964 release, *Goofy's TV Spectacular*, again featuring the original voice of Goofy, Pinto Colvig. Colvig may well have had input into the writing of this LP, which contains inside jokes about his life and career. For example, Goofy reads a fan letter from "Jayville, Oregon," and remarks, "Why, that's my old hometown!" Colvig hailed from Jacksonville, Oregon. In another segment, Goofy plays four different tunes on four clarinets at once (two in his mouth and one in each ear). Colvig had begun his show business career in 1905 with a comedy clarinet act, and he likely played at least some of Goofy's instruments for this routine.

In all, *Goofy's TV Spectacular* does a good job of summing up the character's stated philosophy: "Laughter is the best medicine they is. It don't cost nothin', and it never leaves a nasty taste in your mouth." Colvig appeared as Goofy on only one more LP, *Children's Riddles and Game Songs* (1965), which expanded on the same idea.

Marni Nixon: The Star behind the Stars

After hearing Marni Nixon's performances of *Mary Poppins* songs for the Disneyland second cast album, Jimmy Johnson remarked, "She sounds more like Julie Andrews than Julie Andrews." Many years later, Nixon laughed at the comment: "They wanted somebody to sound like Julie Andrews, but not just do an imitation. It has the same flavor."

An accomplished opera and musical comedy star, Marni Nixon is perhaps best known to movie fans as the singing voice for Audrey Hepburn in *My Fair Lady* (1964), Natalie Wood in *West Side Story* (1961), and Deborah Kerr in *The King and I* (1956). Kerr was kind enough to reveal Nixon's backstage work even though studios had told the singer to keep her performances secret. Offscreen singing was a common practice in musicals when the actors had limited range, but it was not widely publicized before Nixon gained fame.

Born in Altadena, California, Nixon's life was always filled with music. "My parents, three sisters and I had a family orchestra," she recalled. "I was playing violin in the Peter Meremblum Orchestra and sometimes I would stand up and sing an aria." Nixon was only twelve years old when Louis B. Mayer's secretary witnessed one of those stand-up orchestra-singing performances. By 1948, Nixon was doing her first off-camera work for the studio, singing a Hindu lullaby for Margaret O'Brien in *The Secret Garden*. All the while, she was picking up small child roles in films. "My voice was very high coloratura," she said of her bell-clear soprano. "I don't think it was particularly big, but it carried." Equally adept at group singing and solos, Nixon was one of the original members of the Roger Wagner Chorale and sang with such major vocal arrangers as Johnny Mann, Norman Luboff, Robert Shaw, Walter Schumann, and Randy Van Horne and great conductors including Leopold Stokowski, Leonard Bernstein, and composer Igor Stravinsky.

For Disney, Nixon did a lot of "incidental things," many of which now escape her memory, though she recalls voicing a squirrel named Pepe. Her first Disneyland Record was *Great Operatic Composers* with Tutti Camarata, singing selections from Engelbert Humperdinck's *Hansel and Gretel* that would soon be repurposed for the story album of the fairy tale. Around the time she was singing for the cockney geese in the *Mary Poppins* "Jolly Holiday" sequence, Nixon was asked to do the *Poppins* LP with Bill Lee, who enjoyed a similar Hollywood off-screen singing career. *Ten Songs from Mary Poppins* was a huge seller, and Nixon has the gold record to prove it.

Today, Marni Nixon is busy as ever, just finishing a run on Broadway in *Nine*. She has recorded several classical albums as well as CD tributes to Jerome Kern and George Gershwin. She especially enjoyed teaching at the Music Academy of the West in Santa Barbara and her position as director of the vocal department at Walt Disney's beloved California Institute of the Arts. Her autobiography is scheduled to be released by Watson-Guptill Publications in the spring of 2006. "A lot of people come to me and say 'You're my teacher,' even if I'd never met them before, because they learned to sing with *West Side Story* or these children's albums. That makes me very happy. I just lucked out having a nice clear voice."

○

As *Mary Poppins* was gearing up for its premiere, Camarata put together a second cast album of its songs featuring Hollywood ghost singers Bill Lee and Marni Nixon (so named because they often sang off-camera for film actors), Pamela Shannon, and last-minute addition Richard Sherman, who made his Disneyland Records singing debut with "I Love to Laugh." "We had a singer who was trying to do Uncle Albert but he just wasn't hilarious—it didn't work," Sherman remembered. "Tutti said, 'Go in there and just sing to show him what you want.' I sang it once, and Tutti said, 'That's the master!' We paid the guy and I was on the record." Assisting Sherman in his performance was recording

Marni Nixon's bell-clear soprano graced the *Mary Poppins* second cast album. (Courtesy of Marni Nixon)

engineer Brian Ross-Myring, who "squeaked as the squeakelers do."

Nixon remembered the participation of Israeli harpsichordist Amindav Aloni, "a wonderful arranger and composer" who was an old college friend of Nixon. Aloni received his sole Disneyland Records credit on *The Great Composers* for his piano and harpsichord work. It is likely, however, that he played harpsichord for the *Poppins* LP as well as *The Scarecrow of Oz*, *Winnie the Pooh and the Honey Tree*, and many other Disney LPs that featured the instrument. Camarata may also have employed Aloni's arranging skills for these records.

○

The pre-premiere industry buzz on the *Poppins* film was so positive that several major record companies expressed interest in releasing the soundtrack album. George Marek of RCA Victor Records asked to meet with Roy Disney. When Johnson entered the meeting, Marek spoke his case. "I know you've got your own record company now," he said. "But we've heard great things about *Mary Poppins* and we know we can do a job with the soundtrack album that will be better than you could do. After all, we've had tremendous experience in handling these big show albums." Roy answered, "We'll listen to any reasonable proposition." Columbia Records made a similar pitch, and Roy Disney asked Johnson by asking which proposition should be accepted.

Neither. "Roy, we've been in the record business for seven years now," an anguished Johnson replied. "And while we have had some very tough times, we've turned the corner now. We have built a very strong sales force and are now with some of the finest independent distributors in the country. We've got to have this big hit to put on top of our basically strong catalog. This is what

we've been waiting for!" He continued, "With our Disney know-how in merchandising we can run rings around what RCA or CBS might do. We've got to keep the album on Buena Vista!" "That's what I thought you were going to say," Roy chuckled. "Go ahead. Sell the hell out of it!" Although the finished album did appear on the Buena Vista label, RCA released an identical LP on its label for the RCA Record Club.

○

As head of music publishing, Johnson created a sales kit to entice record executives and performers to produce their own versions of the *Poppins* songs. Initially, only Kapp Records responded with an album by the Do-Re-Mi Children's Chorus featuring Disneyland Records veteran Mary Martin (who, along with Bette Davis, had received consideration for the film role, which eventually went to Julie Andrews). A myriad of cover versions of the score gradually appeared, featuring an eclectic group of artists from Ray Conniff to Duke Ellington. Perhaps the most curious version turned up on Hanna-Barbera's in-house record label starring TV's Fred Flintstone and Barney Rubble. Johnson also enlisted singer Louis Prima to record "A Spoonful of Sugar" and "Stay Awake" with Sam Butera and the Witnesses. The single got frequent radio play and "Sugar" became the closing number of Prima's Las Vegas act. Prima, of course, would have a lot to say about Disney music over the next few years.

Mary Poppins's effect on the Disney organization cannot be overstated. The record and music publishing divisions felt the impact from the film's limited release in late 1964 and especially the windfall that occurred after wide release the following year. "Shortly after 1965 began, the *Poppins* boom happened with a big bang," Johnson wrote. "[Charles] Hansen's presses just could not keep up with

Jimmy Johnson and assistant Rose Mussi examine the gold record for the original soundtrack LP of *Mary Poppins*. (Courtesy of Grey Johnson)

the fantastic demand of *Mary Poppins* music books of every kind. We had three times the number of different publications than did Chappell, the publisher of *My Fair Lady*." During the first year after its release, the *Poppins* soundtrack album sold more than two million copies, the second cast album sold almost a million, and the Storyteller version, narrated by an unusually low-key Dal McKennon as Bert, sold nearly a half million.

○

The Sherman brothers won two Oscars and international fame. Their status as Academy Award–winning songwriters was enough to support an album called *Tinpanorama*. The seven tunes they had written for the ani-

mated short *A Symposium on Popular Songs* were augmented by five additional compositions built fancifully around changing pop music styles. "We were kind of salable then," Richard Sherman remembered. "So Jimmy Johnson said, 'If you guys can fill this album out then we'll make it from this Oscar-winning team from *Mary Poppins*.' Our success with *Poppins* gave us the clout." Sherman described the songs as "great Tutti productions. We had everything from the different eras, up to folk singers. We even had something like the Beatles. That was fun."

Another Sherman triumph lay just ahead. Although not as splashy as Mary Poppins, it was pleasantly stuffed with fluff.

Bill Lee:
Singer of a Thousand Voices

Perhaps no male soloist was heard on Disneyland Records more often than the versatile Bill Lee. But that work constituted only one small part of a long and remarkable career.

Lee spent his childhood and teenage years in Des Moines, Iowa. He originally aspired to be a trombone player, an activity he pursued while attending college. During the same period, he sang in school groups, soon realizing that his voice was the instrument that held the key to his future.

After serving as an ensign during World War II, Lee relocated to Hollywood with his wife. He became baritone for the MelloMen, a male quartet formed by Thurl Ravenscroft, and remained throughout the group's existence. Ravenscroft and Lee were the only members of the MelloMen to line up extensive solo work while with the group. A quick study, Lee could vary his range and pitch to match virtually any project. Much of his work consisted of radio and TV commercial jingles. "They sound pretty silly," he said of the jingles, "but it is a good living and allows me to do the things I want."

In addition to a solo album, *My Port of Call*, Lee got the lead role in composer/conductor Gordon Jenkins's *Seven Dreams*, a musical created for Decca in 1953. The album was a sensation in its day and sold for many years. Its cast included Jeanette Nolan, Dick Beals, John McIntire, Ernie Newton, and Ravenscroft in a lavishly mounted yet somewhat dark and disturbing production.

Lee's first work for Disneyland Records was as one of the MelloMen, but his earliest identifiable solo occurs during "Jungle Tree" in *A Christmas Adventure at Disneyland* (1958). His ability to take on various dialects and character voices served him well for *Mary Poppins* (1964), in which he sang for the barnyard sheep in the "Jolly Holiday" sequence and as Bert and Mr. Banks for the second cast recording. He assumed a charmingly dimwitted attitude while singing for Goofy on the album *Children's Riddles and Game Songs* (1965) and for Melvin the moose head in the Country Bear Jamboree at Walt Disney World and Disneyland. He also appeared briefly on-screen in the 1965 TV production of *Rodgers and Hammerstein's Cinderella*.

Lee's talent for singing within an actor's character gave him his most famous if uncredited film roles. He sang for Tom Drake in MGM's *Words and Music* (1948), John Kerr in *South Pacific* (1958), Cary Grant in *Father Goose* (1964), and most notably for Christopher Plummer in *The Sound of Music* (1965). He even sang for Yogi Bear in Hanna-Barbera's first animated feature *Hey There, It's Yogi Bear!* (1964). (Frequent Disney co-performer Ernie Newton sang for little buddy Boo-Boo.)

The demand for group singers declined in the early 1970s, and after the MelloMen disbanded, Lee was heard less frequently, though his peers and even his competitors universally admired him. He died of a brain tumor on November 15, 1980, at age sixty-four, leaving not only his family but also millions of fans who knew his work even if they did not know his name.

7

In Which Pooh and Friends Come to Disney Records

The release of *Snow White* in 1937 had made Walt Disney Productions aware of the value of getting tie-in merchandise into stores well in advance of a film's theatrical debut. In that tradition, the record division released its first titles to promote the upcoming animated featurette *Winnie the Pooh and the Honey Tree* in the spring of 1965.

The fact that no one would see Pooh and his friends on the screen until February 1966 made no difference; Disney had been marketing Pooh toys since 1964, primarily through a lucrative agreement with giant retailer Sears, Roebuck & Co. Children's departments in Sears stores nationwide were suddenly transformed into additional acreage of the Hundred Acre Wood. The public was being well prepared for Pooh's animated debut.

As part of this merchandising blitz, the Disneyland Storyteller LP version of *Honey Tree* presented dialogue from the upcoming film's soundtrack, with additional narration recorded by Sebastian Cabot to explain visual gags that might be lost in the translation to audio. Replacing Buddy Baker's background score, which either had not been completed at this time or was cost-prohibitive to use, were Camarata's versions of the Sherman brothers' Pooh songs. Another LP, *All the Songs from Winnie the Pooh*, ran all of fifteen

minutes and featured the theme song three times. A 45-rpm Little Gem featured the theme on one side and "Little Black Rain Cloud" on the other. Sears even marketed its own "Winnie the Pooh"/"Little Black Rain Cloud" Little Gem record and would be responsible for more record tie-ins in coming years.

The Shermans referred to their Pooh songs as "hums," after the term originated by Pooh creator A. A. Milne. In the film, they were featured quite incidentally. Camarata's interpretations expanded on the film versions, rounding them off with musical bridges and various musical styles. The orchestrations are simple but bold, opening the theme with a

Of his countless Disney performances, Sterling Holloway is most remembered as the distinctive voice of Winnie the Pooh. (Courtesy of Will Ryan)

The Jack Halloran Singers: All Together Now

Jack Halloran first organized a male quartet while attending Northwestern University in Evanston, Illinois. After undergoing several personnel changes over the next few years, the group eventually consisted of Halloran and friends Bill Kanady, Bob Tebow, and Bill Cole. Heard often in Chicago radio and television commercials, they secured a regular spot on comedian Pat Buttram's radio program for Wrigley's gum. When Buttram moved his show to Los Angeles in 1956, the Jack Halloran Quartet moved with it. After Halloran began adding female vocalists to his male quartet, the group became the Jack Halloran Singers. The choir's makeup varied from job to job, depending on who was available for work and how many singers were required for a particular recording.

Halloran himself kept quite busy with activities apart from the rest of his loosely knit group, becoming one of Hollywood's top choral directors and arrangers. His work with Dean Martin on the hit song "Volare" led Halloran to a nine-year stint with Martin's TV program

as well as to roles directing chorus and orchestra for several Bing Crosby albums. Halloran was also responsible for the first recording of the perennial Christmas song "The Little Drummer Boy" in 1957, although his version was not released until after the competitive version by the Harry Simeone Chorale.

The Jack Halloran Singers appeared on numerous Disney records of the 1960s, including the *Winnie the Pooh* songs, but were seldom credited (a rare exception was *Black Beauty*). During this time, most of the individual members remained busy with additional solo careers. Of the original quartet, Kanady did the most Disney work, lending his deep, somewhat gruff voice to several records between 1964 and 1967. He could be glimpsed on-screen (as could Disneyland Records regular Bill Lee) in the 1965 TV production of *Rodgers and Hammerstein's Cinderella*. Bill Cole joined the MelloMen in 1961 and was also a member of the male quartet that sang TV's *Gilligan's Island* theme in its second and third seasons. Cole made his biggest mark on Disney history in 1971, when he performed several different voices for the Country Bear Jamboree Audio-Animatronics attraction. Bob Tebow had fewer Disney solo connections than the others, although he was frequently a part of the choral groups heard in the studio's films. Still working in the late 1980s, Tebow and Kanady sang jointly in Disney's *The Little Mermaid* and Steven Spielberg's *An American Tail.*

By that time, the Jack Halloran Singers were no longer using the group name. Halloran continued to work as a contractor, lining up singers for productions whenever needed, until his death on January 24, 1997. Kanady passed away in 1996, but the other Halloran singers continue to make occasional appearances. Cole was reunited with the other members of the *Gilligan's Island* quartet for a special on the TV Land channel in 2003, and Tebow has remained active as well. Their work for Disney is understandably foggy in their memories, as it represented just another assignment in a business they all truly loved.

rumbling timpani and trumpet fanfare, escalating into a multioctave "aah" by the Jack Halloran Singers before the melody begins, with B. J. Baker singing the "Deep in the Hundred Acre Wood, where Christopher Robin plays" verse. This rendition of the theme would be recycled for countless future record releases. Disney's voice for Pooh, Sterling Holloway, performed his solos especially for the records. "Up, Down, and Touch the Ground" is probably the most symphonic of the three; "Rumbly in My Tumbly" becomes a tango, with a heavy emphasis on the harpsichord; and "Little Black Rain Cloud" is a delicate creation using tinkling bells as its musical backdrop.

The back cover illustration on the *Honey Tree* LP sleeve sports one of the studio's earliest line drawings of the characters (a variation had been used on a 1964 Pooh game from Parker Brothers as well). The illustration shows Piglet and Tigger, though they don't appear in the first Pooh film. Both characters more closely resemble the Pooh books' Ernest Shepard illustrations than Disney's later redesigns. These future stars' presence made for an unusual situation for Jimmy Johnson. Louis Prima was visiting with his four-year-old daughter when Johnson gave the girl a copy of the *Honey Tree* LP. She spotted Tigger on the jacket art and demanded, "Where's Tigger on this record?" Johnson later recalled, "Tigger played a big part in the second and third Pooh films, and I made sure that Louis's kids had copies of those records."

Prima became involved in the forthcoming animated feature *The Jungle Book* at Johnson's suggestion. "Phil Harris had just been cast as the voice of Baloo the bear, and I felt that Louis would be great as a foil in the part

This inner sleeve from a Disneyland LP showcases the Magic Mirror Storyteller series. (© Disney Enterprises, Inc.)

of King Louie," Johnson wrote. "So I recommended him to Walt, who at first was a bit dubious. But Louis really wanted the part, so he brought his entire band down to Burbank at his own expense to audition for Walt and the animators. They set up on one of the sound stages and went into their regular Vegas act. As part of the act, Louis's drummer puts on a rubber ape mask and drums away with a whole fistful of sticks, flipping them into the air, catching them, then drumming all over the room on chairs, on the floor, on other instruments. It's a hilarious bit and the animators broke up. . . . Some of the other antics of Louis and his crew also found their way into the film."

○

In 1965, Disneyland Records released *The Further Adventures of Cinderella's Mice*, the first of several sequel albums. While the Disney organization has found success in recent years with sequels to its animated classics, Walt Disney himself usually avoided them in those days before home video. The few exceptions include a handful of theatrical short subject follow-ups to 1933's *Three Little Pigs*.

Publications were a different story, however—and they frequently told different stories. Disney books and comics had been revisiting classic Disney animated features throughout Walt's day, even combining characters of diverse origins in unlikely ways. The record division's sequel to *Cinderella* occurred nearly three decades before *The Return of Jafar* opened up the video sequel market and almost four decades before the *Cinderella II: Dreams Come True* video.

Cinderella's Mice finds the new princess, the prince, and the mice all living happily ever after in the palace. One day, there is a knock at the castle door. Who is it? No, it isn't opportunity; nor is it the Big Bad Wolf—it is none other than would-be 1957 Disneyland Records star Ludwig Mousensky! In a convoluted reuse of previous recordings, the story unravels into two threads. Mousensky organizes the castle rodents into various glee clubs (bringing back those *Christmas Concert* selections), while Cinderella's stepmother banishes Lucifer the cat from her chateau. The fickle feline plays on Cinderella's good nature to ingratiate himself into a new home in the castle. This leads the mice to devise a method of putting a bell around Lucifer's neck to warn them of his approach. These two diverging storylines come together in the final scene, when Mousensky's set of jingle bells are fitted onto Lucifer like a harness. "From then on," narrates Robie Lester, "it was Christmas every day around Cinderella's castle."

In addition to Lester doing triple duty as narrator, Cinderella, and Lucifer, Jimmy Macdonald re-creates his speeded-up mouse voices for Mousensky, Jaq, and Gus, receiving label credit this time. Sterling Holloway is heard as "guest caller" in a Camarata composition called "Mouse Square Dance," which was originally part of an LP titled *The Country Cousin* and was later reappropriated by Pinto Colvig for his 1964 *Goofy's TV Spectacular* LP.

For 1965, Colvig (as Goofy) hosted the album *Children's Riddles and Game Songs*, trading quips with a group of children (some of whom sound as if they are in their teenage years). It would prove to be Colvig's last performance on vinyl; he died of lung cancer two years later at age seventy-two.

○

The concept of a children's book-and-record combination in which the disc followed the text word-for-word did not originate with Disney. Among the most successful early examples of the genre were Capitol's "Record-Readers," conceived by company president Alan Livingston in 1946. A full-color book was bound inside these 78-rpm record albums, with printed dialogue on the left-hand pages and accompanying illustrations on the right-hand pages. Capitol's first Record-Readers starred Livingston's creation Bozo the Clown and then expanded to include titles by Margaret O'Brien, Harold Peary (radio's "Great Gildersleeve"), Bugs Bunny, Woody Woodpecker, and others. The series even included Disney titles, including *Mickey Mouse's Birthday Party*, in which Stan Freberg voiced Mickey. Golden Records picked up on the same concept several years later and packaged 78- and 45-rpm records with some of its famous Little Golden Book titles. Again, this series mixed in a few Disney subjects, and other record companies released read-alongs in one format or another as well.

With the exception of the LP *A Christmas Adventure in Disneyland*, which had a book that followed the verse on the record, no Disneyland read-alongs were released until November 1965. That's when the first eight

As the Disneyland Story Reader, Robie Lester began her long-running series of read-alongs in 1965. (Courtesy of Robie Lester)

entries in the "See the pictures, Hear the record, Read the book" series were released: *Sleeping Beauty*, *Mary Poppins*, *Three Little Pigs*, *Peter Pan and Wendy*, *101 Dalmatians*, *Alice in Wonderland*, *Lady and the Tramp*, and *Cinderella*. All Disneyland "read-alongs" were seven-inch records played at 33⅓ rpm, perhaps as a result of Johnson's disdain for the 45-rpm record format. They became known as Little LP's, or the LLP series. The accompanying twenty-four-page books were adapted from the Little Golden Books versions of the same stories. Some of the texts veer a bit from the final film versions because they were prepared long before the film was finished. The *Alice in Wonderland* book, for example, includes a Jabberwock character that was cut from the film storyline. Despite this cancellation, the Jabberwock lived on in tie-in merchandise. *101 Dalmatians* does not contain the film story at all; it's actually a Little Golden Book called *Lucky Puppy*.

Robie Lester became the official "Disneyland Story Reader," and the series would be hers alone for the next five years. The first records in the series opened with an introduction: "This is a Walt Disney original little long-playing record, and I am your Disneyland story reader. I am going to begin now to read the story of [title]. You can read along with me in your book. You will know it is time to turn the page when you hear Tinker Bell ring her little bells like this [chime sound]. Let's begin now." No other sound effects or music accompanied Lester's readings. She concluded with: "That is the end of the story of [name]. But now we are going to hear another song from Walt Disney's motion picture." The early books included printed lyrics to the two songs heard on the record.

In the years following, the lyrics disappeared and the opening was slightly altered to begin "This is a Disneyland original little long playing record and I am your story reader." The concluding comments were removed. Walt Disney's passing may have been the reason behind the opening's revision, and music publishing fees may have prevented the further printing of lyrics. At any rate, all subsequent read-alongs followed the same format except for *Peter and the Wolf*, the sole title with music backing up Lester's reading.

Lester recalled the recording sessions for these read-alongs as even more hurried than usual. She would record stories in batches of three or four at a time, so the eight original releases were likely the product of two separate sessions. She would not be told what she was going to record until she arrived at the studio, at which time she would be handed her scripts and would then "have five minutes at the most to scan over them and see what I was doing." There was no video playback or any other reference to demonstrate the original voices for Lester. She was entirely on her own in reading the text and coming up with improvised character voices on the spot. Lester rose to the challenge and invented a myriad of vocal variations, using a reassuring, maternal warmth for the overall narration.

●

The legendary Maurice Chevalier lent his own brand of warmth to another type of narration for *A Musical Tour of France* in 1966. "Of all the great artists I had the pleasure of working with," wrote Jimmy Johnson, "I have never found one more professional than Chevalier." To prepare for the album, Chevalier asked Johnson to send tapes of the songs to Paris, and the Frenchman sang along with them each morning in his bed. When the time for the recording session arrived, Johnson noted, "Chevalier did the entire thing in two hours. It was one take all the way."

Another venerable figure to record for Disney at this time, though from a very different field, was Professor Julius Sumner Miller, a student of Albert Einstein whose lively science lectures appeared on the 1962 *Mickey Mouse Club* revival. Miller did four science albums about Benjamin Franklin, Michael Faraday, Isaac Newton, and Galileo that were perhaps intended for school use.

Two voices from the early Disneyland days returned for new records in the mid-1960s. Mary Martin told and sang *The Sound of Music*, narrating an adaptation based on the film rather than the Broadway show. Annette Funicello, whose beach party film songs were gracing the Buena Vista label at the time, told and sang *Tubby the Tuba*.

Disneyland regular Thurl Ravenscroft contributed narration for *The Ugly Dachshund*, based on the theatrical situation comedy released with *Winnie the Pooh and the Honey Tree*. Side 1 of the modestly produced *Ugly Dachshund* LP features Ravenscroft as the title character, a Great Dane named Brutus who is raised with a litter of wiener dogs. The only music occurs when he sings an incidental "Ugly Dachshund" ditty by the

Sherman brothers that was not heard in the film. Side 2 is a reissue of selections from the 1959 *Shaggy Dog* album.

○

Disneyland Records' second sequel to a classic Disney animated feature was *Thumper's Great Race*, bringing back the characters from 1942's *Bambi* and adding a few new ones. In this twist on the fable of the tortoise and the hare, the animals compete to see which is the swiftest, with Bambi and the Owl as judges. Thumper wins, but not before helping an overturned Toby Tortoise get set to rights.

Robie Lester narrates as Bambi and puts on an impossibly squeaky voice as Thumper, sharing the microphone with Disneyland regulars Dal McKennon and Junius Matthews. Two songs from 1963's *Peter Cottontail* LP were worked in, Lester's squeaky-voiced "Hippety Hop" and the "Thumper Song," with Thurl Ravenscroft singing through his front teeth. Original lyrics and music by Johnson and Camarata include "On the Ice" and "If You Can't Say Something Nice, Say Nothing," sung by Ravenscroft, Bill Lee, and Sally Sweetland in folk-guitar style.

The trio of Lee, Sweetland, and Ravenscroft also appear on *All about Dragons*, showcasing the tune "Puff, the Magic Dragon," which they sing à la Peter, Paul and Mary, who made the song a hit in 1963. Ravenscroft, with an affected British accent, hosts *All about Dragons* as the Reluctant Dragon, singing the title song from the 1941 feature. He gives a brief history of his species, describes how to make a do-it-yourself dragon ("Now you can walk right out and frighten your parents!"), introduces the "wizard's

duel" segment from the 1963 *Sword in the Stone* LP, and closes with Johnson and Camarata's "The Loch Ness Monster" song, in which he demonstrates that his bass voice can go to even greater depths than that "wild, eerie lake" in Scotland.

○

The second group of read-along book-and-record sets was released in 1966 and included *Bambi*, *Pinocchio*, *Snow White and the Seven Dwarfs*, and *Mother Goose*. These followed the same basic format as the original eight with one slight difference: all continued their stories on both sides of the record instead of finishing entirely on side 1.

Lester's range of characterization was put

Sally Sweetland, Bill Lee, and Thurl Ravenscroft harmonized on songs for *Thumper's Great Race* and a rendition of "Puff, the Magic Dragon" for *All about Dragons*.

to the test on *Mother Goose*. With limited preparation time, she entered the recording booth and read thirty-one rhymes in thirty-one different flavors, using her natural voice only to announce the title of each. Though she would never have to come up with so many voices in one sitting again, she came close when she did all the vocal attitudes for *The Seven Dwarfs and Their Diamond Mine*,

Robie Lester:
I Am Your Story
Reader

It is impossible to calculate how many lives Robie Lester touched by singing, acting, and narrating on more individual Disneyland records than any other performer.

Lester was born in the microscopic town of Megargel, Texas, but moved at an early age to northern Ontario, Canada. At age fourteen, Lester left home and made a new life for herself in Detroit. She loved the escapism of the great movie musicals of the 1940s, and she and a friend "would go to see every musical that came to the theater, and then we would walk down the sidewalk singing all the songs from the movie at the top of our voices. People thought we were strange!"

Lester spent a year and a half in the U.S. Air Corps before attending UCLA and majoring in music. Blessed with a clear, powerful voice, Lester was equally adept at singing for dramatic or comedic purposes. Her comic timing came in handy for Henry Mancini's novelty LP, *Terribly Sophisticated Songs*. Girl singers were far from rare in Hollywood, so Lester broadened her horizons by developing an uncanny knack for vocal impersonations. Her ability to sing as well as speak in character was put to frequent use in radio commercials and animated cartoons, from Hills Brothers coffee ads (accompanied by the MelloMen) to episodes of the *Famous Adventures of Mister Magoo*. Before her Disney days, Lester appeared on several pop singles for Liberty label. On A&M Records, she can be heard singing the Spanish verses in the Sandpipers' hits "Guantanamera" and "Canción de Amor."

Lester also worked as a demo singer, performing compositions to assist aspiring songwriters. In this capacity, the Sherman brothers brought her singing and acting talents to the attention of Disney's record division. Lester was initially cast as the sped-up voice of Dale of the chipmunk team Chip 'n' Dale, but by the early 1960s she was narrating Disneyland LPs of various types and doing numerous voices within the stories. She also sang the theme song over the opening credits of Disney's *The Three Lives of Thomasina* (1963).

When Disneyland Records launched its first "See . . . Hear . . . Read . . ." seven-inch 33⅓ rpm book-and-record sets in 1965, Lester was the original Disneyland Story Reader, which added considerably to her quantity of Disneyland Record performances. "Robie could handle anything I would give her to do," said Tutti Camarata. She was often handed scripts and asked to wing it with virtually no preparation, but she would make the performance work.

In December 1970, audiences enjoying the new Disney animated feature *The AristoCats* were hearing Robie Lester singing for Eva Gabor's character, Duchess. When they listened to the Storyteller LP, they heard Lester speaking and singing the role. "She's a wonderful gal," said Richard Sherman. "She did a beautiful recording of 'She Never Felt Alone.' In the picture, Eva just talked a few lines, but this was the whole song. It was great to hear that song done the way my brother and I had written it. [Lester] did a great job." It is one of the few Lester performances that has been reissued on compact disc.

That same December, the Rankin-Bass stop-motion animated Christmas special *Santa Claus Is Comin' to Town* premiered on ABC. Lester played opposite Mickey Rooney's Kris Kringle as Miss Jessica, the schoolteacher who eventually becomes Mrs. Santa Claus. Her earnest performance included the show-stopping "My World Is Beginning Today," demonstrating why she was one of the best soloists in Hollywood. Lester's final Disneyland LP performance was in *The Orange Bird* (1971). She continued to work in radio advertising and animation, but recuperation from two 1972 open-heart surgeries put her out of commission, and "by the time I was ready to go back to work, all of my former producers and directors had changed jobs or died, and no one knew who I was," she said. Disney's animators had not forgotten, though, and when Gabor was cast in *The Rescuers* (1977), Lester was called in to sing "Rescue Aid Society" for Miss Bianca.

In the years that followed, Lester wrote the novel *Heaven's Gift* and busied herself with her family and several charitable causes, primarily animal welfare and the Random Act of Kindness program. She continued to write and perform and was on hand to cheer her friend Tutti Camarata when he was honored at the Walt Disney Studios in 2003. Her final appearance was in an episode of the acclaimed children's radio drama, *Adventures in Odyssey.* She lived quietly in California's citrus country with her husband, Geoff, and her many animal friends until her death on June 14, 2005. Lester took great pleasure in knowing that she had a legion of fans who grew up enjoying her work.

the third Disneyland Records animated feature sequel. Taking place two years after Snow White's visit with the little men, *Diamond Mine* is a self-described "mystery story" in which the dwarfs hear odd noises coming from their mine. Strange messages instruct them to be at the mine at midnight for a great surprise. It turns out that Snow White has sent all her royal carpenters and stonemasons to build a grand ballroom adjoining the mine. The only music on the LP is "Music in Your Soup" and "You're Never Too Old to Be Young," two songs written by Frank Churchill and Larry Morey for sequences that Walt Disney felt slowed down the story and were ultimately deleted from the final *Snow White* film. Sung by Lee, Ravenscroft, and Bill Kanady with Lester affectionately providing commentary as Snow White, these modest renditions likely constitute the world premiere recordings of these tunes.

Around the same time, Lester also solo narrated *Black Beauty*, the first Disneyland album adapted from classic literature that was not also a concurrent Disney film. The album features no supporting cast or musical background, save for three Johnson/Camarata songs performed by the Jack Halloran Singers.

O

The first Disneyland album that could be described in today's terms as "interactive" was 1966's *A Happy Birthday Party with Winnie the Pooh.* The songs tied to traditional birthday party games, with Pooh and friends demonstrating the instructions inside the book. This Storyteller LP marks the studio's first use of Pooh and friends in original material outside the Milne books or Disney films. Sterling Holloway is Pooh, of course, but the other characters seem oddly cast. Instead of reprising his film role of Rabbit, Junius Matthews plays Owl. Rabbit is given a raspy little boy voice by Robie Lester, who also speaks for Kanga, Christopher Robin, and Roo. It is unclear who plays Eeyore, although it very well could be Jimmy Macdonald or whoever else was handy at the time.

Johnson and his writers seem relatively unfamiliar with the world of Pooh in this recording, as the characters in the script do not always ring true. For example, Christopher Robin would have never called Eeyore "sawdust head," as he does in this story, and even the other characters seem bent on insulting each other until they come across as a sort of Friar's Club Roast in the toy box.

Once again, Piglet and Tigger appear in the artwork long before receiving animated treat-ment, although they are not heard in the recording. Their depiction here does not resemble the original Shepard book illustrations as much as they did in early Disney publicity art: Piglet looks more like a real pig wearing an old-fashioned striped bathing suit, while Tigger has beady eyes, a toothy grin, and a shaggy black mane. This would remain his Disney look for various pieces of merchandise until the release of the next Pooh featurette in 1968.

Carol Lombard, Al Capps, and Ron Hicklin, accompanied by folk guitar, recorded new songs for *Birthday Party.* The remaining selections come from earlier records, except the very unusual version of "Winnie the Pooh" that opens the album. "Once upon a time there was a lovable bear named Winnie the Pooh," says Louis Prima as the music begins. After inexplicably calling his buddy "Winnie" instead of the more familiar "Pooh," Prima launches into a half sung/half scat performance with other characters joining in, including Lester giggling and doing some mean scatting for Roo. Prima acts as informal host for the rest of the record. For all its quirks, *A Happy Birthday Party with Winnie the Pooh* was a long-selling success and received a Grammy nomination.

Prima was rapidly finding a second career in Disney records. For the 1966 Christmas season he recorded a 45-rpm single consisting of two novelty songs, "Santa, How Come Your Eyes Are Green When Last Year They Were Blue?" and "Señor Santa Claus." Both capture his effervescent stage presence, and the former includes some creative ad-libbing during the lyrics ("Don't you look at me with those bloodshot eyes, Santa Claus!").

O

In 1966, anticipation was high for the newest Disneyland attraction, Pirates of the Caribbean, which was to open the following

The inimitable Louis Prima promotes his 1966 Disney single "Señor Santa Claus." (Courtesy of Gia Maione)

spring. Disneyland Records created a vinyl version of the ride, with some variations on the original. In the attraction itself, Paul Frees performs most of the pirates. Other voices include Dal McKennon, Ginny Tyler, Thurl Ravenscroft, and Xavier Atencio, the Disney Imagineer who wrote the script. (He warns, "Dead men tell no tales.") Frees charged a premium price for his vocal services, and it is likely that his attraction performances were not licensed for recordings. Ravenscroft handled the record narration in Frees' place, along with Lester as the mayor's wife ("Don't tell heem, Carlos! Don't be cheecken!") and several other uncredited performers.

Disneyland guests were supposed to catch only snatches of the voices as their boats glided past in the attraction; Walt Disney compared it to hearing bits and pieces of conversations during a cocktail party. The dialogue was never intended to be heard all in one sitting, so the individual scenes, dramatized in their entirety for the record, seem rather drawn out. The album includes some of the attraction soundtrack music, particularly "Yo Ho! (A Pirate's Life for Me)" by Atencio and Buddy Baker, performed by Ravenscroft and the MelloMen. Sound effect montages were borrowed from *Chilling, Thrilling Sounds of the Haunted House* recording, including screams and the unmistakable *Lonesome Ghosts* groan. Despite its extended story line, *Pirates of the Caribbean* only fills one LP side. Side 2 recycles the sea chanteys recorded by "Admiral" Ravenscroft for the 1962 *Little Toot* album.

O

TV soundtracks rarely appeared on Disneyland Records of this period. An exception was *A Nature Guide about Birds, Bees, Beavers, and Bears*, featuring excerpts from the November 1966 *Wonderful World of Color* episode "A Ranger's Guide to Nature." Radio veteran Bill Thompson played Ranger J. Audubon Woodlore, conducting a nature hike for Donald Duck's nephews Huey, Dewey, and Louie. By this time, the three youngsters were no longer using Clarence Nash's sped-up voice but had been recast with Gloria Wood, Robie Lester, and Dick Beals.

O

It is not known how aware Walt Disney was of these, the final recordings produced in his lifetime. Walt's last few months had been preoccupied with getting plans under way for his mammoth new entertainment complex in Florida plus as many other projects as he could fit between doctor's appointments. Shortly after he underwent surgery to remove one entire cancerous lung, the seemingly immortal Walt Disney died on December 15, 1966, in the hospital across the street from his studio. "'Gone,' 'gone,' 'gone' was the gloomy word that echoed through the corridors of the buildings, and in the offices and on the sets," Johnson wrote. "It was strange that no one said Walt had died. He was gone!"

Bill Thompson's voice turned up on Disneyland Records in selections taken from the soundtracks of his many animated films. His characterizations included Mr. Smee in *Peter Pan* and Ranger J. Audubon Woodlore on the Disney TV show. (Courtesy of Richard Huemer Jr.)

Walt Disney had had minimal involvement with merchandising entities such as the record division, so there was no question that they would continue as they had without him. The bigger question was whether the Disney name and its creations as a whole would be able to survive without their public face. Disney stock went up nine points the day after Walt's passing. "Wall Street evidently figured that Walt had been the gambler and the spender, and that the company would now not build, not innovate, just cash in," Johnson stated. "They didn't reckon on Roy."

8

The Jungle Book Goes for the Gold

As the world mourned the loss of Walt Disney, those he left behind at his studio were in shock. "There were few creative organizations in the history of the world that were more of a one man show than Walt Disney Productions," Jimmy Johnson wrote. "What would happen now?" Some at the studio found that their growth was stunted because they had relied heavily on Walt for their creative direction, while others blossomed during this period. Through it all, Roy Disney was determined to carry on Walt's dreams, especially the Walt Disney World resort in Florida. "The financial derring-do was all Roy's," asserted Johnson. In addition to enlisting corporate partners for the immense Walt Disney World project, Roy issued debentures, bonds backed by the strong momentum and publicity of the company. Ninety million dollars in debentures were converted into common stock over a two-year period. (By 1971, *Forbes* magazine was reporting that "Walt Disney Productions will end up building and owning nearly all of a $320 million piece of property, without having incurred a penny of long term debt in the process.")

Financial problems were held at bay, but creative challenges mounted in Walt's absence. Animated features took longer to produce and projects overall were subject to group thinking and the ever-present "What would Walt do?" examination. The public saw little apparent difference between pre- and post-Walt projects. Indeed, he had initially supervised many of the films released in the years after his death. By and large the public still flocked to Disney films and bought as much merchandise as ever, including records.

The first seven-inch read-alongs released in early 1967, such as *Winnie the Pooh and the Honey Tree*, differed from earlier versions somewhat in that Robie Lester dropped her usual character interpretations and narrated at a markedly slower pace, perhaps to better assist preschool-age children in learning to read.

○

One clear letdown for the studio and the record company in particular was the box office disappointment of 1967's *The Happiest Millionaire*, a lavish musical intended to capture the same audience as *Mary Poppins*. In an era of lengthy, opulent family musicals, this entertaining film with its affable Sherman brothers score was lost in a sea of big-budget tunefests. Buena Vista's *Millionaire* soundtrack LP included an eleven-page book of lyrics and photos. For some reason, however, the album's sound quality was marred by an excessive echo chamber, perhaps inspired by RCA Victor's best-selling (and equally reverberating) *The Sound of Music* soundtrack LP.

Disneyland Records issued a second cast

The Mike Sammes Singers lent their distinctive, impeccable sound to Disney music at London's Abbey Road studios in the late 1960s and early 1970s.

Millionaire LP featuring Bill Lee, Bill Kanady, Joseph Pryor, and Carol Lombard. Richard Sherman also sang two songs with a Rudy Vallee–style megaphone sound. Jean Kanady recalled that her husband, Bill, received a call from Camarata to do the songs. Kanady rose to the occasion despite a head cold, delivering capable—though postnasal—performances of "Detroit" and "Are We Dancing?" The Kanadys had no idea how the recordings were going to be used until they spotted the album listing Bill's name in a store some time later.

Selections from this LP rounded out a Storyteller LP entitled *George and The Happiest Millionaire*, the only record released in the United States that was narrated by British choral director Mike Sammes. Dropping his natural accent, Sammes narrates from the point of view of George, one of the alligators kept as pets by the eccentric Biddle family in the film. Because *The Happiest Millionaire* was essentially a romantic, somewhat sophisticated musical comedy, the company decided to market the album to children by

Brian Fahey and the Mike Sammes Singers: British Invasion

The contributions of the Mike Sammes Singers to popular music, particularly in Europe from 1955 to 1975, are virtually incalculable. The volume of their work is overwhelming. Yet the man behind the music was as unpretentious as they come. "Mike Sammes was a very 'un-showbusinessy' person," said arranger/conductor Brian Fahey, who arranged and/or conducted the Sammes music heard on Disneyland and Buena Vista Records. "He was charming, studious, avuncular, polite and gentlemanly. And he had an outstanding talent for creating and molding groups of singers."

A veteran of the Royal Air Force, Sammes joined fellow musician Bill Shepherd in forming a male vocal group called the Coronets. Shepherd lost interest, but Sammes got the bug for providing backup vocals, and he was soon singing in as many as four recording sessions a day, six days a week, with Valerie Bain, Enid Hurd, Marion Gay, Ross Gilmour, Mel Todd, and Mike Redway. They did so many recordings, movies, and TV shows that sometimes they would sing the same song for different recordings on the same day.

In addition to their Disney records, the Mike Sammes Singers were heard in the United States on such imported records as Tom Jones's "Green, Green, Grass of Home" and Engelbert Humperdinck's "The Last Waltz" and on TV series including *Thunderbirds* and the *Benny Hill Show*. They backed up Tony Bennett, Barbra Streisand, Andy Williams, Ray Charles, and Sammy Davis Jr. The group also recorded under the name of the Knightsbridge Singers. As a soloist, Sammes was heard offscreen in *The Road to Hong Kong* and TV's *The Avengers*, among many other productions. He also recorded under a different name, Redd Wayne. Perhaps the Mike Sammes Singers' most famous (or infamous) work came when producer Phil Spector enlisted them to back up "The Long and Winding Road" for the Beatles. The group disapproved of the vocals, but the record became their best-selling single.

Mike Sammes died in 2001, but Fahey recalled the joy of working with him and the group. "All the sessions were happy and enjoyable," he said. "It was always a pleasure to work with Tutti Camarata. His background was in some ways similar to my own, rooted in the big band era. I remember him telling me that Abbey Road [studio] was the only place he could walk in at 10 o'clock in the morning with nothing, and walk out at 5 o'clock in the evening with recordings for a complete LP under his arm!" For the Disneyland/Buena Vista label, the team would create sparkling versions of music from *Finian's Rainbow*, *Fiddler on the Roof*, *Bedknobs and Broomsticks*, *Chitty Chitty Bang Bang*, *Oliver!*, and many others.

Fahey played piano and cello as a child and graduated to arranging, composing, big band, and jazz. He spent six years in the British army during World War II, including a long

Mike Sammes performed many solos on Disney records in addition to directing his group of singers.

spell in German prisoner-of-war camps. After the service, he toured as pianist with Rudy Starita's band, where he met his wife, Audrey Laurie, the band singer who became his orchestral contractor.

Like Sammes, Fahey worked for Chappell music publishing for many years but left to freelance for record labels and the BBC. From 1967 to 1972, he toured with Shirley Bassey as musical director. He has composed countless melodies for commercials, TV themes, and orchestral works. Fahey recalled that the sessions for Camarata were "always made up of the elite London session musicians. The recordings were made in straight stereo without the benefit of multitracking, overdubbing, remixing, etc. These techniques were in their infancy at the time. We recorded for three hours in the morning and three hours in the afternoon. First we would achieve an orchestral and vocal balance. Then we would rehearse and record each item separately—all playing together as if in an actual performance. The ensemble sound when the six voices [three women and three men, including Sammes himself] were occasionally spread over a range of three to four octaves was thrilling to my ears. . . . Usually at EMI an LP would be recorded in three three-hour sessions."

Through it all, Sammes was the consummate professional. "Mike achieved his results in a very quiet manner. It was obvious that he was trusted and admired by his colleagues, as, indeed, he was by me." Sammes died on May 19, 2001, at age seventy-three.

Robie Lester makes a TV appearance as the Blue Fairy in a musical version of *Pinocchio* (costarring Paul Winchell and Jerry Mahoney). She also played the role on *The Further Adventures of Jiminy Cricket* LP, Cliff Edwards's final performance as Jiminy. (Courtesy of Robie Lester)

playing up the alligators, which were also illustrated in whimsical cartoon style for books and other merchandise. This story angle was also employed in a seven-inch read-along *George* book-and-record set read by Lester.

A footnote to *The Happiest Millionaire* lore was its "lost" song, a ballad called "It Won't Be Long 'Til Christmas." Sung on-screen by Greer Garson and Fred MacMurray, it was cut from the film shortly after a preview and was not included in the *Millionaire* soundtrack album or in any of the second cast versions. In the fall of 1969, it suddenly emerged as a Buena Vista 45-rpm single recorded in England by big band singer Anne Shelton, backed by the John Alldis Singers with musical direction by Camarata.

◖

The internationally renowned Mike Sammes Singers made their Disney LP debut in 1967 with *Camarata Conducts Man of La Mancha*, the first in the Buena Vista Fanta-Sound series of albums. Borrowing the name from the Oscar-winning stereophonic sound process created in 1940 for *Fantasia*, Fanta-Sound records were aimed squarely at the adult audiophile market. They were packaged with elegant artwork and lyrics and touted as a custom product for the connoisseur. Most were recorded in Europe and consisted of either classical music played by the Symphonie-Orchester Graunke, including the Grammy-nominated *Carnival of the Animals*, or show music sung by the Sammes group and arranged by Brian Fahey, including the sole Disney score in the series, *The Happiest Millionaire*.

On the Disneyland label, the Mike Sammes Singers began to appear on many records, including their version of the score from 1967's *Doctor Dolittle*, another mega-musical that failed to be another *Mary Poppins* or *The Sound of Music*. Had events unfolded differently, *Dolittle* might have been a Disney animated feature at some point. Jimmy Johnson recalled that when he was a young employee of the studio's publicity department in 1938, he gave tours to many notable people, "including Hugh Lofting and his wife," he wrote. "Walt was very interested in *Doctor Dolittle*, and Lofting was interested in the Disney studio. But the author's ideas of what *Doctor Dolittle* was worth as a motion picture property and what Walt could afford to pay for a story in those days were far apart. So no deal ever came about."

Among all these cheerful records launched in 1967, one sad release signaled the close of a chapter in Disney history. *The Further Adventures of Jiminy Cricket* brought back a shadow of the character's former self. Deteriorating health had caused Cliff Edwards's diction to become slurred and his brilliant comic timing to virtually evaporate in what would be his last Disney recording.

This odd tale, punctuated by Camarata/Johnson songs, concerns Jiminy and his new friend, a young pine tree named Alwyn (Lester) who wishes to be a blue jay. Jiminy helps by enlisting

Jimmy Johnson tirelessly promoted Disneyland Records throughout the world. Here he addresses a gathering in France during the European release of *The Jungle Book*. (Courtesy of Grey Johnson)

the help of the Blue Fairy (also Lester) to grant Alwyn's wish. Alwyn the blue jay becomes obnoxious and eventually begs to be a tree again, but first the Blue Fairy turns him into a telephone pole to perform some character-building community service. Alwyn proves himself brave, truthful, and unselfish—no, wait, that was another wooden friend of Jiminy's—by standing firm as a forest fire rages all around him and is finally restored to his fine pine form.

Nineteen sixty-seven was the year of the *Jungle Book* premiere, a success that reaffirmed Disney's preeminence in animation following the loss of Walt Disney. The last animated feature to benefit from Walt's personal supervision, *The Jungle Book* showcased snappy character dialogue and solid songs that proved just as effective on vinyl as on the movie screen.

The Jungle Book Storyteller LP, edited from the film soundtrack by Larry Blakely at Sunset Sound, was a smash, earning a gold record for outstanding sales from the Record Industry Association of America. Dal McKennon narrates, skillfully transitioning between his performance as Bagheera the panther and the soundtrack dialogue of Sebastian Cabot in the same role. A similar album, without narration and fewer dialogue passages, was marketed to an adult audience on the Buena Vista label.

The second cast version, *Songs from the Jungle Book and Other Jungle Favorites*, was a bit of a stylistic departure for the Disneyland label. Steeped in late-1960s grooviness, the arrangements have a decidedly pop flair. Camarata's name does not appear on this album, creating speculation that another uncredited arranger/conductor influenced this particular disc. In any case, no other Disneyland albums of the period had this distinctive sound. The instrumentation features an electric organ, bass guitar, and brass, and the vocals credited to "The Jungle VIPs" are

Songbirds of the South, North, East, and West:
Loulie Jean Norman, Sally Sweetland, Carol Lombard, and Sally Stevens

Left to right: Loulie Jean Norman, Sally Sweetland, Carol Lombard, and Sally Stevens were all featured soloists on Disneyland Records.

The Hollywood music industry consumed musical talent at an incredible rate, especially when one considers the sheer volume of commercial jingles, background vocals, and television and movie themes that were churned out on a regular basis. A relatively small group of singers was responsible for much of this output, and when it came to female voices the field was even more limited.

The grande dame of the core studio singers was Loulie Jean Norman. A native of Birmingham, Alabama, Norman migrated to the bright lights of New York in the 1920s to study music. By 1935 she was a featured singer on network radio shows, and she would never be without work thereafter. In most cases she was placed firmly behind the scenes, receiving little or no credit for her contributions. She died on August 7, 2005, at age ninety-two.

Norman's first brush with Disney came as a member of the Jud Conlon Singers, vocalists on *Alice in Wonderland* (1951), *Peter Pan* (1953), and other animated features. Her legendary high soprano voice could be heard on numerous Disneyland Records beginning in the late 1950s. During the same period, Norman dubbed the singing for Diahann Carroll in the 1959 film *Porgy and Bess* and got a rare chance to deliver comedy dialogue for the LP *Spike Jones in Stereo*, in which she played the morbid Vampira opposite Paul Frees as Count Dracula. ("Oh, Drac, you slay me!") In the 1960s, Norman continued her work in television themes with the title song for *Flipper*, and "aahhing" in her highest register in the theme for *Star Trek*. In the Haunted Mansion at Disneyland, she was the opera singer in the graveyard scene.

Sally Sweetland's career somewhat resembled Norman's. During the 1940s, Sweetland provided the singing for actress Joan Leslie in a string of musicals, including *Yankee Doodle Dandy* (1942) and *Rhapsody in Blue* (1945). With her husband, Lee Sweetland, she became a vocal coach and continued that work alongside her various television shows, movies, and records, including songs for such children's labels as Golden and CRG. Her Disneyland Records of the mid-1960s were among her last before retiring from active performing to concentrate on her coaching. Well into her nineties and proud of it, Sweetland continued to teach vocal classes into the twenty-first century.

Carol Lombard constantly endured being confused with Carole Lombard, noted actress and wife of Clark Gable. Carol Lombard got her big break when accepted as a member of the Skylarks vocal group on Dinah Shore's television program. The group went on to sing backup on many other variety shows of the era, and Lombard was often heard as a member of the Jack Halloran Singers as well. Her Disneyland Records work represented the bulk of her appearances as a soloist rather than as a member of a group. In the 1960s, Lombard formed a children's choir known as the Carol Lombard Kids, and they recorded the theme for a Japanese animated cartoon import, *Prince Planet*. Today, although still occasionally called on to sing in groups for such films as *The Matrix*, Lombard devotes most of her time to her children's group, which is still in demand.

Sally Stevens was just beginning in the music business when her Disneyland Records solos on *The Jungle Book* second cast LP and ensemble work as part of the Jack Halloran Singers first appeared. Stevens's parents were studio singers, and her mother was one of the sped-up voices for the Munchkins in *The Wizard of Oz*. (Coincidentally, thirty years later, Sally Stevens would solo on the Disneyland Records LP *The Tin Woodman of Oz*.) Although she sang with a number of ensembles, Stevens's main work has been as a vocal contractor for some four hundred theatrical films and television series and as choral director for the annual Academy Awards telecasts from 1997 through 2003.

handled by Carol Lombard, Ron Hicklin, and Al Capps (who warbles "The Bare Necessities" in a deep bass).

Two non-Disney tunes round out the album: "The Abba Dabba Honeymoon," from the MGM musical *Two Weeks with Love*, which became a 1950 hit for Debbie Reynolds and Carleton Carpenter, and "Civilization," from the 1947 musical *Angel in the Wings*, its most famous performance by the Andrews Sisters with funnyman Danny Kaye. (The VIPs also recorded two other tunes, "The Vulture Song" and "Whatcha Gonna Do," that were not included on the LP but turned up on a Disneyland 45-rpm single.)

○

Beginning in the fall of 1967, the Gulf Oil Company assumed sponsorship of Disney's Sunday-night anthology TV series, now retitled *The Wonderful World of Disney*. Gulf stations nationwide began offering Disney premiums, including plastic placemats and record albums. The first Disneyland promotional album for Gulf was *Walt Disney's Happiest Songs*, selling for one dollar with a gas tank fill-up. Compiled from master tapes housed at Sunset Sound, *Happiest Songs* was a sampling from the past ten years of Disneyland Records inventory. Like other compilation albums of the 1960s sold through retailers such as True Value Hardware and Goodyear Tires, the album boasted numerous stars, including Mary Martin, Julie Andrews, Burl Ives, and Phil Harris. The album was so popular that a second collection, *Walt Disney's Merriest Songs*, was released the next year.

From 1968 to 1970, *Wonderful World of Disney* magazine was also available at Gulf stations. This glossy quarterly largely comprised recycled material created under Jimmy Johnson's supervision when he was editor of *Mickey Mouse Club Magazine* (later called

Veteran radio, movie, and television actor Sam Edwards was heard on numerous Disneyland Records. His performance of "The Wonderful Thing about Tiggers" was reused numerous times. (Courtesy of Sam Edwards)

Walt Disney's Magazine) a decade earlier. Material from the *Wonderful World* magazine also showed up in slipcased Disney children's book sets sold by mail, another project masterminded by Johnson. One of the regular artistic contributors to the magazine was Paul Wenzel, whose album covers for Disneyland and Buena Vista Records were appearing more and more frequently.

○

Sometimes when the Disney studio bought the rights to a series of stories, it gained control over more material than it could possibly use in one movie. Though Walt Disney purchased the entire *Winnie the*

Pooh series from A. A. Milne's estate, parts of only two of the twenty-three stories had been incorporated into the initial *Winnie the Pooh and the Honey Tree* featurette, and another handful of tales was adapted for 1968's *Winnie the Pooh and the Blustery Day*.

The *Blustery Day* Storyteller LP appeared in stores nearly a year before its film release. No soundtrack material was used, perhaps because none was ready at production time; instead, the story and music were recorded at Sunset Sound with the Disneyland stable of actors and the Jack Halloran Singers. The only voice actors to reprise their movie roles were Sterling Holloway as Pooh, Barbara Luddy as Kanga, and Jonathan Walmsley as Christopher Robin. Walmsley was a Hollywood child actor transplanted from his native England. In his *Pooh* appearances, his accent was in the process of disappearing. It would be completely gone five years later, when he became Jason on TV's *The Waltons*.

Sam Edwards emerged to the forefront with this album, filling in for Paul Winchell as Tigger and also playing Owl ("Today's weather report called off on account of bad weather"). Tigger was one of Edwards's favorite performances, combining manic energy with just a touch of goofiness. Edwards's version of "The Wonderful Thing about Tiggers," originating on this LP, became the only version ever heard on Disneyland vinyl records. For the years his Tigger performance was available, Edwards was often credited with his name alongside the title, a rare event for most cast members except Sterling Holloway, whose *Blustery Day* solo was (what else?) "A Rather Blustery Day." The other two songs, "The Rain, Rain, Rain Came Down, Down, Down" and "Hip Hip Pooh Ray," were performed by the Jack Halloran Singers and featured Sally Stevens and Bob Tebow among the identifiable voices. One song left off the *Blustery Day* album was "Heffalumps and Woozles," again likely because the album was produced far ahead of the film and the song might not yet have been written.

The story portion of the *Blustery Day* suffers a bit from a lack of postproduction. Side 1 seems unfinished, with empty spaces taking the place of missing sound effects. There is also some misplaced dialogue: in one scene, the wind noiselessly destroys Owl's house and Piglet is supposed to reproachfully ask Pooh, "Did you do that?" to which Pooh replies, "I don't think so." Due to an editing error, this exchange comes before the house falls. Sound effects are only heard on side 2.

Making use of the wealth of Milne stories, Disneyland next released a Storyteller LP called *Winnie the Pooh and Tigger*. Scriptwriter Johnson combined the tale of Tigger's first meeting with Pooh and a chapter about Tigger and Roo becoming stuck at the top of a tall tree (which would become part of the 1974 film *Winnie the Pooh and Tigger Too*). Brief musical moments on this album and subsequent Pooh adaptations combined Milne verse and Camarata music, sung by either the Jack Halloran or Mike Sammes Singers (neither of which receives album credit).

A single Milne story inspired the *Winnie the Pooh and the North Pole Expotition* LP, in which the characters journey to "discover the North Pole," even though most of the "expotition" has no idea of what that might be. The Disney studio brought this episode to the screen thirty-five years later in *Piglet's Big Movie*. The last Storyteller LP adapted directly from Milne stories was *Winnie the Pooh and the Heffalumps*.

○

Election year 1968 saw the release of the third major Sherman-scored Disney musical,

The One and Only, Genuine, Original Family Band. This project had begun under Walt's personal leadership, based on Laura Bower Van Nuys's autobiography, *The Family Band: From the Missouri to the Black Hills.* Three albums were released as tie-ins.

The soundtrack LP on Buena Vista followed the album-and-book format of *The Happiest Millionaire* release. The second cast version is of particular interest because of the rich orchestrations and vivid performances that went into what was essentially a budget album. "I think Tutti went to England to record that one where he could really spend some money on it," said Richard Sherman. "He loved it and he really did some great stuff on it." The vocalists were among the best in Hollywood: Bill Lee, Loulie Jean Norman, Gene Merlino, and Ernie Newton. Sherman was delighted with the results, from Merlino's towering rendition of "Dakota" to Newton's stirring interpretation of "Drummin' Drummin' Drummin'." More than thirty-five years later, Sherman said that it still "gives me gooseflesh when I hear it."

The Storyteller version of *Family Band* featured the same second cast songs wrapped by narration by Robie Lester as Mayo Bower (played in the movie by Bobby Riha). In a departure from the typical single-narrator Storyteller format, Lester's plot account received a comic boost from precocious side comments by Laura Bower (played on-screen by Pamelyn Ferdin). Cast as Laura on the LP was Jimmy Johnson's daughter, Gennifer, whose delivery was punctuated by a pronounced (and genuine) lisp. Gennifer Johnson Choldenko is today an award-winning children's book author, and in that capacity she had at least one occasion to recall her solitary appearance on vinyl: "In 2001, one of my books got made into a book on tape with Listening Library, and I sat in for the recording.

The producer was not wild about having me there, and she said to me, 'I'll bet you've never even been in a recording studio.' I didn't set her straight on this, but I thought about telling her about my debut/swan song."

O

The Enchanted Tiki Room, the first Disneyland Audio-Animatronics show, made it onto a record in 1968, five years after its debut. Its complete soundtrack easily fits on one side of an LP, so for side 2, Thurl Ravenscroft narrated an in-studio re-creation of the Jungle Cruise attraction, backed up by Camarata's Adventureland music from 1956's *Walt Disney Takes You to Disneyland.*

In addition to rides and attractions, Disneyland also featured live concerts featuring

Popular ghost singer Gene Merlino was a standout performer on the second cast songs from *The One and Only, Genuine, Original Family Band.* Merlino is seen here with Robie Lester, who narrated the Storyteller LP. (Courtesy of Robie Lester)

Gene Merlino: Sir Sing-a-lot

One of Hollywood's busiest singers began his career in San Francisco, on CBS radio in the 1950s. With his wife, Lois Draper, Gene Merlino moved to Los Angeles to work in the song-poem trade, recording tunes submitted by amateur songwriters. "They were paying two dollars a song," he said. "We would do thirty to fifty songs in a couple of hours, one time through. I was willing to do *anything*!" He estimates that he recorded ten thousand such songs over the next twenty years.

His singing gigs began to increase after he joined the quartet on the *Red Skelton Show*. His voice could be heard on TV variety shows with such stars as Dinah Shore, Danny Kaye, Dean Martin, Jerry Lewis, Donny and Marie Osmond, Carol Burnett, and Sonny and Cher. On records, he backed Frank Sinatra, Julie Andrews, Henry Mancini, Michael Jackson, Barbra Streisand, Bette Midler, and many others. Behind the movie screen, Merlino provided the singing voice for John Kerr in *Tea and Sympathy* (1956) and Franco Nero as Sir Lancelot in *Camelot* (1967). The latter was a bit of a coup for the singer, since good friend and singing rival Bill Lee usually captured the plum roles in Hollywood musicals. "They wanted Sergio Franchi to sing for Lancelot," Merlino recalled. "But Franchi wanted to be on camera too, and they cast Franco Nero, who did not sing. I remember when I finished the audition and [vocal director] Ken Darby said, 'I think you're going to get this one!' As I was leaving the audition, who should walk out but Bill Lee, so I thought I'd lost another one to him. But he said, 'I think this is yours,' and it was." Merlino sang the classics "If Ever I Would Leave You," "Soliloquy, C'est Moi," and a duet of "I Loved You Once in Silence" with Vanessa Redgrave.

Merlino was also one of the last members of the legendary MelloMen with Bill Lee, Bill Cole, and Thurl Ravenscroft, appearing on camera with them in the Elvis Presley musical *The Trouble with Girls* (1969). Though he sang theme music for TV series as diverse as *Rawhide*, *Alien Nation*, and the *Road Runner Show*, one of Merlino's most eye-opening works was as one of the quartet that sang "The Ballad of Gilligan's Island" in the show's second and third seasons. This particular credit has earned him a cult following when he speaks to college students. "I'll tell about the Grammy awards and the big bands and other things I've done, but I always end with *Gilligan's Island* when they're falling asleep," Merlino laughed. "Then their faces all light up and they think it's the greatest thing in the world! There was even a poll that named it the most recognizable theme of all time."

He also enjoyed a long association with the Anita Kerr Singers, the vocal group that received a Grammy Award for Best Performance by a Vocal Group. "When we won, nobody believed it!" he recalled. Their a cappella version of "A House Is Not a Home" was a mammoth international hit. When Kerr did the music for Rod McKuen's best-selling series of poetry albums for Warner Brothers Records, Merlino was called upon to narrate *The Sea*, which charted for 140 weeks.

For Disney, he not only recorded such memorable selections as "Dakota" for *The One and Only, Genuine, Original Family Band* second cast LP but also sang in the chorus of such animated classics as *The Little Mermaid*, *Aladdin*, *Beauty and the Beast*, and the 1982 digital Irwin Kostal re-release of *Fantasia*. He coached the Kids of the Kingdom at Disneyland Park and sang on many theme park attractions such as *Mickey's Philharmagic* at Walt Disney World. Merlino still sings every year on the Academy Awards broadcast and continues to sing in movies, including *The Matrix* and *Van Helsing*. "When you're a studio singer you rarely get known [to the public]," he said, "which is okay, but after fifty-plus years, I'm sure I've recorded more music than any other studio singer in town—and that's some kind of accomplishment."

big bands, low-key teen pop, and Dixieland jazz. Since 1961, phenomenal trumpet virtuoso Louis Armstrong had been a frequent "Dixieland at Disneyland" headliner. He also appeared in an episode of *Walt Disney's Wonderful World of Color* called "Disneyland after Dark." In 1966, Walt Disney personally asked Armstrong to record an album of Disney songs, but the album was not made until after Walt's death. Jimmy Johnson fondly recalled the 1968 sessions: "The dates with Louis were among the happiest I can remember. He had been quite ill and had gone on a rigorous diet. He was very thin but looked well and was full of energy. He not only sang on the album, he blew his horn, something he hadn't been doing much of in recent days." Armstrong enjoyed recording *Disney Songs the Satchmo Way* so much that he wrote to Camarata,

This goldarned "Wish upon a Star" is so beautiful and more than that, man—I listen to that tune three or four times a night. Man, did you know I'm a doggoned long-time wishing cat? Well I am, man.

Tell Maxwell [Davis, the album arranger] what a great job he did. That man's got soul. (A soul Br'er!) Tutti you are in there yourself. Being one fine trumpet man yourself, you're bound to get the right sounds 'n everything 'nice' musically in your inimitable way. (Did that come out of me?) That's it Daddy—nobody mess with those 'ears' you have for music.

I haven't enjoyed anything better than our recording sessions since—well, I can't remember when.

○

Mickey Mouse celebrated his fortieth birthday in 1968. His image had just become fashionable again, as celebrities and members of the counterculture sported his wristwatches for the first time since the 1930s. August 1968 saw the release of *Mickey Mouse and His Friends*, a compilation LP of many old Mickey tracks lifted from past recordings, including some of the original 1955 *Mickey Mouse Club* songs. The album also featured a newly recorded version of Carl Stalling's 1929 classic "Minnie's Yoo Hoo," performed as a rinky-tink 1930s ditty. It appeared on the "Mickey's Fortieth Birthday" TV special, turned up on the B side of Phil Harris's Buena Vista single of the 1930s song "What? No Mickey Mouse?" and would serve as theme music for the syndicated *Mouse Factory* series in 1972.

○

In another of Disney's Euro/American productions, Johnson and Camarata created an adaptation of Johanna Spyri's *Heidi*. Like the Hollywood-produced Disney records, the London recordings made good use of the pool of voice talent available from the worlds of radio and animated cartoons. English actress Brenda Dunnich narrated as grown-up Heidi; Carole Lorimer played Heidi as a child; British Broadcasting Corporation veteran John Witty was Heidi's grandfather; and

British cartoon voice artist Ysanne Churchman was a London-based Disney record performer during the late 1960s. (Courtesy of Ysanne Churchman)

Ysanne Churchman, whose career went back to pre–World War II experimental television days, played the invalid Klara Sesemann. Stella Kimball had the dual roles of Heidi's somewhat ditzy Aunt Dete and tyrannical tutor Miss Rottenmeier. For some reason, Ginny Tyler and a British actress share the role of Peter the goatherd. Camarata wrote music and lyrics for five of the six songs, performed by the Mike Sammes Singers. The sixth, "Miss Rottenmeier's Rules," was a Johnson/Camarata collaboration that boasted one of Camarata's famous tempo changes, from minuet to jazz.

○

Sunset Sound: Bruce Botnick, Larry Blakely, and Friends

Sunset Sound Recorders began as a veritable extension of Disneyland/Buena Vista Records, with Tutti Camarata employing its facilities primarily for his Disney projects. Very quickly, it grew to be one of the most influential recording studios in pop music history.

"Alan Emig built that studio from the ground up," said legendary engineer Bruce Botnick. "He was an incredible mixer and a great technician. He designed and built all his own consoles and amplifiers." Emig and Brian Ross-Myring handled the early Sunset work; Botnick arrived in 1963 as the studio was beginning to expand. It was a full-service facility where records could be recorded, mixed, and mastered. "There was a record that needed to be done at Disneyland of the Ward Gospel singers," Botnick recalled of the days when he eagerly pursued a position at Sunset. "I would not take no for an answer. I told them that Ted Keep [of Liberty Records] had a mobile recording studio, so they hired Ted. I did that project and that was it. That was the album that got me into the fold. I went from being an apprentice to doing recording right out of the box." Botnick became a fixture at Sunset through most of the 1960s.

Camarata was an amazing innovator with incredible creative range, said Botnick: "His contribution was enormous. Tutti invented the idea of the isolation booth. He said, 'I want to take the mastering room and turn it into a big iso booth where we could put strings or a chorus or whatever.' No other studio had one. It set the industry on edge because all of a sudden you could do a session and isolate things 100 percent. Up until that time, everybody was recording everything in one room, live."

The studio was so successful that it began to crowd out its own founder, which was just fine with him. "Sunset was becoming a commercial studio," said Botnick. "When Tutti couldn't get in, he kept building more studios. He kept one room for himself and was eventually chased out of that one, too." This may be one reason that so much music for late-1960s Disney records was recorded in Europe.

By the mid-1960s, Botnick's typical day started early in the morning and continued until late at night: "I would come in at 8:00 and do a commercial for Midas, and by lunch or late morning I was doing a Disney Storyteller. In the late afternoon, about 4:00, I'd start on the Doors, the Beach Boys or Baja Marimba Band, and work into the night." Botnick's workload required Sunset to hire more engineers for the Disney work, including Jimmy Messina, later of Loggins and Messina.

One of Botnick's most renowned Sunset projects was the Doors' third album, *Waiting for the Sun*. Years later, he found himself working on Disney projects again with his own company, Digital Magnetics. "I was doing *Beauty and the Beast*, *Aladdin*, and *The Lion King*," he said. "I can't get them out of my life, and I'm delighted."

One of the young engineers brought to Sunset Sound in 1966 was Larry Blakely, who had his own recording studio in Dodge City, Kansas. Blakely worked on *A Happy Birthday Party with Winnie the Pooh* and numerous soundtracks including *The Jungle Book*, *The Gnome Mobile*, and *The One and Only, Genuine, Original Family Band*. "When we would do a movie soundtrack album, the Disney studio would send in the whole movie and the music on quarter-inch stereo tape," Blakely explained. "My job was to cut it down and assemble a twenty- or thirty-minute record from a two-hour movie. I had no script or visual guidelines from the movie. So, with an editing block and a razor blade, I'd soon be up to my knees in edited tape! At that point, we'd have a stereo master tape. We would cut a master disc, they'd ship it to the processing plant and make the records."

Blakely also recalled Sunset as a happening place to be. "It was an incredible time," he said. "That was the record industry heyday in Hollywood, with Herb Alpert and the Tijuana Brass, Jackie De Shannon, the Monkees, the Turtles, Buffalo Springfield, Ricky Nelson—it was unreal. At one point, about thirty-five of the one hundred top albums listed in *Billboard* were recorded at Sunset."

Camarata was always involved with the goings-on. Blakely recalled, "Tutti's one of the most self-effacing men in Hollywood. People like Sinatra and Mantovani would drop by the studio. We'd be talking and he'd suddenly mention in passing working with Billie Holiday or Ella Fitzgerald, and I'd be awestruck, yet he never blew his own horn."

Blakely left Sunset in 1973 and had a successful second career in marketing and sales of recording equipment and technologies. He has written more than three hundred articles and columns about the industry. Blakely's dream project was *The Power and the Glory*, an album of Latter-day Saints hymns that reunited him with Camarata and Botnick more than thirty-five years after their Disneyland Records days. Four years in the making, the project brought Camarata out of retirement to arrange and conduct in London, saying, "Larry, I'm going to help make this dream come true for you." "That's the kind of person Tutti is," Blakely said. "A true gentleman."

Nineteen sixty-eight was the biggest year yet for read-along entries, with a record thirteen productions released. Most notable were *Acting Out the ABC's*, which repeats its entire text on the record twice; *It's a Small World*, a story about an orphan boy who visits the famous Disneyland attraction; and *Mickey Mouse, the Brave Little Tailor*, based on the animated short, which featured Robie Lester's only take on Mickey's voice.

One of the most elaborate Disneyland album sequels, *More Jungle Book*, also was created this year. Jimmy Johnson wrote: "Although there wasn't and probably won't be a sequel on film to *Jungle Book*, we did do a sequel on story-telling records called *More Jungle Book*. I asked [radio comedy veteran] Larry Clemmons, who had been the chief story man on the film, to write a sequel. We started the project out with a luncheon attended by Phil [Harris], Larry, Tutti Camarata and myself." Johnson continued, "Phil was very excited about the project and began setting the story line as he saw it. He reasoned very rightly that one of the strengths of *Jungle Book* had been the close and warm relationship between Baloo and Mowgli, the man-cub. Now Mowgli [played on the record by Ginny Tyler] had gone back to the Man Village and Baloo missed him sorely. With the help of Bagheera the Panther [Dal McKennon] and King Louie of the Apes [Louis Prima], he gets Mowgli back for a few more adventures." Johnson gave much of the credit for the album to Harris: "Phil's sense of what is right for him, and won't play, is very keen. He was a big help on the story of the sequel story album."

The songs included "Baloo's Blues," "Jungle Fever" (not to be confused with the 1930s hit song), "If You Want to See Some Strange Behavior (Take a Look at Man)," and "It's a Kick." Both Harris and Prima had ample opportunities to ham it up with these numbers. More than three decades later, Walt Disney Pictures released *Jungle Book II* to theaters. The plot had some natural similarities, but there was no direct connection between the record and the film.

Johnson and Camarata were now hitting their stride in turning out Disneyland Records, whether drawing from the studio projects, theme park attractions, or literary adaptations. Now that they had brought Pooh and Baloo to vinyl, they prepared to venture into more fantastic horizons, including the Land of Oz.

9

The Road to Oz and the End of an Era

By the late 1960s, Jimmy Johnson had proven to be an accomplished scriptwriter for dozens of Disneyland Records. "Turning a motion picture into a story telling record for children is not as simple as it sounds," Johnson wrote. "Films are visual, records are not. Disney films in particular are full of sight gags which bomb completely when one tries to explain them in words on a phonograph record." He went on, "I think I did a good job at it. No less artists than Peter Ustinov and Walter Slezak congratulated me on my scripts for *Blackbeard's Ghost* and *Emil and the Detectives*. I will admit that Peter embellished my script on *Blackbeard*, but he did say that I had caught the character very well in the narration I had written."

Especially difficult to adapt were the Disney live-action film comedies. Audio could capture vivid dialogue, but no matter how skillful the narration, it could not convey the special effects and facial expressions so essential to the humor. *Blackbeard's Ghost* has merit as a soundtrack album because of the superb verbal sparring between Ustinov and Dean Jones, though it cannot do justice to the film's visual comedy.

The Love Bug may not have fared so well on vinyl. The comedy about a Volkswagen beetle with a mind of its own became the stu-dio's biggest smash of the post-Walt era and the highest-grossing film of 1969. Had the studio known what a hit the film would be, the record division might have lavished a bit more attention on the tie-in LP. As it happened, the record was very low-key and did not even include the signature George Bruns theme music. Buddy Hackett, one of the film's stars, does a creditable job as narrator, but his performance sounds somewhat stilted since reading a script in a sound booth is very different from doing stand-up comedy. He projects a bit more energy into the album's reenacted film scenes.

Like Jimmy Johnson's *Blackbeard's Ghost* LP script, the *Love Bug* album begins with a short monologue. In this case Hackett, as Tennessee Steinmetz, talks about his unusual name and sings a few bars of "The Ballad of Davy Crockett" because it mentions the state in the lyrics. He then talks briefly about automobiles and running boards before he gets to the film's story. Disneyland Records regulars Robie Lester and Dal McKennon play supporting roles, joined by Gerry Hoff in the Dean Jones role of Jim Douglas. Hoff's acting experience, especially played against such seasoned pros, is clearly limited. There is no soundtrack material save for Hackett's Japanese lines on side 2.

Misty the Mischievous Mermaid is a Storyteller LP that invites speculation about its source material. Hans Christian Andersen's *The Little Mermaid* was one of the last stories Walt considered as a feature film, so it is conceivable that a good amount of concept work may have been done between that period and the film's eventual release in 1989. Some of this early material may well have made its way onto the *Misty* LP. The story, recorded with a British cast, concerns itself more with pirates and treasure than the Andersen tale, but Misty has her share of undersea friends and even has the same red hair as Disney's Ariel (though Misty wears it in a 1960s-style hairdo).

One of the most eagerly anticipated attractions in Disneyland history was the Haunted Mansion. It had been announced in the early 1960s but remained unfinished while other projects took precedence. When the attraction finally opened in 1969, there was a Disneyland Records Storyteller LP to complement it. Unlike earlier albums based on attractions, *The Haunted Mansion* is the only Disney LP that builds additional story material around the ride. In addition to original scenes and effects that never made it into the final attraction, the record featured a subplot about two teenagers returning home from a date.

Though most of the LP's dialogue was recorded at Sunset Sound, the music comes from the ride's soundtrack, including the theme music played by famed Hollywood organist Gaylord Carter and the Madame Leota sequence in which Eleanor Audley (voice of *Cinderella*'s stepmother and *Sleeping Beauty*'s Maleficent) speaks as the disembodied medium. Thurl Ravenscroft handles the narration in his most funereal tones, with

Pete Renaday performed many different roles on Disneyland Records from the late 1960s onward, most notably as *The Haunted Mansion*'s Ghost Host and as Mickey Mouse.

teenagers Karen and Mike played by Robie Lester and future Oscar-winning director Ron Howard (shortly after *The Andy Griffith Show* and during his involvement with Disney film and TV projects such as *Smoke* and *A Boy Called Nuthin'*). Performance fees prevented the use of Paul Frees from the attraction soundtrack, so Pete Renaday performs the Ghost Host lines from Xavier Atencio's attraction script, with additional material created especially for the record. Rather than attempting to duplicate the inimitable Frees, Renaday creates his own host, and engineer Larry Blakely added a unique touch by "doubling" all of Renaday's lines, running them through a series of recording and playback heads in the tape machines. The doubled voice takes on a stereophonic life of its own, sometimes coming from the center, sometimes bouncing from left to right channels.

The album's attic sequence describes something that no longer appears on the attraction. After seeing the ghostly bride with the beating heart, Mike and Karen encounter a cloaked figure whose head disappears from his body and reappears in a hatbox. Shortly after this LP was produced, the hatbox ghost was removed from the ride: the effect, which depended so much on the right balance of light and dark, just never worked well enough to be convincing. The cemetery scene

Pete Renaday:
Vinyl Mickey Mouse, Other Ghost Host, and More

Disney enthusiasts are well aware that Walt Disney did the voice of Mickey Mouse until 1947, when he asked sound-effects master Jimmy Macdonald to take over. In recent decades, Mickey's falsetto has been given perhaps its widest range and depth by the remarkable Wayne Allwine. What is not commonly known is that other actors also played Mickey along the way, including Stan Freberg for Capitol Records. But the actor who talked and sang as Mickey most often besides Disney, Macdonald, and Allwine is Pete Renaday.

Pierre L. Renoudet was born in New Iberia, Louisiana, but changed the spelling to phonetic Renaday in the mid-1970s. "I started off as a messenger at the Disney studio," Renaday recalled. "Then I worked for the art props department, which also handled scripts. There was so much live action and television going by then, the library became its own department." Between duties at the studio, Renaday pursued an acting career. One of his first screen tests was for a Disney TV production called *Willie and the Yank* with James MacArthur. Outside the studio, Renaday took on a French character role on the TV series *Combat*.

He also did a lot of plays, many of them within the Disney studio gates. "There was a theater group called the Disney Players, which raised money for one of Walt's favorite charities, the John Tracy Clinic. Walt played polo with Spencer Tracy, and this was a speech and hearing clinic that Spencer and his wife started because of their son, John, who was deaf. "We did plays like *Light Up the Sky*, *Mary, Mary*, *The Whole Darn Shooting Match*, and *The Man Who Came to Dinner* on the orchestra stage in the main theater," he said. "One day the director was approached by Walt, who said, 'You know, we've bought this Broadway show, *The Happiest Millionaire*, and I've never even seen the thing. Maybe the Disney Players will put it on and we'll have a look at it.'" Walt called on Brian Keith to play the lead, since *Millionaire* was not conceived as a musical until after *Mary Poppins*'s success. For this live production, seen only by Disney employees and their families, Renaday was cast as Angier Duke and Roberta Shore as Cordy, roles played years later in the film by John Davidson and Lesley Ann Warren.

Renaday continued to enjoy the best of both wonderful worlds as a Disney studio employee and working actor. "I stayed at the studio for many years because one didn't stop me from doing the other," he explained. "They let me come and go and never stopped me." Until he left the studio in 1992, Renaday worked as a dialogue coach, assisting film actors with script reading, including Dean Jones in *The Horse in the Gray Flannel Suit* and the children in *The One and Only, Genuine, Original Family Band*. He also played small roles in numerous films, including the treasury agent in *$1,000,000 Duck* and the policeman who sees Herbie attempt suicide in *The Love Bug*. When *Who Framed Roger Rabbit?* was in the planning stages, Renaday played Eddie Valiant in the test footage.

He also did a number of Disney voices, including Henry the Bear in the Country Bear Jamboree attraction, the milkman in *The AristoCats* (1970), and even some whistling and humming for the lead character in *Robin Hood* (1973). His debut on Disneyland Records was as the Ghost Host for *The Haunted Mansion*.

Jimmy Macdonald asked Renaday to do Mickey's voice for various functions when Macdonald was unavailable, such as Mickey's phone calls to children. When Jymn Magon and company ushered in the second golden age of Disneyland-Vista Records, Renaday became Mickey on all of the albums, including *Yankee Doodle Mickey*, *Pardners*, and *Merry Christmas Carols*. In addition, he was the voice of Talking Mickey Mouse, an electronic toy that told adventure stories in the fashion of Teddy Ruxpin. Renaday's Mickey performances were confined mostly to records and cassettes, though he did voice Mickey for the 1972 syndicated TV series *The Mouse Factory*.

Pete Renaday remains one of Hollywood's busiest actors, both on- and offscreen. His many roles included John Jacks on *General Hospital* and the voices of Splinter and Vernon on *Teenage Mutant Ninja Turtles*. He performed voice work as a dragon monster in the English version of *Nausicaa of the Valley of the Winds*, an animated feature by Hayao Miyazaki (*Spirited Away*), and is frequently heard on the syndicated children's radio drama, *Adventures in Odyssey*.

features the song "Grim Grinning Ghosts," penned by Atencio and Buddy Baker and sung by Ravenscroft. Heard faintly in the background are Bill Lee as a phantom king, Loulie Jean Norman as a screechy opera singer, and deep-voiced Candy Candido as a shackled prisoner.

The Storyteller version of *The Haunted Mansion* has developed quite a cult following, becoming one of the most sought-after Disney records. Fans enjoy hearing the most comprehensive description of the popular ride and prize the accompanying artwork by Collin Campbell.

O

Walt Disney was well aware of the popularity of the Oz books, initiated by L. Frank Baum in 1900 and continued by various successors after his death in 1919. Disney had first inquired about the movie rights to the Oz books around the time *Snow White and the Seven Dwarfs* was completed in 1937, but MGM was planning the well-known Judy Garland live-action musical version, which was released two years later.

In the 1950s, Disney achieved some success in obtaining the Oz series. In 1956, the first book, *The Wonderful Wizard of Oz*, entered public domain, so anyone could have access to it. The rights to the second book, *The Marvelous Land of Oz*, had been sold to another producer. After many legal twists and turns, the Disney studio acquired twelve of the fourteen original Baum Oz books. Disney executives decided to turn the books into a live-action feature starring some of the *Mickey Mouse Club* Mouseketeers. In a *Disneyland* fourth anniversary TV episode from the fall of 1957, the Mouseketeers enacted scenes from their "forthcoming" feature, *The Rainbow Road to Oz*. Annette Funicello was cast as Princess Ozma, Darlene Gillespie as Dorothy, Bobby Burgess as the Scarecrow,

Doreen Tracey as the Patchwork Girl (with the singing voice of Gloria Wood), and Lonnie Burr as farmhand Zeb. Buddy Baker and Tom Adair composed the songs. This "preview" of the film was as far as the project went, as Walt became dissatisfied and halted the project.

The Oz books languished on the Disney shelf until 1965, when Ray Bolger reprised his MGM role for an LP based on Baum's 1915 book, *The Scarecrow of Oz*. The record is relatively faithful to the somewhat convoluted book story. A girl named Trot, an old sailor named Cap'n Bill, and a trouble-prone boy named Button-Bright find themselves in an unpleasant section of Oz known as Jinxland. Glinda the Good sends the Scarecrow to help them, but he runs afoul of ambitious King Krewl and Prime Minister Googly-Goo, who have enlisted Blinkie the witch, who turns Cap'n Bill into a grasshopper and freezes the heart of Princess Gloria.

Robie Lester plays Button-Bright, Princess Gloria, and Glinda (whose storybook illustration resembles the real-life Lester in 1965). Dal McKennon is Cap'n Bill and a British, birdlike creature called the Ork. Martha Wentworth gave her final Disneyland Records performance as Blinkie. As for the uncredited actors who played Trot and Pon, they are believed to be Pamela Shannon (of the *Mary Poppins* second cast LP) and Michael Donohue (from *Hansel and Gretel*). The musical background is performed mostly on harpsichord, likely because of budgetary limits. The sole original song, "Happy Glow," is an odd minor key tune sung by Bill Lee; the record concludes with a children's choir singing "Over the Rainbow," from the MGM film.

The next Disney/Oz production was one of the best: a full cast adaptation of Baum's *The Wizard of Oz* book, with songs from the

Sam Edwards: From Radio Row to the Land of Oz

Sam Edwards was one of a special group of performers who could truthfully claim that they had been in show business for their entire lives. Edwards was born in Macon, Georgia, where his parents were active in vaudeville and dramatic stock, and it must have been a given that young Edwards would also go into the entertainment field. His first experiences on stage involved playing child roles in his parents' stock company.

In the early 1930s, the family migrated to San Antonio, Texas, where his parents created a children's radio serial, *The Adventures of Sonny and Buddy*, for KTSA. Sam, his brother, and his sister were in the cast, and they continued their roles when the show moved to the West Coast. Edwards became a very active part of Hollywood's burgeoning radio scene and expanded into animated cartoons, appearing as the voice of the adolescent version of Thumper the rabbit in Disney's *Bambi* (1942).

One of his earliest film roles included playing sidekick Chuck Ramsey in Columbia's serial version of the radio classic *Captain Midnight* (1942). Around 1943 he began his longest-running radio role, playing bumbling boyfriend Dexter Franklin opposite Janet Waldo on *Meet Corliss Archer*. He appeared regularly on the *Lux Radio Theatre*, *The Cisco Kid*, *Red Ryder*, *Yours Truly Johnny Dollar*, *The Whistler*, *Escape*, and *Dragnet* and was part of the *Gunsmoke* stock company, appearing in dozens of episodes during the series' radio run.

His movie work ran concurrently with his radio appearances. He put on a thick southern accent for Gregory Peck's *Twelve O'Clock High* (1949) and had an emotive role as Junior in John Wayne's *Operation Pacific* (1951). The script called for Edwards to drown during a climactic battle on the open sea, but according to him, the water in the tank that was being used for filming was so cold that he nearly performed his death scene for real.

On television, Edwards appeared on *I Love Lucy*, the *Andy Griffith Show*, and in Jack Webb's stock company for *Dragnet*. "They used us over and over again," he recalled, "until the audience started noticing that the same suspects were turning up in every show!" Behind the screen, he was heard on such animated series as *The Adventures of Jonny Quest* and *Rod Rocket*.

Edwards's Disneyland Records career ranged from playing the Big Bad Wolf in *Three Little Pigs* (1958) to the crusty-but-benign father on *The Orange Bird* (1971), with lots of Pooh and Oz characters in between. He subsequently took on his last continuing TV role as town banker Anderson on the long-running *Little House on the Prairie*.

By the early 1980s, Edwards and his wife, Beverly, were ready to retire from show business, and after finishing up his *Prairie* episodes, Sam moved to a mountaintop home in Colorado. Beverly was a well-known travel writer for many different camping and RV magazines, and Sam was more than happy to sit back and leave the driving to her as they traveled over the entire United States in their motor home.

Edwards's final public appearance was at one of his beloved old-time radio conventions just one month before his death on July 28, 2004, at age eighty-nine.

MGM version performed by the Mike Sammes Singers. In one of her most effective performances, Lester narrates as Dorothy. Dal McKennon takes on the roles of the Scarecrow, using his self-described "standard dumb voice" crossed with a bit of Ed Wynn; the Guardian of the Gate, a role he also voiced in the Filmation animated feature *Journey Back to Oz* (1974); and the Wizard, whose dialogue shifts tone in midscene, perhaps because of editing of separate takes. Two newcomers to Disney's Oz were Sam Edwards as both the Cowardly Lion and Tin Woodman and Ginny Tyler as Glinda, Aunt Em, and the Witches of the North (good) and West (wicked). This particular version adheres more closely to the first Baum book than many other vinyl versions before or since.

Even though *The Rainbow Road to Oz* was never produced, two of its Buddy Baker/Tom Adair songs, "The Oz-Phabet" and "The Pup-Pup-Puppet Polka," were rescued for the *Cowardly Lion of Oz* LP. Four additional songs by the team (which may have also been intended for *Rainbow Road*) are also included. There is no evidence that the story on this record has any relationship to the screenplay of *Rainbow Road*, nor does it resemble the Ruth Plumly Thompson book of that title, even though the album cover credits the book as its source.

Like *The Scarecrow of Oz*, the serpentine plot of this LP chronicles a struggle for the throne. Glinda summons the Cowardly Lion because the peace of the neighboring Prattling Country is threatened when King Maydor's son, Prince Paul, is kidnapped. It's an evil plot by Archduke Grimble, who also employs Smarmy the witch to transform Prince Paul and fiancée Princess Flora into marionettes, hauled around Oz by sinister puppeteer Glarm (a dead ringer for *Pinocchio*'s Stromboli). The Lion is assisted in his mission by Forget-Me-Not, an absent-minded young girl. Edwards reprises his Bert Lahr impersonation as the Cowardly Lion, with vocal support from Lester, McKennon, and Tyler. The vocals for the *Cowardly Lion* songs were recorded with Mike Sammes singing in London for the Cowardly Lion and Carol Lombard singing in Hollywood for Glinda and Smarmy. The Mike Sammes Singers and Brian Fahey's orchestrations also came from the United Kingdom. Whereas Sammes makes no effort to sound like Edwards (and most likely never heard the U.S. dialogue), Lombard recalled working very closely with Tyler to match the speaking and singing voices as closely as possible.

The final Baum book to be produced by Disney for records was 1970's *The Tin Woodman of Oz*. In Johnson's adaptation, a teenager named Woot the Wanderer is searching for his true love. The Tin Woodman, looking for his lost Munchkin girlfriend, joins Woot, accompanied by the Scarecrow and the Cowardly Lion. After a detour in the land of balloon-like Loons, they encounter the giant Mrs. Yoop, who changes them into various creatures. Another of Mrs. Yoop's victims is Polychrome the fairy, who is turned into a canary. Eventually Ozma, the Queen of Oz, restores everyone, and Woot and Polychrome become engaged. The Scarecrow, the Tin Woodman, and the Lion all get married by the end of the record. This ending is not in Baum's book, but it does draw a curtain over the Disney records of Oz.

Once again, Edwards plays the Tin Woodman and the Cowardly Lion, with Lester,

McKennon, and Tyler returning as well. Ron Howard marks his second Disneyland Records performance with Woot, though a very grown-up sounding Bill Lee sings his song, along with Sally Stevens as Polychrome (for Lester) and Lombard as Mrs. Yoop (for Tyler). The songs from *Wizard*, *Cowardly Lion*, and *Scarecrow of Oz* were later combined on one LP.

○

The first time Disneyland Records ventured outside the Disney realm for an animation soundtrack was when *Goldilocks* came to the label in 1970. *Goldilocks* was a half-hour NBC-TV special produced by DePatie-Freleng Enterprises (of *Pink Panther* cartoon fame). It starred Bing Crosby and his family, including Mary Frances in the title role (she would go on to be the person who shot J.R. on the hit TV series *Dallas*). Animation voices included Paul Winchell and Avery Schreiber. The Sherman brothers, who wrote the songs and coproduced the special, were responsible for getting the soundtrack on Disneyland Records. "We went to Jimmy Johnson and said it would mean a lot to us and we'd like it to come out as one of the Storytellers," recalled Richard Sherman, "I think it was the only time Bing Crosby recorded for the Disneyland label." The LP was also released without the Disney name as a special premium album sold by dealers of the show's sponsoring product, Armstrong Evans-Black carpets.

○

Johnson took another crack at Disney big-screen comedies with *The Boatniks*. The film—about bumbling jewel thieves, bumbling Coast Guard rescuers, and zany California boat enthusiasts—was neither as successful nor as inspired as *The Love Bug*, but its LP version is a tour de force for Dal McKennon, who uses skillful timing and nuanced inflec-

Dal McKennon's superb comic timing enhanced the Disneyland Records adaptation of *The Boatniks*. (Courtesy of Tammy Rock)

tion to make Phil Silvers's Harry Simmons character his own. Robie Lester and Sam Edwards turn in especially inspired performances, and Gerry Hoff is quite suitable this time around, sounding quite a bit like the actor for whom he is substituting (Robert Morse).

One of the last times several of these actors would work together was on the Grammy-nominated *AristoCats* Storyteller, which arrived in stores two seasons before the animated feature's Christmas 1970 release. The movie cast glamorous Eva Gabor as pampered feline Duchess, but she was not a singer (as evidenced in her "talk-sing" performance of the theme to her hit TV series, *Green Acres*). For the film, Robie Lester sang several bars for Gabor. On the album, Lester

both speaks and sings for Duchess. Phil Harris and Sterling Holloway reenact their film roles as Thomas O'Malley the Alley Cat and Roquefort the Mouse, respectively. Sam Edwards as Edgar and Candy Candido as Scat Cat round out the studio cast. Soundtrack dialogue of Pat Buttram, George Lindsey, Monica Evans, and Carole Shelley is also included, but Holloway sounds as if he is battling health problems: distinct differences exist in the quality of his performance in the narration and in the dialogue sections, which of course were recorded on different dates. (At one point he even blows his lines by referring to "Madame and the kittens" instead of "Duchess and the kittens.") Three names are credited for Duchess's kittens, Marie, Toulouse, and Berlioz: Gregory Novack, Susan Novack, and Victor Sweier. However, on the recording, only two of the kittens are played by children, while Lester plays the third. It is possible that the third child actor listed originally recorded the part and then Lester re-recorded the dialogue.

The vocals by Harris, Lester, and the children, with the Mike Sammes Singers and London musicians providing backup, were also released on another LP, *The AristoCats and Other Cat Songs*, which also included the first album appearance of the Wellingtons' 1964 single "Thomasina" from *The Three Lives of Thomasina*.

○

With the 1970s under way, Disney found that its supremacy as the source of children's entertainment was being challenged as never before. One of the biggest landmarks hit TV screens for the first time in November 1969. *Sesame Street* took elements proven successful in commercial children's programming and adapted them for educational purposes, including catchy, fast-paced "commercials" that sold kids on the alphabet and counting rather than cereal and toys. Jim Henson's Muppets, which had been making memorable TV appearances since 1957, hit their stride with the new PBS series. *Sesame Street* songs became children's standards, with "Rubber Duckie" charting as a pop novelty single. Every children's record company produced its version of songs from the series, and Disneyland was no exception.

Seven of the show's earliest musical numbers were recorded for a Disney LP called *Rubber Duckie and Other Songs from Sesame Street*. Released three months short of the TV show's first anniversary, this album was one of the last to feature some of Disneyland's most durable performers, while introducing new ones. One of these newcomers was Jeromy Stuart, a pianist and songwriter who was also featured in the late 1960s rock group the Electric Prunes (which certainly put a new wrinkle in his career). Throughout 1970, Stuart would also be responsible for composing and performing several one-shot songs for the flip sides on the ongoing "readalong" series. Another new arrival was powerfully voiced singer Katie Briggs.

Together again were Lester, singing in a childlike voice, and Ravenscroft. "Hi, I'm a frog," growls Ravenscroft in his unmistakable Tony the Tiger tones just before launching into Joe Raposo's now-legendary theme for Kermit, "Bein' Green." Even odder is when Ravenscroft joins Stuart, Briggs, and Lester in "I've Got Two." When he rumbles, "I wanna sing some tunes! I wanna sing some tunes!" and Stuart replies, "Go right ahead, Thurl," it may be the only time Ravenscroft was ever referred to by name on a Disney record.

More pressing than giving Ravenscroft credit in the script was the opening of the gigantic Walt Disney World resort in Florida, a vacation complex twice the size of Manhat-

Robie Lester finished her long run as the Disneyland Story Reader with the 1970 *Pecos Bill* read-along. (Courtesy of Robie Lester)

tan Island that Roy saw completed only months before his death in 1971. As he had done with the Disneyland park, Roy and his Walt Disney World team partnered with many major organizations, including the Florida Citrus Growers' Association. To that end, Disney artists created a new cartoon character called the Orange Bird to advertise Florida-grown orange juice. Designed to be as cute and cuddly as possible, the new character had an oversized head shaped like an orange and wings that resembled shiny green leaves. He was animated for television ads encouraging viewers to "think orange," as live-action Anita Bryant sang, "Come to the Florida sunshine tree." An area of Adventureland in the Magic Kingdom featured the "Sunshine Tree Terrace," where the Orange Bird swung to and fro as citrus refreshments were served below.

Vince Jefferds, who headed Disney's consumer products division, clearly wanted his Orange Bird to catch on. He receives a story credit on *The Orange Bird* Storyteller LP, which promotes Walt Disney World on the back cover. Anita Bryant, then a Florida resident and frequent TV spokesperson, narrates the story of the Orange Bird. Communicating only through orange puffs of smoke, he is rejected by other birds and threatened by a cat before a picnicking family adopts him. The album does not overtly promote citrus products or Florida tourism, only making reference to a "sunny place in the South" and finishing with a ballad called "Orange Tree." The songs by the Sherman brothers were written especially for the album, with one exception. "'I'll Fly the Skyway' was written originally for *The AristoCats*," said Richard Sherman. "It was called 'My Way's the Highway,' actually Thomas O'Malley Cat's song. [An O'Malley song by Terry Gilkyson was chosen instead.] So when Jimmy Johnson wanted songs for this Orange Bird thing, we rewrote the song. This sort of thing happens to all songwriters. Why throw away a perfectly good tune when you can use it for something else?" Sherman continued, "We wrote several songs for the Orange Bird because Johnson wanted to promote the character. It didn't go very far but they had big hopes for it."

Ron Howard, Sam Edwards, and Robie Lester would all make their final Disneyland Records appearances on *The Orange Bird*. Lester had already been phased out of her long-running "read-along" series. One of her last little book-and-records was *The Haunted Mansion*, a solo journey through the attraction, with "chilling, thrilling" sounds on side 2. Lester's two final productions, *Pecos Bill* and *Susie, the Little Blue Coupe*, were released in December 1970. Lester recalled that one day she received a telephone call from Gypsy Belew, Camarata's secretary, regretfully informing her that her services would no longer be required. Lester had always wondered if this was a result of a

British singer and actress Lois Lane became the Disneyland Story Reader in 1970. (Courtesy of Lois Lane)

ACT NOW!
GET 5 FREE RECORDS
Limited Time Only...

Buy 10 Rec

THIS RECORD **FREE**

THIS RECORD **FREE**

THIS RECORD **FREE**

10 DAY FREE TRIAL

RECORDS THAT TEACH AS THEY ENTERTAIN

Here's the way to make learning fun! Whether it's a new song, a classic rhyme or a new game, you'll be thrilled at how quickly your children understand when they can listen to a record. You'll be pleased at how much enjoyment a record album "teacher" can bring. For example, learning to sing a song about *Puff, The Magic Dragon* is only a part of the excitement in store on the album "All About Dragons".

Imagine the eager look on your youngsters' faces when they find out that they can actually become a dragon—the record tells them how! This is just one of the educational creative exercises that Disney music experts turn into play. Another is the Play-Along At Home Rhythm Band on the "More Mother Goose" album. Every song is a happy musical lesson with the help of these Disneyland records!

RECORDS THAT

Your child will be held spellbound with classic Walt Disney's vast collection of stories by th master story tellers. These are the most belo fables, legends and lore that have always th fascinated children. Every record is a wonderf tation of the kind of entertainment that childrer

Direct mail remained an effective way to sell Disney records, as this advertising flyer from the 1970s illustrates. (© Disney Enterprises, Inc.)

dispute over her receiving screen credit for *The AristoCats*, but it was most likely a financial move.

Twenty-six-year-old Lois Lane, who had begun her career as a singer, recorded the read-alongs in London from that point forward. Under her original name of Lois Wilkinson, she was 50 percent of a duo billed as the Caravelles. When she decided to go out on her own in 1966, she deliberately chose the name Lois Lane after the fabled girlfriend of Superman. Most of her work for the British Broadcasting Corporation remained in the musical realm, and it eventually led to her role as the new Disneyland Story Reader.

Lane did not re-record anything Lester had done but simply added a few more stories that remained in the Disney canon. Ironically, at least two of Lane's first releases were condensations of LPs narrated by Lester, *Thumper's Race* and *Mickey and the Beanstalk*. Lane made no attempt to give each character in the story a different voice, as Lester had done. All of her characterizations had British accents, even those in *Brer Rabbit and the Tar Baby*. This leads one to suspect that Lane originally started doing read-alongs for British Disney records and company executives subsequently decided that it would be more cost-effective to reuse her narrations in the United

States. Lane's tenure as Story Reader lasted exactly one year, with her final set of stories—virtually the only Disney productions not yet included in the series—released in May 1971.

Another long-running section of the Disneyland Records catalog that came to an end at the same time was the Little Gem series of 45s. Their final installment was also released in May 1971, a pairing of Anita Bryant's "Orange Bird Song" and "Orange Tree" from the *Orange Bird* LP. The Disney 45-rpm single would be revived in new formats in years to come.

○

There was one last big project ahead while at least a few of the original Disneyland Records crew remained on board: *Bedknobs and Broomsticks*, an ambitious live-action/animated musical strongly reminiscent of *Mary Poppins*. (So similar was the subject matter that Walt Disney had originally purchased the rights to the *Bedknobs* stories when it appeared that he might not be able to come to terms with Pamela Travers, the infamously stubborn creator of *Poppins*.) Though *Bedknobs* turned out to be solid Disney entertainment with a good many outstanding attributes, its production was dogged by Walt's absence. Creative decisions were being made by a group of studio executives known to the Shermans as "the Committee." Songs were discarded as concepts changed. The biggest blow to the Shermans came when the film was discovered to be too long to suit the show schedule at Radio City Music Hall and a great deal of music and expository material had to be cut. (It has recently been restored, in part, for home video.)

The soundtrack LP is distinguished by the fact that it contained many of the songs and sections cut from the film's initial release. "With a Flair" was excised after initial showings to cut down on running time, while "A Step in the Right Direction" took a wrong turn somewhere and never showed up in the finished movie except as a background theme.

The Storyteller LP version of *Bedknobs* featured Dal McKennon as professor Emelius Browne, with a British accent similar to the one he used as Bagheera the panther in the two *Jungle Book* story LPs (he had also voiced the Fisherman Bear in the *Bedknobs* film). By the time this album was produced, McKennon had moved his family back to his ancestral homeland on the Oregon coast and was commuting to Los Angeles for his work in animated cartoons. This LP would be McKennon's final new material for Disneyland Records, although he would continue to provide vocals for various attractions in the theme parks for at least another decade. This Storyteller LP and the second cast LP of *Bedknobs* contained the last songs produced in London by Tutti Camarata with the Mike Sammes Singers, featuring Sammes in most of the solos.

The most fascinating selection from these albums is "Substitutiary Locomotion," whose female soloist did indeed have a British accent but whose name was mysteriously missing from most issues of the record label and album jacket. Other issues were sold with sticker material covering the credit on that particular name. Those who scratched it off discovered that the singer was Judy Carne, the "sock-it-to-me" girl on NBC-TV's *Laugh-In*. How her voice ended up on the *Bedknobs* second cast songs remains a mystery, although it is known that she did audition for the lead role of amateur witch Eglantine Price (played in the film by Angela Lansbury). Carne's "Substitutiary Locomotion" was apparently taken from one of her test recordings, with a children's chorus and an impressive arrangement that progressively builds from a slow creep to a rousing march.

After finishing his work on the *Bedknobs* songs, Camarata came to the conclusion that he would be better off working as a freelance music producer and arranger than being tied exclusively to Disneyland Records, and he and Jimmy Johnson reluctantly parted ways. Within a year's time, Disneyland Records had lost much of its long-established talent. Future records would have a completely different sound and flavor. Most of the existing material remained on sale in stores and through mail-order, so it is likely that few members of the general public noticed that Lester, McKennon, Edwards, Sammes, Camarata, and their compatriots were now being heard only in reruns.

10

Scrooge McDuck Strikes Again

The loss of Tutti Camarata's involvement, combined with certain budgetary issues and the drifting creative focus of Walt Disney Productions as a whole, caused Disneyland Records to become somewhat less productive in the early 1970s than in years past. While occasional new records benefited from such Disney musical directors as Buddy Baker and Bob Brunner, the catalog relied heavily on reissues and compilations.

January 1972 saw the launch of the "four complete songs" seven-inch 33⅓-rpm LP line to replace the departed Little Gem 45-rpm series. All the selections came from existing albums, including soundtracks, second cast versions, and some original works such as *Heidi* and *The Orange Bird*. This series would continue through the 1970s, although a handful were also converted to 45-rpm format with similar picture sleeves in 1978.

○

The October 1971 opening of Walt Disney World had some effect on the record division, but it was not as dramatic as that of the Disneyland park. The first Walt Disney World attraction soundtrack came in September 1971 with the *Country Bear Jamboree* LP. Side 1 contained the complete audio of the Audio-Animatronics comedy, with no additions made for the record, though references to the show's corporate sponsors, Pepsi-Cola and Frito-Lay, were deleted. While not cre-

ated specifically for Disneyland Records, *Country Bear Jamboree* brims with members of the company's talent stable: Pete Renaday as Henry; Thurl Ravenscroft as Buff the buffalo; Bill Lee as Melvin the moose; and Dal McKennon as Zeke the bear, with contributions from Loulie Jean Norman and Bill Cole, late of the MelloMen. Side 2 of the Storyteller LP contained atmospheric background music (known in Disney circles as BGM) from the Frontierland Mile-Long Bar.

The other Walt Disney World soundtrack to grace an LP was the original incarnation of *The Hall of Presidents*. The attraction itself, of course, has been updated over the years, but the album contains narrator Lawrence Dobkin's original presidential roll call, ending with Richard Nixon. Also from Florida came an entire LP devoted to the *Walt Disney World Band*, under the direction of James Christensen. Many of its tracks have made their way onto subsequent compilations.

Though it was not a park soundtrack, a Storyteller album called *Mickey Mouse: This Is My Life* was marketed as a companion piece to the beloved attraction known as the Mickey Mouse Revue. This show, now housed at Tokyo Disneyland, chronicled Mickey's career and featured Audio-Animatronics re-creations of musical Disney moments with arrangements created just for the production. *This Is My Life* was presented

Mike Curb:
The Great Congregator

Such Disney recordings as the "Mickey Mouse March" and "It's a Small World" have been only a footnote in the meteoric, eclectic career of Mike Curb, who was as capable in the recording booth as he was in the governor's mansion.

Curb's music career began at the age of nineteen, when the Savannah, Georgia, native started a record label that featured film soundtracks. His work with the company led to projects for MGM, Warner Brothers, Disney, and American International, for which Curb produced the *Thunder Alley* LP with Disney legend Annette Funicello. He was also in his teens when he formed the Mike Curb Congregation, a vocal group that scored hits on its own ("Burning Bridges") and with major stars ("The Candy Man" with Sammy Davis Jr.).

In the late 1960s and early 1970s, Curb led MGM Records to success, guiding the early careers of the Osmonds both as group and solo artists. He also wrote songs for such notable singers as Roy Orbison, Anne Murray, Liza Minnelli, and Andy Williams. When Disney's *Pete's Dragon* was in production in 1977, Curb produced Helen Reddy's single version of "Candle on the Water" for Capitol Records. Intended for pop appeal and radio play, this rendition included a choral backup and faster tempo than the soundtrack version.

He also transitioned from the music business to politics and was elected California's lieutenant governor in 1978 and served as acting governor for a year in the absence of Governor Jerry Brown. Curb has chaired national commissions, served on corporate and college boards, raised millions for campaigns, and received honorary degrees. In 2003 he established the Mike Curb College of Entertainment and Music Business at Belmont University in Nashville, Tennessee, and the Curb Center for Art, Enterprise, and Public Policy at Vanderbilt University.

Since starting his Curb Records label in 1974, Curb has signed a stellar roster of performers, including Wynonna, Tim McGraw, LeAnn Rimes, Lyle Lovett, and many more. After forty years in entertainment and public affairs, he's still breaking new ground.

as an interview with Mickey (Jimmy Mac-donald) that concluded with the same lineup of Disney songs as the attraction. However, the songs on the record come from existing Disney albums rather than the attraction soundtrack. Nevertheless, this LP was packaged with a *Mickey Mouse Revue* sticker attached to the cover when sold in the Magic Kingdom park. (The only soundtrack material from the Mickey Mouse Revue ever released in the United States was the overture, which opens a 1978 Ovation Records album set called *The Magical Music of Walt Disney*.)

The 1972 syndicated Disney TV series *The Mouse Factory* also brought forth tie-in albums that were not genuine TV soundtracks. *The Mouse Factory Presents Mickey and His Friends* was a character compilation very similar to 1968's *Mickey Mouse and His Friends*. It includes "Minnie's Yoo-Hoo," which was used on the new show, but it was the recording made in 1968. *Stories from the Mouse Factory* was a collection of four read-along Little LP stories with the page-turning signals removed and a few added songs in stereo. The albums bore only a passing resemblance to the TV series, which consisted of half hours themed to specific subjects with celebrity guests and vintage cartoon snippets.

One of the highest-profile Disney records of 1973 was a contemporary version of "It's a Small World" by the Mike Curb Congregation. This group had impressed the Disney brass with their work with Sammy Davis Jr. on the hit single "Candy Man." "The new version of 'Small World' worked for all kinds of purposes—parades and so forth," Curb said. "When it was released as a single, it hit the Top 10 on the Adult Contemporary charts! We used three different drummers to make that distinctive sound, three different

pianos and vocals in unison. It's very hard to reproduce." By the time of Curb's Buena Vista LP *It's a Small World: Walt Disney's Greatest Hits* (which still sells well today as a CD on Curb's label), his group was considered the official Disneyland and Walt Disney World singers. He also helped bring such performers as Lou Rawls and the Osmonds into the parks. "They'd move us to Tomorrowland at the California and Florida parks," Curb added. "[Disney executive] Bob Jani was very innovative. He'd say, 'Let's do a version for the parade in different languages.'"

Disney's big Christmas theatrical release for 1973 was the animated feature *Robin Hood*. The Storyteller album hit stores several weeks ahead of the premiere. The record

Lois Lane received her sole Disneyland opportunity to demonstrate her singing as well as narrating talents on a Storyteller LP combining soundtrack dialogue from the non-Disney films *Born Free* and *Living Free*. (Courtesy of Lois Lane)

company anticipated sales success along the lines of *The Jungle Book*, so special emphasis was given to the impressive voice cast, including Peter Ustinov and Terry-Thomas, as well as Phil Harris in his third Disney animated feature appearance in a row.

Robin Hood's Storyteller album does *Jungle Book* one better by having a voice talent from the film, Roger Miller, tell the story; however, it lacks a musical background and sound effects. Neither the film nor the album had the same impact as *The Jungle Book*, although they performed admirably.

○

One of Disney's most unusual albums of the early 1970s was *The Sounds of Christmas* (1973), hailed on its cover as "the first Christmas sound effects record." Jimmy Johnson conceived it as a yuletide answer to the bestselling *Chilling, Thrilling Sounds of the Haunted House*. This album had a similar format, with a sound-effects-laden story on side 1 and the effects by themselves on side 2. Unlike the earlier album, *The Sounds of Christmas* also features a small cast and original songs, told, sung, and directed by actor and longtime Disney studio staffer Pete Renaday, who also wrote the title tune. "Jimmy Johnson had called me in to do the album," Renaday recalled. "I had a dream that night and the song ran through my head! So I jumped out of bed, grabbed the guitar and the tape recorder, and played as much as I had in my head from the dream. When I got to work the next day, I wrote it all down except for the bridge, because I didn't dream the bridge." Pat Boone also recorded the song for another label. Renaday credits Bob Brunner's beautiful arrangement for much of the song's appeal. There is one point in the performance, when Renaday sings about "the sound of laughter," in which his voice cracks emotionally. Upon hearing the song again

recently, Renaday said the effect was unintentional: "I thought it might be a problem and they would want another take, but they left it that way!"

Another song on the album is "Here He Comes," a cheery anticipation of Santa's arrival. It was written just before World War II by Bob Brunner's parents, Francis and Barbara. "Even 'White Christmas' hadn't been written yet," recalled Brunner, "and my parents couldn't find any Christmas songs for my sister and me. So they decided to write one themselves." The talented Brunner youngsters made a big hit with servicemen by performing "Here He Comes" at USO camp shows during the war. While arranging the music for *The Sounds of Christmas*, Brunner said to Renaday, "I can't get Jimmy Johnson to publish any songs!" Renaday complied by working "Here He Comes" into the album script and recording it for the first time.

The supporting cast included Florence Daniel, a Walt Disney Music Company employee since 1958, as Renaday's spouse, a role she later assumed for a time in real life. Dana Laurita, who was at the studio providing the voice of Sister Rabbit in *Robin Hood*, played the daughter. Though the actor playing the boy is not known, Renaday recalled that Joshua the dog was played by Johnson's pet pooch: "He insisted on using his dog for the bark and recorded it at home," Renaday chuckled. "I tried to tell him that it didn't quite sound like a real dog!" Renaday assumes that the meows of Jedediah the Siamese cat were also recorded at the Johnson menagerie.

Despite its fanciful story of a family enjoying holiday festivities, a reprise of the MelloMen's howling rendition of "Home Sweet Home" from *Lady and the Tramp*, a visit from Santa (also played by Renaday), and a bevy of sound effects from bells and toys to

Jerry Whitman: Found Horizons

Some enter the performing arts with dreams of fame; others simply for the joy of doing what they love. "Having my name in lights wasn't the route I wanted to take for many reasons," said Jerry Whitman. "The variety and anonymity of studio singing appealed to me, plus being able to work with a lot of wonderful composers and musicians." As one of the most sought-after studio singers in the music business, Whitman could do it all, whether in a solo, a trio, a twenty-voice chorus, or in the style of popular singing stars.

Whitman started singing professionally in a quartet while in college in his native Dallas, Texas. Playing clubs, he came to the attention of one of the preeminent radio jingle companies of the 1960s, Futuresonic, and was set to work on station IDs and other production music. In the Air Force, he was accepted into the Singing Sergeants choir until getting a solo gig with the Airmen of Note, a continuation of the military band founded by Glenn Miller.

After touring the country as backup for Danny Kaye, Whitman's first big Hollywood job was as part of the Jack Halloran Singers on the *Dean Martin Show*. This led to TV work for Sonny and Cher, Carol Burnett, Tom Jones, and Pearl Bailey, for whom he was vocal contractor. He was married for a time to Halloran alumnus Diana Lee, daughter of studio singing giant Bill Lee. Their records together included such Disney LPs as *Songs from Sesame Street 2*, *Songs from the Electric Company TV Show* and *What a Wonderful Thing Is Me!*

The couple also sang offscreen for Peter Finch and Liv Ullmann in *Lost Horizon*, one of Hollywood's most notorious flops. Ullmann told interviewers she did not sing, although studio ghost singers were forbidden to reveal their work: "They don't want you capitalizing on it or putting out a press release," Whitman explained. "The movie turned out to be such a bomb I don't think anyone would care if I talk about it now." Ironically, Whitman and Lee also sang on the Disneyland LP of *Lost Horizon* songs, *The World Is a Circle*.

No one was more surprised than Whitman when he got top billing on a Disneyland album, *Jerry Whitman Sings Songs from the Mister Rogers TV Show*. "That was really unusual," Whitman said. "I didn't even expect that. It was not some deal I made with them; I just showed up and sang the songs. I didn't know until the album came out."

Henry Mancini tops Whitman's list of favorite music people, and he made the first recording of Mancini's last song, "King's Dilemma." Composer/lyricist Leslie Bricusse asked Whitman to sing demos for *Scrooge* and other musicals. For musical director Walter Scharf, Whitman did demos for a stage production of *Willy Wonka and the Chocolate Factory*. "That was produced in England," he said. "It was a totally different version, more like the book. Walter always thought the [1971] movie didn't do justice to the story. I did all the demos, and they produced it on stage about eight or ten years ago."

A veteran of many successful music businesses, the semiretired Whitman sings occasionally for TV and film, from *The Hunt for Red October* to *King of the Hill*. But to 1970s-era kids who grew up listening to Disneyland Records, Jerry Whitman may have had more of an impact than he expected. During a recent phone call to FedEx, he was giving his name to the customer service person when she asked if he had done any record albums. "I mentioned recording *Mister Rogers*," recalled Whitman, "and she said, 'When I was a little girl I played that album over and over until I ruined it!' That's the closest brush I had with fame."

weather and laughs, *The Sounds of Christmas* did not enjoy the sales bonanza of *Chilling, Thrilling Sounds*. The reason may be that the first LP had a practical use for Halloween parties, storytelling, and trick-or-treat atmosphere. During Christmas activities, listeners are more likely to trim trees, wrap presents, and throw parties with merry music rather than sound effects playing in the background. A noble experiment nonetheless, *The Sounds of Christmas* must have seemed like a good idea to others in the industry; Pickwick also released an album called *Fun and Sounds of Christmas*.

О

With limited budgets, Disneyland Records of the early 1970s frequently combined new selections with previously released items. The album *"Candy Man" and Other Sweet Songs* offers a fine rendition of the hit song

Jerry Whitman appeared on several early 1970s Disneyland Records LPs, including a collection of songs from *Mister Rogers' Neighborhood*. (Courtesy of Jerry Whitman)

The Finest From 50 Happy Years
8 Great Storyteller Albums
Disney's Best-Loved Stories Plus Your Favorite Songs in a Magnificent Collection of 12" Long-Playing Records with Beautifully Illustrated, Giant Size, Full-Color Books

Many of Hollywood's most talented artists and musicians have been brought together to re-create the brightest, happiest, most memorable moments from 50 years of unmatched Walt Disney entertainment. From films, from Disneyland, from television—from all the wonderful worlds of Walt Disney—comes this prized commemorative selection of records and books. And, with this Special FREE TRIAL offer, you can easily introduce your children to the magnificent Anniversary Collection.

Here's a rare entertainment treat for children of all ages—a unique library of long-playing records and fully illustrated "giant size" books—each in full color. These exciting albums contain the finest in Walt Disney music selected from the best in Walt Disney movies—you'll hear songs from the original films, including Academy Award Winners like Zip-A-Dee-

Doo-Dah! You'll even take a record and book tour of the famous fun-filled and fanciful Disneyland attraction, "It's a Small World"!

Now—you can own the world's greatest children's classics. The Anniversary Collection brings your child wonderful hi-fidelity records to play...."giant size" books to read...beautifully illustrated full-color pictures to see...all-time favorite stories to hear...the finest in music to listen to...and hours of stimulating musical entertainment. Each album has its own durable, handsomely illustrated hard cover with page after page of lavish full-color illustrations and large, easy-to-read type. Each album is a true joy for any child, of any age, to treasure forever.

Books to Read! Pictures to See! Records to Play! Stories to Hear! Music to Listen to!

Disney's record division participated in the fiftieth anniversary of the Disney studios with this direct mail offer as well as a compilation album called *50 Happy Years of Disney Favorites*. (© Disney Enterprises, Inc. Winnie the Pooh: Based on the "Winnie the Pooh" works by A. A. Milne and E. H. Shepard)

Bob McGrath: Street Smarts

Few performers have the opportunity to be part of a cultural phenomenon as immense as *Sesame Street*. Since 1969, generations have been entertained and educated by this landmark children's series, and Bob McGrath was an original member of the cast. During the decades, McGrath also headlined on stage and recordings not only for *Sesame Street* but for Disney as well.

McGrath grew up on a farm in Ottawa, Illinois. Though money was tight (McGrath was six when his home first got electricity), his mother made sure all of her children were exposed to music. One day she was playing piano and five-year-old Bob started singing along. "She said I had a good ear," recalled McGrath. "My dad was working in the fields, and by the time he came in for lunch my mom had taught me 'In the Good Old Summertime.' I sang it for him at lunchtime and I was off and running from that time on."

By high school, McGrath was juggling football practice and singing on his own radio show. After stints at the University of Michigan, in the army, and at the Manhattan School of Music, he ventured out into the business. One of his biggest early gigs was singing on Mitch Miller's TV show, which led to his first album on Columbia Records. By the time of *Sesame Street*'s creation, McGrath had already performed with such giants as Pablo Casals and Igor Stravinsky, even finding himself a teen idol in Japan.

The landmark series was a perfect vehicle for McGrath's affable persona and soaring tenor voice, which trilled such now-classic songs as "People in Your Neighborhood" and "Sing." In addition to his work on the Grammy-winning *Sesame Street* albums, he recorded albums for various children's labels, including Disneyland. His likable persona and farm-bred work ethic made McGrath a popular live headliner, performing in concerts, festivals, and other musical events to scores of children and adults. He came to the attention of Walt Disney World Entertainment as a prime candidate for the mammoth Epcot theme park in Florida. During summers in the mid-1980s, Epcot hosted the All-American College Orchestra, an assemblage of outstanding student musicians. Celebrity guests appeared on the America Gardens Stage with them, and McGrath became a fixture. "I did that for four or five years," McGrath said. "We put together a new show every year. Those musicians were just out of this world, and there were some amazing moments. One day, during rehearsal, I remember a jazz pianist was just noodling around and started playing 'The Rainbow Connection,' so I went over and started humming and singing. All of a sudden the rhythm section pulled in and then all the strings and brass. By the time we got to the end of the first chorus the whole orchestra was playing it. Then I modulated up half a step and they followed and finished out the thing. We were all kind of stunned; it sounded so beautiful. They had played a full arrangement of the whole thing without any music on their stands! We ended up performing it every night." During the Epcot shows, McGrath would "speak" to the voices of Big Bird and Oscar, who were "phoning in" to say hello. It was perhaps the first time Muppet characters were represented at a Disney park.

McGrath continues to perform and runs into former All-American College Orchestra alumni as he sings with symphonies throughout the United States and Canada. He speaks on the impact of music on young minds and cognitive development. And of course, he's still a resident of *Sesame Street*, reaching out to millions of youngsters. He's also a father of five and grandfather of six.

The secret to his continued success is a simple philosophy: "You just do the best you can every day and hope you're on the right track," he said. "When you do live performances, you know from the kids whether you're doing it right. That's why I love doing live concerts like the International Children's Festival. I have to work very, very hard at what I do. But the reaction of kids and their parents makes it very invigorating."

from the 1971 film *Willy Wonka and the Chocolate Factory* plus "I'd Like to Teach the World to Sing," "Sweet Gingerbread Man," and "Lollipops and Roses" as well as four tunes from the vaults. *"The World Is a Circle" from Lost Horizon* contains three songs from the legendary Hollywood flop sung by Jerry Whitman and Diana Lee (daughter of the ubiquitous Bill Lee), who also sang offscreen for the film's stars Peter Finch and Liv Ullmann. The album's remaining four songs come from the 1958 Disneyland LP *Little Gems from Big Shows*. British Disneyland Story Reader Lois Lane told and sang the stories from the films *Born Free* and *Living Free*, marking the first time dialogue from non-Disney films was heard on Disneyland Records and including a rare Lane singing performance for the label.

A few remaining records still bore the Camarata touch. Several of his compositions appeared on *Silly Symphonies*, which has no relation to the Disney cartoon series but instead contains songs from various read-along Little LPs.

Singer Jerry Whitman also recalled working with Camarata on the *New Zoo Revue* LP. The immense success of *Sesame Street* influenced records almost as much as it revolutionized television. Every children's record label scrambled for similar TV properties to showcase. Disneyland negotiated an album based on the *New Zoo Revue*, a daily children's TV series with human and puppet characters. Several original cast members recreated their roles for the LP, which was released as a single LP and a Storyteller book-and-record set.

The only educational title of this period

that was not based on a TV show was *What a Wonderful Thing Is Me!*, a collection of original songs about the human body featuring Jerry Whitman and Diana Lee, with Ida Sue McCune and Tom Bahlor (who were part of TV's *Partridge Family* studio vocal group). These vocalists also appeared on the Disneyland Records version of songs from the *Electric Company*, another series from the makers of *Sesame Street*. Disney's LP was nominated for a Grammy in 1973; Warner Brothers' original cast album took the award a year earlier. This LP and several others in the new educational crop were touted on TV commercials.

The push to get a piece of the *Sesame Street* action reached its zenith when Disneyland Records brought in one of the show's original stars for his own album, *Bob McGrath Sings for All the Boys and Girls*, produced by Buddy Baker. "We picked the top songs of the times," McGrath remembered. "I performed these songs for a quite a while afterward, especially on telethons throughout Canada." The album was a bicoastal production. Lee Norris's arrangements were charted on the East Coast; McGrath was flown from New York to Los Angeles for sessions with the Jimmy Joyce Singers. The resulting LP was lavish for Disneyland's somewhat lean times, although it contained a total of only six songs. "It was amazing that they even allowed me to do this," added McGrath. "And I was tremendously thrilled to be asked."

○

One of the last members of the Johnson/Camarata repertory group to cut a Disneyland record in the 1970s was Ginny Tyler on *Trick or Treat* (1974). It's really only half an album, because side 2 contains an edited version of 1969's *Haunted Mansion* Storyteller. *Trick or Treat* was originally a 1952 Donald Duck cartoon in which the mean-spirited mallard

keeps tricking instead of treating his nephews until Witch Hazel teaches him a lesson. For the film, June Foray voiced Hazel in one of her earliest sessions. Rather than bringing in Foray to narrate the album, Johnson called on his longtime witch voice, Tyler. She performed the difficult task of providing continuity, replacement lines, and even overlapping dialogue alongside Foray's soundtrack.

○

Yet another soundtrack derived from the Disneyland park was *America Sings*, a now-defunct Audio-Animatronics salute to popular music that opened in 1974 in anticipation of the Bicentennial. The voice of Burl Ives hosts the show as Sam the Eagle, with Sam Edwards as his owl sidekick. (Edwards recalled that he and Ives never actually met; their dialogue and singing were recorded separately.) The vocal cast also included Disneyland Records regulars Jerry Whitman, Gene Merlino, Rex Allen, Diana Lee, Bill Cole, Bill Lee, and Betty Taylor.

Edwards's 1968 version of "The Wonderful Thing about Tiggers" bounced up again on *Winnie the Pooh and Tigger Too*, a Storyteller based on the third theatrical Pooh featurette. This LP was a blend of soundtrack dialogue and additional Sebastian Cabot narration. Like the *Honey Tree* Storyteller, this LP used Camarata's earlier second cast songs rather than soundtrack music, so listeners heard Paul Winchell speaking and Edwards singing as Tigger. The resulting LP was nominated for a Grammy, but in promoting this fact late in life, Winchell, who died in June 2005, was careful *not* to note that his signature song was the Edwards version. *Winnie the Pooh and Tigger Too* was released as a seven-inch Little LP book and record read by Lois Lane and as a cassette and book in a new Disneyland "Story Tape" line with narration by Thurl Ravenscroft.

Ravenscroft also narrated *The Island at the Top of the World*, a Storyteller version of the Jules Verne–like Disney epic released to theaters on a double bill with *Tigger Too*. The album contains generous passages of soundtrack dialogue, but the stirring Maurice Jarre orchestral score never made it to vinyl. Instead, famed Hollywood organist Clare Fischer plays Jarre's music under the dialogue. While not as rich as full instrumentation, it's an advantage over other story albums that have no music at all. Fischer returned to the keyboard to play Johnny Mandel's music for the Storyteller of *Escape to Witch Mountain*, narrated by Eddie Albert. In this instance, the otherworldly nature of the story and score well suits the organ sound.

O

The Mike Curb Congregation scored another successful single for Buena Vista, a contemporary, groovin' version of the "Mickey Mouse March," featuring the group's unique multidrum march time beat. The new single enjoyed frequent airplay and tied in beautifully with the *Mickey Mouse Club* revival that was to come.

Local stations began daily syndicated broadcasts of the *Mickey Mouse Club* in January 1975, using the same edited half hours shown in 1962. The record division's primary contribution to the substantial marketing and merchandising campaign was *Mickey Mouse Club: Mousekedances and Other Mouseketeer Favorites*. With some added echo for stereo effect, this collection of the Mickey Mouse Club–related songs dated back to the original discs from the show's 1955 premiere, with the 1974 pop version of "Mickey Mouse March" added to the mix and touted by a special sticker on the shrink-wrap.

To help promote the new LP, a thirty-second TV commercial was inserted into the syndicated prints. Produced in black and white and voiced by Disney's oft-heard announcer Dick Tufeld, the spot matched the rest of the show so closely it almost seemed to come from the 1950s.

Three different versions of this album were pressed. The first version begins side 1 with Curb's "Mickey Mouse March"; the second begins with the 1955 MelloMen rendition and closes side 1 with the Curb version; a third version brings out the original soundtrack theme for the first time and again closes side 1 with Curb. The follow-up to this bestselling LP, a Storyteller with an accompanying photo album, *Mickey Mouse Club Song Hits*, contained more soundtrack material than ever, including the premiere of the original versions of "Talent Roundup," "Fun with Music," "Anything Can Happen," and "Today Is Tuesday."

O

While the Mouseketeers were once again making merry on TV screens nationwide, internal changes at Disneyland/Buena Vista Records were occurring that would alter the course of the division and its products. In March 1975, Jimmy Johnson and the Walt Disney Music Company amicably parted ways. Though the issues behind the parting remain unclear, Johnson's account of his tenure with Disney in his unpublished autobiography was highly positive and complimentary to all concerned.

Merrill Dean, who, like Johnson, had risen through the ranks of the company's publications division, replaced Johnson. After taking the helm, Dean took a close look at the record company's recent output and realized that some changes would have to be made. One of the first things he did was promote Gary Krisel to oversee the product line. Among Krisel's first duties was to come up with a Christmas album starring Mickey Mouse and other Disney characters.

Alan Young: From Talking Horses to Talking Ducks

Alan Young (left) during his days as an ABC network radio star in the late 1940s.

As if gaining pop culture immortality as Mister Ed's best friend and Scrooge McDuck's voice weren't enough, Alan Young is also an accomplished writer, comedian, and actor with two Emmy Awards among his credits.

Born Angus Young in northern England, he spent his formative years in Canada, where he wrote and performed in his first radio show at age seventeen. The show was brought to the United States, where he also began his stand-up "comedy with bagpipes" career. On the big screen, he was appearing in such films as *tom thumb* and *The Time Machine*; on live TV, he was writing and starring in the award-winning *Alan Young Show*.

Of course (of course), *Mister Ed* really launched Young into TV legend status. The whimsical fantasy about a talking horse attracts new generations of fans in perpetual reruns. Young and a stand-in Mister Ed traded some new dialogue in the 2005 *TV Land Awards* special.

Young gained another fan base after becoming the voice of Uncle Scrooge starting with the 1975 Disneyland Storyteller album *Dickens' Christmas Carol Featuring the Walt Disney Players*. But even though he wrote, coproduced, and did the voices of Uncle Scrooge, Mickey Mouse, and Merlin on the LP, Young almost missed out on being cast for the 1983 film version, *Mickey's Christmas Carol*. "I was working with an actor who was doing a Scottish accent," remembered Young. "He gave me the script, and lo and behold, it was the one I had written for the album! So I called someone at Disney and said, 'Can I audition for Scrooge McDuck?' They said, 'Yes, but we didn't think you would want to do it.'"

With his natural Scottish burr (long suppressed for American acting roles) and his seasoned comic timing, Young became Uncle Scrooge for *Mickey's Christmas Carol*, for which he also received on-screen writing credit. Young was delighted with the big-screen animated version of his original script and particularly pleased with the voices. "The cast was very good," he said. "I know the fellow who does Mickey now [Wayne Allwine] and he's a dear man. I know them all. It was perfect with me, because the characters are so good."

Years of Uncle Scrooge projects followed, including many TV episodes and a feature film of *DuckTales*, various recordings, theme park shows, and animation projects such as 2004's *Mickey's Twice upon a Christmas*. In the regular role of Jack Allen, Young even returned to his golden age radio roots by joining the cast of the long running *Adventures in Odyssey* series.

Young prefers to look forward rather than back, but when confronted with the fact that millions of people have been entertained by his work, he simply said, "That makes me very humble and grateful. I love a lot; I love my business and I love people. So there you are."

"It really began when Krisel had just come out of college and I gave him a job in something I was doing," recalled legendary actor/writer Alan Young. "I didn't see him for a while after that, but one day he called when I got out to L. A. He thanked me for getting him a job a few years before and said, 'I want you to help me.'" Drawing on Young's experience in the golden age of radio, Krisel asked him to write a script around album art that had supported an earlier, unsuccessful recording that had not sold well. The artwork depicted various Disney characters taking on roles in Charles Dickens's *A Christmas Carol*. "As it happened, I used to belong to a Dickens society before I came to America," said Young, a native of Canada. "So I got a friend of mine who was then doing a thing called *Wait Till Your Father Gets Home* for Hanna-Barbera." The friend was Alan Dinehart, veteran scriptwriter for such shows as *The Flintstones* and *Gilligan's Island*, associate producer of *Top Cat*, and voice actor/director for many series.

Child star Virginia Wilder was also an old friend of Young's. She opened the doors of Hollywood's Wilder Brothers recording studio for him. The tonal quality of *Carol* was not the only thing that made the LP sound different. As producers, Young and Dinehart enlisted some veteran voice actors who were new to the Disneyland record label, including Janet Waldo (of *The Jetsons* and countless other Hanna-Barbera cartoons) and Walker Edmiston (a leading voice in *H. R. Pufnstuf*, *Sigmund and the Sea Monsters*, and numerous other Sid and Marty Krofft live-action shows).

Titled *Dickens' Christmas Carol with the Walt Disney Players*, the 1975 album boasted the largest assemblage of major Disney characters gathered for a recording. Mickey "played" Bob Cratchit, Uncle Scrooge McDuck "portrayed" Ebenezer Scrooge, and Alan Young provided both of their voices as well as that of Merlin from *The Sword in the Stone* (as the Ghost of Christmas Past). Young also wrote the entire script, although he shared the writing credit with Dinehart on the strength of an additional quip in which Willie the Giant (the Ghost of Christmas Present) says to Scrooge, "We have a long way to travel and we must fly. Take hold of my robe—Duh, not back there, unless you want to fly tourist!"

This album provided Disney with more than impressive sales: it inspired the Oscar-nominated 1983 featurette *Mickey's Christmas Carol* and led to Young's permanent status as the voice of Uncle Scrooge on the series *DuckTales* and other TV and theatrical cartoons, recordings, and theme park shows.

○

The greater infusion of classic Disney characters into records was only one of Dean's new directions. Because new Disney animated features came out only every four years or so and few of the studio's live-action films would work as records, Dean sought more properties outside the Disney realm for records and tape products.

One of Dean's first attempts at diversification was a direct result of his long-standing work in the publishing department. One of Disney's oldest allies was legendary Western Printing and Lithographing, the company that had produced the vast majority of Disney books for decades. In the 1970s, Western also published the popular Little Golden Books line, with such beloved titles as *The Poky Little Puppy* and *The Saggy Baggy Elephant*. Dean made a deal whereby Disneyland Records would bump up its read-along line by producing non-Disney stories from the Little Golden Books catalog. (Golden Records had had its own version of Little Golden Book read-alongs up until the mid-1970s, but they were now off the market.)

Krisel was responsible for putting together a lot of Little Golden Books and Records in a

Janet Waldo is a legend in the cartoon voice world, but her solitary (though unforgettable) appearance on Disney Records was as all the female characters in 1975's *Dickens' Christmas Carol.* She is seen here with Disney records regular Sam Edwards, her costar on the radio comedy *Meet Corliss Archer.* (Courtesy of Sam Edwards)

very little time. To reach sales targets, a staggering twenty-four books had to be adapted, cast, scored, and produced in only a few weeks. To get the job done, he turned to someone he knew and trusted from college, his old roommate Jymn Magon. Magon's arrival in the Disney fold ushered in the second "golden age" for Disneyland and Buena Vista Records.

11

Mickey Mouse Goes
Double Platinum

In addition to the new Golden Book and Record line, the fall of 1976 saw the release of *Winnie the Pooh for President*, a combination record and coloring book commemorating Pooh's second run for president of the United States. This sort of promotional stunt was somewhat of a tradition for cartoon characters: Alvin the Chipmunk had campaigned in 1960, Yogi Bear competed against Magilla Gorilla in 1964, and Snoopy sought the office in 1968—and of course, Pogo Possum ran comic strip campaigns every four years.

Winnie the Pooh's first Presidential campaign took place in 1968 as part of "On Stage, U.S.A." at Disneyland. A larger celebration took place in 1972, conducted primarily through Sears department stores. For the 1976 election, the marketing plan included a 45-rpm Disneyland Record produced for Sears. The resulting recording was an historic mix of debuts and farewells. British actor Laurie Main made his debut as narrator of side 1, replacing Sebastian Cabot, who was either too expensive or in declining health (he died in 1977). It was a role Main would continue on film, TV, and recordings for decades. Also making his first Disney record was singer/songwriter Larry Groce, who had a big novelty hit at the time, "Junk Food Junkie." His "Pooh for President" tune made up side 2

of the disc. Another Disney records newcomer was Billy Simpson as Christopher Robin, a young actor who would also do voices for the Golden Book and Record series. From the original cast came John Fiedler as Piglet and Sterling Holloway as Pooh, in what would be his final performance for the label. Soon thereafter he suffered a heart attack that essentially put him into retirement (although his distinctive voice could be heard sporadically in TV commercials until his death in 1992).

Groce's prolific talent for songwriting came in handy when he wrote one or two original songs for each of the first twenty-four titles in the Golden Book series, which brought with it a noticeably new breed of read-along and the beginning of Jymn Magon's remarkable Disney career. Magon grew up in Dearborn, Michigan, the son of professional dancer/teachers. While he was attending Principia College, a friend dared him to write and produce a radio show. The resulting program, *Green Nurd Theater*, parodied classic radio drama and pulp fiction with narration, character dialogue, and sound effects. One of the student performers was Gary Krisel, who never forgot the quality of Magon's work and told him years later, "When you're done with the Navy, you should come out to California. We could really use someone like you." Magon thought Krisel was kidding. "There are so many talented people in California," he thought. "Why would they need some English major from Michigan?" After Magon submitted a few spec scripts to show how he could write for Disney characters, Krisel continued to urge him to relocate. So Magon visited on vacation and Krisel convinced him to write and produce all twenty-four Little Golden Book and Record sets in roughly a month. Forgoing many a good night's sleep, Magon ended up producing them at a rate of one new recording every day or two. "It was really bizarre," Magon remembered. "I had never been in a professional studio, I had never worked with professional actors, and I had to rewrite all these books because they didn't work as recorded scripts."

In the original Golden Books, the narrative phrase "he said" or "she said" interrupts the character dialogue. For the read-alongs, Magon took out those remarks and let the narrative naturally lead to the characters' lines (e.g., "The Engine was worried. 'Who will help me?'" instead of "The Engine said, 'Who will help me?'"). This style of writing continues in every Disney read-along to this day.

○

With Groce on board to write the songs, the next hurdle was finding voice actors. Fellow cast member Les Perkins, who later created the Disney Character Voices department, handed Groce a tape that a sixteen-year-old aspiring actor had submitted some time earlier. The actor was Corey Burton, and Magon was blown away. "There were all these amazing voices, from Captain Hook to Fred MacMurray," said Magon. "I hired Corey when he was nineteen and asked him to suggest other people. He suggested Tony Pope,

Pat Parris was one of the students in Daws Butler's voice acting workshop who landed numerous roles on the 1976–77 Disneyland Records read-alongs. (Courtesy of Pat Parris)

Linda Gary, and Pat Parris." Burton took Magon to one of the renowned voice acting workshops conducted by Daws Butler, the legendary talent behind Yogi Bear, Huckleberry Hound, Elroy Jetson, and many others for Hanna-Barbera as well as memorable work with Stan Freberg and Jay Ward. "Daws had a garage or office in the back of his house where he held the workshops," Magon recalled. "I met the actors at his evening class and started using them for the records."

Like Robie Lester, Thurl Ravenscroft, Dallas McKennon, Ginny Tyler, and others before them, these new performers became part of a regular stable that also included veteran voice actor/narrators Hal Smith and Bob Holt. In a nod to the past, Sam Edwards was called in to play Tigger and Rabbit in the remake of Lois Lane's final read-along, *Winnie the Pooh and Tigger Too*. Lucille Bliss, absent from Disneyland Records since 1963's

Corey Burton: The Voice Actor's Voice Actor

Corey Burton has known his career path since he was four years old, trying to mimic the voices and vocal effects he heard in cartoons. "*Rocky and Bullwinkle* was a huge inspiration to me," Burton said. "The Jay Ward shows were what made me want to do cartoon voices to begin with. Paul Frees, June Foray, Bill Scott, Hans Conried, William Conrad—it's like the greatest cartoon character actors of all time were thrown together with that brilliant writing and fast pace."

Tape recorder always handy, he practiced for years on his own, then studied with voice acting legend Daws Butler. While still in his teens, Burton started to gain a name for himself as an announcer. "[Engineer] George Charouhas was highly responsible for my career," said Burton. "The first session I did with him was for an album by the Ramones, and we just clicked. He recommended me to other record promo producers and really got me started at the time. I always recommended him every chance I got."

Burton's first Disney job was a filmstrip called *Chef Ahmalette's Health Diet* for Walt Disney Educational Media Company. They needed a Hans Conried voice, but Conried was out of town doing a play. Burton stepped in, and his performance led to more educational projects as well as to his first work for Disneyland Records, the Little Golden Book-and-Record series.

With an exhausting repertoire of voices from original creations to on-target impressions of numerous talents such as John Huston, Orson Bean, and Ed Wynn, Burton appeared on dozens of Disneyland and Buena Vista read-alongs, including a stint as Luke Skywalker on the *Star Wars* records that impressed Mark Hamill. "It may have been Tony Pope who told him that I did the impression for the read along, and Tony had copies with him," Burton remembers. "The next time I saw Mark he said, 'Boy, you sounded exactly like me! How do you do that?'"

Burton has become one of Hollywood's most sought-after voice actors, doing animation for film (Molière in *Atlantis: The Lost Empire*) and TV (*The Transformers* was his first), commercials (Old Navy), and theme park attractions (announcer for "It's Tough to Be a Bug!"). On radio, he played Star Lab Controller Jerry Lyden on *Alien Worlds* and Cryin' Brian Dern (among many others) on *Adventures in Odyssey*.

He is also Disney's official voice of Captain Hook, Professor Ludwig von Drake, Dale, and Grumpy. And he has never stopped doing read-alongs for children, including narration for *Dr.*

Seuss' How the Grinch Stole Christmas, for which he received a Grammy nomination, and *The Adventures of Rocky and Bullwinkle*, which brought him full circle from his childhood.

Burton is always conscious of his young audience when recording for children. "I always resented as a kid when I was being pandered to. So from a child's standpoint, I always try to give an adult performance. I never liked the saccharine or patronizing tones. You can hear the reality in a characterization even without a trained ear. It just seems genuine."

Peter Cottontail, also narrated a few Golden Books in her husky voice.

Drawing on his college radio drama experience, Magon produced each title with a full cast, sound effects, and, for the first time, music (the sole previous exception being *Peter and the Wolf*). When the first twenty-four were finished, Krisel assigned Magon to create four additional Christmas Golden Book titles, followed by a long-range plan to modify the existing read-alongs based on classic Disney favorites.

Little LP titles such as *Sleeping Beauty* and *Cinderella* were re-recorded with the new stable of actors. Background music came from the films and from some Camarata music tracks. And thanks to the ingenuity of engineer George Charouhas, special care was taken to re-create the sound quality of the original movies. "The read-alongs were engineered differently," said Charouhas. "There was a conscious decision made on the part of Jymn and myself to try to make the Little LPs sound like the old optical film soundtracks. So what we did was fatten them up and filter them. We took off some high and low end. We didn't want them to sound too hi-fi. It was fun. I was always into experimenting."

Unlike Disneyland Story Reader Robie Lester in the 1960s, who was handed multiple scripts with no character voice references, Krisel and Magon would screen film footage so that the actors could study the voices. When the actors entered the recording studio, roles would be assigned by consensus. "We'd ask each other, 'Who does a better impression of this or that character?'" said Burton. "We'd say, 'Let's hear yours, and let's hear yours,' and so on. Then it would be, 'Okay, you do this one and you do that one.' We'd just sort of distribute them to whoever was strongest in any character." He continued, "We'd run through the script and sometimes halfway through the script, we'd reassign the voices. Then we'd get on mike, tape would roll and we would pretty much go straight through the show, backing up whenever a mistake was made. You were expected to just pop in when your cue came up and just nail that character voice in one take and not slow down the progress. There were not a lot of retakes; they were done pretty efficiently. We'd record five or more in a session."

Charouhas remembered the lighthearted mood of the recording sessions. "Jymn loved to have fun at the studio. It was always like a

party when the talent was in the room, with lots of goofing and joking. Jymn led the way, but he always kept his producer and business hats handy. He wanted to get the best performances and wanted everybody to feel good about what they had done." "We just enjoyed ourselves," said Burton. "We joked around a lot, especially in the read-throughs, usually egged on by Bob Holt's wry sense of humor. We Daws Butler students were probably more reserved, but Bob and Hal came from those old showbiz traditions and kept all of us laughing. On more than one occasion I suffered a little loss of vocal control because all that laughing wore out the voice!"

O

Magon graduated to long-playing records with *The All-New Mickey Mouse Club*, a TV soundtrack album of songs from the 1977 incarnation of the series. It was packaged with a poster including profiles of the new Mouseketeers and was the first album in what was soon to be known as the Disneyland Premier Series. These premium-quality albums largely comprised new material and sold at a slightly higher retail price than the DQ series. Krisel was so pleased with the album that he sent a note to the Mouseketeers:

Linda Gary and Charles Howerton: A Match Made in Voice Heaven

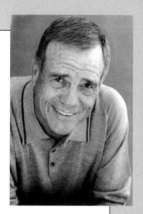

When the Disney read-along series was revised starting in the late 1970s, Linda Gary was the primary female narrator (and voice actor) on such titles as *Alice in Wonderland* and *Three Little Pigs*. It was a mere footnote in her vast acting career, a career she enjoyed for many years beside her husband, Charles Howerton, who did a fine share of acting work as well.

Gary started her acting career as a child. Her mother, a Russian immigrant who at age fifteen had taken her family over the Romanian border on a hay wagon, got young Linda involved in theater and early TV. She appeared on such shows as *Mickey Mouse Club*, *Schlitz Playhouse of Stars*, and *Playhouse 90*, under the names of either Linda Gay or Linda DeWoskin (she later borrowed the name of Gary from her actor brother, Paul).

After attending the University of California at Northridge and doing some modeling in New York, Linda Gary returned to Los Angeles to do a play at Northridge, where she met Howerton. Howerton had studied Theater Arts at the University of Texas and had established himself in Los Angeles through years of TV commercials, soap operas, and series.

In 1970 the couple visited Europe for a three-month stay. Actor/director Mel Welles got them started in a new career direction in the art of foreign film dubbing. "We started getting work dubbing in Rome," Howerton said. "Linda was an instant hit because she had such range. That's when she discovered her talent for voice-overs." They worked throughout Europe and ended up staying four years. "Italian actresses would ask for Linda to do their voices," Howerton recalls with pride. "Once she dubbed Lauren Hutton for a foreign film, and even Lauren didn't realize it wasn't her voice."

Upon returning to Los Angeles, she started getting voice work with the major animation companies, including Hanna-Barbera, Rankin/Bass, and Marvel, for which she was the voice of *Spiderman's* Aunt May. On radio, she costarred with good friend Corey Burton on *Alien Worlds*.

She most enjoyed working for Filmation Associates, because of the volume of roles the company offered. "In animation, you have to do two or three roles. Linda wound up doing five to seven," said Howerton. "She was 90 percent of the female characters. There were many times when even I didn't know it was her, she was so good at changing her tone and pitch."

Howerton's career also flourished, on stage, in front of the camera, and behind the scenes. For Disneyland/Vista Records, he is heard as Lando Calrissian in *The Empire Strikes Back*, narrating *The Lion King: The Brightest Star*, and in the lead role on the *Dick Tracy* cassettes.

Gary and Howerton often worked together; some of these projects included the Disneyland Storyteller LP redramatization of *Cinderella* and English dubbing for the Japanese children's TV series *Spectreman*. Other members of the family got into the act when Gary and Howerton's daughter, Dana, played Dorothy to Gary's Aunt Em on Disneyland's *Return to Oz* read-along and was teamed with her sister, Alexis, in the *Peter Pan* read-along, among others. They're even in the Disney theme parks: Gary is the magnificently malevolent Maleficent in the show *Fantasmic!*, and Howerton narrates "Goofy about Health" at the Wonders of Life pavilion.

By the time Gary was doing the Grandma voice in the third *Land Before Time* film, she had contracted a brain tumor and began a tragic physical decline. Howerton remembers her last *Spiderman* session in 1995, during which the production people "were very upset. They wanted her to come in and play Aunt May. She didn't want to do it because she knew she wasn't at her best. I took her there in a wheelchair. They had to feed her the lines because she was almost blind. It was just three weeks before she died."

With Dana and Alexis grown and enjoying success, Charles Howerton continues his busy career on TV shows such as *The West Wing* and *The Matrix* and in animated productions for Marvel and Warner Brothers. Linda Gary is never far from their thoughts. "She was very special. Her agent once told me Linda was probably one of the three most talented clients he had ever had in his life. A lot of other people felt that way too. Me included."

Congratulations on your first album. I hope that it is one of many. We have the highest hopes for the success of this record.

We would like nothing better than to see you individually and collectively become recording stars as well as successful TV performers.

You guys are all great! I hope all of you will stop by my office any time.

Again, congratulations!

Despite Krisel's optimistic appreciation, the company released no further albums by the new Mouseketeers, even though they recorded plenty of additional songs.

○

Nineteen seventy-seven was a comparatively big movie year for Disney and thus a big one for Disneyland Records. Both an animated feature and a lavish musical were scheduled for release.

For *The Rescuers* LP, background music was included with soundtrack dialogue for the first time since *The Jungle Book* Storyteller. The album also marked a return appearance by Robie Lester, who sang for Eva Gabor in "Rescue Aid Society" for the film.

"I remember going and watching pencil tests of the rough animation," Magon said of *The Rescuers*. "Of course, they were still doing cel animation at the time, so for Storyteller book, I had to go get cel setups. I would actually pull the background and the cel and have them shot, then I would give the transparency to Western Publishing so they could put them in the book."

Because he felt the album should emphasize story over songs, Magon decided to trim the music. Tunes such as the Oscar-nominated "Someone's Waiting for You," sung by the wispy voice of Shelby Flint, would play for a chorus and verse or two, then fade out. Complete versions of the film's four songs would not be released on vinyl until a year later on Ovation's boxed set, *The Magical Music of Walt Disney*.

O

Change was in the wind at Disneyland/Vista Records. Even the paper labels that were pressed onto the records had been changed to a new full-color rainbow design, replacing plain yellow, purple, and other solid colors of the past.

Acting on the mission to bring popular, contemporary talent to the label, Merrill Dean was instrumental in negotiations behind singer Helen Reddy's involvement in *Pete's Dragon*, Disney's most ambitious musical fantasy since *Bedknobs and Broomsticks*. Because of Reddy's contract with Capitol Records, the soundtrack of *Pete's Dragon* was issued on Capitol, though the read-along and Storyteller (with edited songs) appeared on Disneyland. *Pete's Dragon* was well received but did not cause the *Mary Poppins* bonanza for which everyone at Disney was hoping. It would take something very different than a traditional musical to rejuvenate the record division for the first time since *Poppins*.

O

Dean also expanded the Disneyland/Vista catalog by negotiating record deals with outside companies. One of the first to benefit from this association was Rankin/Bass Productions. This New York–based production company had been responsible for more perennial holiday specials than any other company. The most renowned Rankin/Bass specials—*Rudolph the Red-Nosed Reindeer*, *Frosty the Snowman*, and *Santa Claus Is Comin' to Town*—had already been released on other labels, so Disneyland/Vista had to choose between sequels or lesser-known titles. Executives chose one of each. The "all-livin'" snowman gets married on *Frosty's Winter Wonderland*, a follow-up to the highly rated original. High Nielsen audience ratings were likely the reason '*Twas the Night Before Christmas* became a Disneyland Record; the special was a consistent ratings winner for over a decade.

Rankin/Bass shows were animated overseas using either stop-motion Animagic or limited animation, with musically rich, star-studded soundtracks that lent themselves well to records. There was almost always a narrator and lots of script exposition, so the soundtracks could stand on their own, intact, without visuals. As album producer, Magon merely had to lay down the soundtracks, make minor edits, and supervise the album covers.

The biggest Rankin/Bass project for Disneyland/Vista was *The Hobbit*, a ninety-minute adaptation of the J. R. R. Tolkien classic first broadcast on NBC in 1977. Six

Hal Smith: Pillar of the Mayberry Community

One of America's finest character actors, Hal Smith may be best known to TV fans as Otis on the *Andy Griffith Show*, but his career actually spanned six decades. Born in the small town of Petoskey, Michigan, Smith started show business as a singer in Joe Callpari's band and performing in vaudeville with his brother while still in high school. He entered radio as a singer, announcer, and newscaster. After serving as an entertainer in the Special Services Division of the Army Air Force, he ventured to California and began a steady stream of work in radio and films in the late 1940s and 1950s. On television, he had recurring roles in early series such as *I Married Joan*, *The Ruggles*, and *The Adventures of Ozzie and Harriet*, where he appeared for seven seasons.

Hal Smith's 1960s and 1970s television and movie credits are too numerous to list here, and his animation voice credits are almost endless, too. For Disney, Smith narrated countless educational materials as well as dozens of read-along records, appearing in several Disney films as well. Smith performed the voice of Goofy on many occasions, including in *Mickey's Christmas Carol*. (Today, the equally skillful Bill Farmer is officially designated as Goofy's voice.)

In his later years, one of his favorite roles was as the original John Avery "Whit" Whitaker on the children's radio series *Adventures in Odyssey*. This was a rare instance in which he played the lead role; he usually intentionally pursued character parts instead of starring roles. That way, he knew he could sustain constant work in a variety of acting parts and, with wise investing, enjoy a balanced lifestyle with his fans, family, and his wife of forty-five years, Louise. Considered one of the nicest people in show business, Smith remained very much in demand until his death from cancer in 1994.

Tony Pope:
Watch Out for
Goofy

When top Hollywood voice actor and impressionist Tony Pope would visit a certain casting agency for auditions, Pat Lentz would flirt with him. "I was much taller than Tony," Lentz said. "After we were married, we would always say that my flirting would go over his head." Pope and Lentz worked together for twenty years, averaging twenty hours a day together, doing voices, promos, and theater. Pope had already made a name for himself with numerous cartoons and a slew of Disneyland/Vista Records.

Pope started out as an impressionist in Cleveland, Ohio, playing nightclubs at fifteen years old. He eventually watched enough movies and cartoons to convince him to go to Hollywood, where he studied in Daws Butler's workshop. (He and Corey Burton started on almost the same day.) Pope was one of the talented actors Jymn Magon hired to do a parade of voices and impressions for the Little Golden Book-and-Records series and the classic Disney read-alongs. One of his most memorable Disney records was the remake read-along of Robie Lester's *Mother Goose Rhymes*, in which Pope performs the verses in various celebrity voices, including a personal favorite, George Burns. His dream project was a one-man show about Burns. "Tony was terribly proud of his Disney records work," said Lentz. "He would get all the gold records. They're all over our house. He really felt like he was part of something special."

His Disneyland Records work led to voicing Goofy for eleven years on various projects. Pope's voice was heard in films, theme park rides, and cartoons. He also voiced enough toys to fill a large playroom, from talking Matchbox cars to Chef Tony for a Mattel kitchen. When Furby, the cuddly interactive creature, took the world by storm in 1998, Pope gave him an international vocabulary. "He recorded Furby in six languages," said Lentz. "They would bring in people from Japan, Italy, and Spain and they would teach him how to say the words."

If Pope had not become an actor, he would most likely have been a baseball player. A fan of the Cleveland Indians and Browns, Pope was a softball MVP at the age of forty-nine and coached his daughters' games. Pope was very much at the top of his game in 2004, when he died of complications from bypass surgery. His memorial service was attended by 450 family members and friends and a veritable who's-who of the voice acting community, and nearly 400 people attended the funeral. "Everybody loved him," Pat Lentz said. "And he was able to do what he loved for a living. He felt truly blessed."

recorded products were released: a seven-inch book and record, a matching book and cassette, a condensed Storyteller soundtrack, a soundtrack song album, and a two-LP boxed set of the complete soundtrack, which was nominated for a Grammy.

The same year, Buena Vista started Charlie Brown Records, a label for albums and read-alongs based on Charles M. Schulz's *Peanuts* TV specials. Magon coproduced with Lee Mendelson, who had produced all the TV specials. Some of the albums, such as *A Charlie Brown Christmas*, were direct lifts from the soundtrack, while others, including *Charlie Brown's All-Stars*, combined soundtrack dialogue with new voice work by the current *Peanuts* child actors.

○

The first *Star Wars* movie created a sensation in 1977, and the Disneyland/Vista team obtained from Lucasfilm the rights to a read-along Little LP (a story album and music soundtrack had already been released on Twentieth Century Fox Records). Magon produced a reenactment of the story using the Disneyland/Vista stable of actors, with soundtrack music by John Williams. To get the authentic sound effects, he met with *Star Wars* sound designer Ben Burtt, who "came down to the studio carrying the sound effects with him," Magon recalled. "He wanted to make sure they didn't get copied and given to other studios. I had to be very careful to hang onto them. I was playing some of our Disney sound effects, which were from the RKO library back from when Disney didn't have its own distribution. He wanted the musket rifle sound from *Davy Crockett*. It's a three-part sound: the hammer coming down, the powder hitting the flint and igniting. I tried to help him because he was a sound effects collector. At one point, I was playing him a lion's roar and he said 'Stop! Wait! That's the lion's roar that was run backward and used for *King Kong*! I've heard snippets of it but I've never heard the whole sentence.' So I made him a copy. It was like trading cards."

○

With several of these non-Disney projects in the works, Krisel also sought new stylistic avenues for Disney product. *Saturday Night Fever* started the disco craze, and the entire recording industry followed the trend. Disney was intrigued but initially noncommittal, although other children's records quickly joined the disco boom. The Sesame Street label released *Sesame Street Fever*; Peter Pan Records parlayed a cover version of Rick Dees's "Disco Duck" into a best-selling album series featuring Irwin the Disco Duck, sometimes played by Hanna-Barbera voice veteran Don Messick. Nashville record producer Paul Whitehead was the force behind an LP titled *Kartoon DisKo* on the Happy Tunes label. Whitehead licensed animation-related tunes and themes, including Disney songs. *Kartoon DisKo* contained modernized renditions of "Zip-A-Dee-Doo-Dah" and "Chim Chim Cheree." Immediately after this album's release, according to Whitehead, he began trying to convince Disneyland/Vista to produce an entire LP of Mickey Mouse disco music. Another supporter for the project was former Sun Rays musician Eddy Medora, by the late 1970s Disneyland/Vista sales manager for the western United States and a key idea man.

Disco in its early days was tainted somewhat by hedonistic images of Studio 54 and other hot spots, so much so that Whitehead recalled Magon telling him that disco was too controversial a format to risk. Disney records toyed with the genre, however. On *The All New Mickey Mouse Club* LP, the song "Discovery Day" includes the lyrics, "D-i-s-c-o, D-i-s-c-o, D-i-s-c-o-v-e-r-y . . . Day!" though it was not set to a disco beat. Later, Buena Vista Records released a 45-rpm single called "Disco Mouse" sung by new Mouseketeers Scott Craig, Alison Fonte, Kelly Parsons, Lisa Whelchel, and Curtis Wong. *New Mickey Mouse Club* viewers were treated to a behind-the-scenes look at the making of this disc from recording studio to pressing plant.

Not until disco was somewhat on the wane, becoming a more comfortable musical style for mainstream audiences, did Krisel say, "Let's do it." Pat Patrick, the owner of a recording studio in Nashville, Tennessee, remembered his initial encounter with Disney as occurring quite by accident. "I was doing a special project for a company called International Horizons," he said. "They had a series of books on tape that were intended to teach children in Japan how to speak English, and they had licensed the Disney characters for this. We must have done a hundred songs for those records. Apparently Jymn Magon heard them somehow, and since he already had this other project in mind, he sent us a list of titles for songs he wanted on *Disco*. One of them was 'The Greatest Band,' and I think I wrote it in three or four minutes."

"Gary found this company called Odyssey Productions in Nashville," recalled Magon. "Great people like Paul Whitehead, Jack Jackson, Pat Patrick, Dennis Burnside, and a whole studio full of musicians who had gone to college together and decided to start a business. It was a very cool, aggressive location and they really wanted to make a deal with Disney. We decided how many tracks we needed. We already had 'Chim Chim Cheree' and 'Zip-A-Dee-Doo-Dah' [from the Whitehead record], so I had nothing to do with those, but everything else was freshly recorded."

Magon again faced a daunting task. "I knew as much about making disco albums as

the elephant next door!" he laughed. "I remember sitting up late in the Holiday Inn, listening to Donna Summer tapes and stuff and saying, 'Look! They use police whistles here! Oh look, they go ooh-ooh!' I was trying to remember all this stuff so at least when I walked into the studio the next morning I'd know something. We were very lucky. We had such talented people for these things. Dennis Burnside had done these terrific arrangements for the songs, including my little song, 'Mousetrap.' He just made that thing come alive. So we recorded all these tracks, and I basically went home with the tracks under my arm."

The title number, "Disco Mickey Mouse," came from Tom Worrall, who had been responsible for much of the music in the *Disney on Parade* traveling arena show of a decade earlier. Charouhas and his songwriting partner, Steve Furman (who died just a couple of years later at age twenty-nine) contributed "Welcome to Rio" and "Watch Out for Goofy." The arrangements were credited to Burnside, a local keyboard player who finished his part of the job within three days. The album may have been titled *Mickey Mouse Disco*, but Mickey's voice is nowhere to be heard. However, Donald Duck makes a memorable appearance in "Macho Duck," Tom Worrall's spoof of the Village People hit "Macho Man," with lead vocals by Nashville studio singer Eddie Frierson. In this song, Jim Tadevic, who was on the Disney studio staff as location spotter, plays Donald.

Tadevic had filled in as early as 1964 when Clarence Nash was unavailable to voice Donald for one reason or another, appearing first in commercials and later in Disney educational products. Tadevic's Donald differed from Nash's because Tadevic generated the voice in his throat rather the back of the mouth, as Nash and most other successors had done. Disney executives believed that Tadevic's vocal process made him more suitable for narration and other duties in which Donald's normally poor diction would have been a hindrance.

For "Macho Duck," Tadevic was called in to listen to the completed song and ad-lib responses. "The version you hear on the album is the result of four different takes, with the best stuff from each edited together," he explained. The end result was so entertaining that Tony Pope was then brought in to add comic dialogue to "Watch Out for Goofy," as the lovable bumbler made a shambles of the dance floor and its patrons.

When *Mickey Mouse Disco* first hit stores in July 1979, it was only a modest success. "We did okay initially," said Medora. "But then we had a sales meeting and we said 'Lets run direct TV,' because the *Mickey Mouse Club [Mouskedances and Other Mouseketeer Favorites]* album had done so well." Using footage edited from classic Disney short cartoons like *Thru the Mirror* (1936) and *Mr. Duck Steps Out* (1940), the *Mickey Mouse Disco* television spot resembled other record album ads of the time, with the song titles crawling on-screen over the footage. A toll-free number was provided so viewers could order the album through direct mail. "After TV, we shipped the album gold [500,000 copies]," Medora explained. "The spot played on TV for months and the reorders kept coming in."

To the surprise and delight of everyone at Disneyland/Vista Records, the Recording Industry Association of America awarded the album Gold Record status in April 1980; a month and a half later it reached the Platinum level. In October 1984, it became the first children's album ever to be awarded Double Platinum recognition (2,000,000 copies sold). For the first time a Disneyland Records release was fueling material in other Disney divisions, including *Mickey Mouse Disco* lunchboxes, posters, and other tie-in merchandise. In the Los Angeles area, gigantic billboards adorned Sunset Boulevard and various Tower Records stores.

Krisel, Magon, and company now had the breakout success they needed. They no longer had to depend solely on Disney films for their material, and the money generated from *Mickey Mouse Disco* gave them the clout to pursue further original album concepts.

12

Mickey Makes a Big Splash

During the same period that *Mickey Mouse Disco* was germinating, Pat Patrick's studio was also responsible for producing the first installment in Disneyland Records' long-running *Children's Favorites* series. These disarmingly simple LPs showcased the folksy style of Larry Groce, who was glad to be able to record his material in Nashville rather than traveling all the way to Burbank, as he had done for his earlier Disney work.

Patrick recalled how trouble-free the *Children's Favorites* recording sessions were; Groce usually recorded each song in one take. For a special touch, a children's chorus was added to most of the tracks during postproduction. Back in Los Angeles, choral direction was put in the capable hands of Betty Joyce, a vocal contractor/arranger who went on to do nine albums for Disney.

A professional singer since age eighteen, Betty Joyce was the widow of premier vocal arranger Jimmy Joyce, who was equally adept at children's choruses (*The Sound of Music*; Frank Sinatra's "High Hopes") and adult choirs (the *Red Skelton Show*). A musical family, the Joyces had five children, all of whom were involved in singing. "Betty was so sweet," said George Charouhas. "She always had the kids ready to go. All I had to do was set the mikes and watch them go. Sometimes Betty would sing with the kids too." "It was always different each time I got the children together," Joyce recalled. "But I would rehearse with them before the session so when they went in they knew what they were to do." Though the group would vary, they were named the Disneyland Children's Sing-Along Chorus.

The *Children's Favorites* series would become more elaborate as time went by, but the first two volumes remained the biggest sellers. Volume 1 received a Gold Record in March 1983, with volume 2 following in October. Three years later, both volumes reached the Platinum level.

On the heels of his novelty hit, "Junk Food Junkie," Larry Groce became the headliner of Disneyland Records' *Children's Favorites* series. Many of the songs are still available today. (Courtesy of Larry Groce)

Larry Groce: From London Bridge to Mountain Stage

Variety is the spice of Larry Groce's musical life. He has thrived on all kinds of music since his childhood in Dallas. He started earning money in a band when he was in junior high and hobnobbed with a number of aspiring musical performers at Adamson High, which for some reason has produced many a music success. At Principia College near St. Louis, Groce met Gary Krisel and Jymn Magon, who would make it possible for Groce to record some of the best-selling children's records of all time.

When Groce graduated from college, he started playing New York clubs, including one called Focus where he alternated with Melissa Manchester and other notable performers. His first record was an album of hymns, *Green Pastures Are before Me*, in 1969. The next year, he made *The Wheat Lies Low* for RCA's Daybreak label. He made one more record for Daybreak when he moved to Los Angeles in 1972, but his big break came with his 1975 novelty tune "Junk Food Junkie," concerning a health food nut who secretly stuffs himself with all manner of forbidden goodies. "We put it out as a single ourselves," said Groce. "It caught on with disc jockeys. It was a success, even though it had no label and no distribution, so Warner Curb Records re-released it in 1976. It was in the Top 10 on radio station KHJ in L.A. That was one of the things that led to Disney albums."

Krisel and Magon used the hit status of "Junk Food Junkie" to convince Disney higher-ups to hire Groce, who was already a popular Disneyland park guest artist, to create original songs for Disneyland Records. Shortly after his first song, "Pooh for President," pleased the folks at Disney, Groce was asked to write and usually perform original songs for their new Little Golden Book-and-Record series. He soon found himself in studios in Nashville and Los Angeles to record the first of four volumes of *Children's Favorites*. These albums were such perennial best sellers that they became the longest-running non-movie Disney titles ever released. The albums combined the best public domain children's folk tunes and nursery rhymes and play-along songs with selections from the Golden Book series and others. "A lot of those songs are great," Groce said. "I'm glad I recorded them, because they're songs children ought to know. Every kid in America should know 'O Susanna,' the songs of Stephen Foster, and others. It's like basic education. It was fun to do and I liked to do it."

While his Disney career was in full swing, including a guest appearance on the *New Mickey Mouse Club*, Groce enjoyed a simultaneous career as a live performer. His role as artist in residence with the West Virginia National Endowment for the Arts led to his starting the *Mountain Stage* show on public radio in 1983. Even as radio music has gradually become targeted to limited, specific audiences, *Mountain Stage* features a consistently eclectic mix of musical acts from around the world, from traditional and country music to avant-garde rock and jazz. *Mountain Stage* is now heard on 110 public radio stations, XM satellite radio, and Voice of America. Groce hosts both the radio and long-running television versions, which have featured Lyle Lovett, Mary-Chapin Carpenter, REM, Sarah McLaughlin, Allison Krauss, Phish, and Bill Monroe, among numerous others.

Groce serves as host, producer and artistic director. He also wrote the theme song. "We focus on traditions and keep them alive, like blues and bluegrass and the people who create and write music—the singers and songwriters," he explained. "The only thing we stay away from is mainstream pop music. You can hear that everywhere else. People tune in to see who they know and then discover ones they had never heard. It's been the first national media exposure for a lot of people who have become famous."

Groce still takes pride in his Disney work and in how it has entertained generations of children. "Believe me, I'm very humbled by that fact, and grateful," he said. "Children are the very best audiences of all. Their minds aren't colored. If they like something, they like it. The fact so many kids have listened to the records and liked them is very inspirational to me. I used to get a big thrill playing at schools. At one school, I sang one of the Disney songs, 'Carrot Stew,' and was amazed when the kids sang along. The teacher told me it was because the song was in their Silver-Burdett third-grade music textbook. Being in a schoolbook that children see in school, alongside people like Woody Guthrie and with songs that had been around forever— it was one of my best contributions to American music."

○

The Disney studio was hoping to capture the *Star Wars* movie audience in 1979 with its own science fiction epic, *The Black Hole*. The film did not live up to expectations, but the Buena Vista soundtrack album of background music by John Barry is significant because it was touted as the first digitally recorded soundtrack on records. The digital process, as opposed to analog recording that relies more heavily on tape, resulted in less background hiss and a purer, clearer sound. It was a sign that Disneyland/Vista was always striving to embrace the next wave of technology. *The Black Hole*, Disney's first PG-rated film, was also adapted into a Storyteller LP with dialogue from the soundtrack.

○

By 1980, more than enough album-ready theme park material had accumulated to compile *The Official Album of Disneyland/Walt Disney World*. For the first time, selections from the Haunted Mansion, Pirates of the Caribbean, Country Bear Jamboree, and other attractions and area music were assembled on one album.

○

Mickey Mouse Disco opened the door for what Disneyland/Vista insiders called "the big three"— a trio of musical albums featuring Disney characters that were recorded more or less at the same time. The first, *Yankee Doodle Mickey*, was a collection of patriotic songs sung by Larry Groce and the children's chorus, with a few archival pieces (with beautiful harmonizing by the Mello-Men) mixed in. And unlike *Mickey Mouse Disco*, Mickey, voiced by Pete Renaday, sings on the album. *Yankee Doodle Mickey* also featured three solos by twelve-year-old Molly Ringwald, then playing Molly Parker on the TV series *The Facts of Life* (alongside former Mouseketeer Lisa Whelchel). No stranger to recording, Ringwald had cut her first album, *I Wanna Be Loved by You, Molly Sings* for another label when she was six. "Molly wasn't a part of the children's chorus," said Jymn Magon. "Her father, Bob, was her agent at the time. He was also a jazz musician and he was blind. I remember standing next to her at the microphone and coaching her. She stood there, arms at her sides and just belted out these songs. I said 'Great!' and she went home. Our time together was very brief."

The second of the "big three" was *Goin' Quackers! Wacky Songs to Quack You Up*, marking the debut of comedy/music duo Will Ryan and Phil Baron. Calling themselves

Will Ryan, Donald Duck, and Phil Baron quack each other up while promoting their *Goin' Quackers!* LP. (Courtesy of Will Ryan; Donald Duck © Disney Enterprises, Inc.)

Willio and Phillio, the pair had gained a loyal following in their native Cleveland, Ohio, and were gaining popularity in Chicago with regular TV, radio, and nightclub performances. They had released one album and were hoping to record their lilting version of "When You Wish upon a Star." The two set off for Burbank, where they "met with Jymn Magon and dropped off our first album," said Baron. "Two weeks later he called and said, 'I really like your stuff. Would you like to write some songs for an album about Donald Duck?' We immediately got to work and submitted half a dozen songs and they bought them all! It was the perfect marriage of what we did and what Disney was trying to do. You can't believe how that felt."

Ryan couldn't believe he was working at the Disney studios: "When I first set foot on the Disney lot, it was so exciting for me to go around and see the wonderful back lot— the *Zorro* set, the Western sets, the midwestern lot, the garage where flubber was invented, 'That Darn Cat's' house, and the

Willio and Phillio: Forever Quackers

The musical comedy duo of Willio and Phillio didn't always play specifically to children, but their material was for everyone to enjoy, whether they were making records, playing nightclubs, or performing at "dayclubs," as they called their matinees.

Will Ryan and Phil Baron discovered the chemistry between them when Baron was asked to supervise Ryan's music for an off-Broadway show. On long car trips between their home base in Cleveland and New York, they started writing songs. "We hit it off," recalled Baron. "We started writing a show together, and before you knew it, we decided we would collaborate some more. A cousin of mine was running a church basement coffeehouse in Cleveland and asked if I wanted to play there. I said, 'Sure.' I was rehearsing with Will one day and told him about this thing coming up, asked him to do it with me."

Willio and Phillio were born. "We based these characters on ourselves, and then we based ourselves on the two characters," Baron continues. "We did a silly act with a bunch of songs we loved. Instead of attempting to please the audience, we decided to do what we thought was going to be fun. Sure enough, the audience went nuts." Within six months, they were practically household names in Cleveland, doing numerous radio appearances and selling out concerts. Then came *The First Willio and Phillio Album,* distributed to the surrounding regions, including Chicago. Soon the team had a regular spot on the Cleveland edition of TV's *PM Magazine*, exploring the funny and silly goings-on around town, and hosted a morning radio show. "We were doing Disney songs long before we worked for Disney," Ryan said. "There hadn't yet been albums of people doing quirky versions of Disney songs, so we just did it for the heck of it."

By the late 1970s, their work came to the attention of Jymn Magon at Disneyland Records, and they were asked to make demos for their first Disney LP, *Goin' Quackers!*, which was followed by *Pardners*. Relocating to Los Angeles, they started playing clubs and doing character voices, including the voices of Chip 'n' Dale with their cover of "The Chipmunk Song" for the album *Merry Christmas Carols*. When the Disney Channel was starting up, public TV producer Christopher Sarson (*Zoom*, *The French Chef*) planned to produce a new series called *Magic Kingdom* with Willio and Phillio but withdrew from the project after budgetary disputes. Another executive slated to become president of the channel also promised them a series but subsequently decided not to relocate from New York.

The team kept performing at clubs such as the Improv, created more song demos, and did more voices. Ryan, who had already been playing various roles on Disney read-along records, landed the part of Rabbit for the featurette *Winnie the Pooh and a Day for Eeyore*. The duo eventually ended up on the Disney Channel on a series called *Welcome to Pooh Corner*, with

Ryan as Rabbit and Tigger and Baron as Piglet. They wrote dozens of songs for other Disney Channel shows, including *Dumbo's Circus* and *You and Me, Kid*.

Baron also became the voice of animatronic plush toy Teddy Ruxpin, with Ryan as a character called Grubby. They reprised their roles on an animated series based on the toy. Ryan also voiced Willie the Giant for the animated featurette *Mickey's Christmas Carol*. Today, Ryan continues to write and perform and remains one of Hollywood's top voice artists. He is the voice of Eugene Meltsner on the *Adventures in Odyssey* radio series, and he's the creator of Elmo Aardvark, the legendary cyberspace cartoon character. After years of composing and scriptwriting, Baron now serves as cantor for Valley Beth Shalom in Encino, California. "I decided to fulfill a lifelong dream," he said. "I'm responsible for all the music at all the services, I supervise the choir and conduct concerts. I'm also writing new material, everything from playing blues harmonica to ukulele for the services. I'm settled in and not changing careers again. Some things are even bigger than Disney."

little church. I would sit under the tree on that street at lunchtime and I was back in Lakewood, Ohio. I used to see this street on the *Mickey Mouse Club*, and I was at home there."

Goin' Quackers! also brought Clarence "Ducky" Nash back to Disneyland Records as Donald Duck. Ryan spearheaded Nash's reemergence as Donald. Baron recalled, "After *Goin' Quackers!* came out, Ron Miller, who was in charge of Disney studios at the time, issued a letter that said Nash would be used as Donald and no one else." The duo became close friends with Nash and his wife.

Ryan and Baron were at Disneyland as the park celebrated the birthday of Donald Duck. In addition to a parade, every child age twelve or under received a 45-rpm single of "Goin' Quackers." "I'll never forget walking down Main Street, U.S.A. and seeing every kid

holding a copy of the record!" Ryan said. "We went where an interview with Ducky was going on. Suddenly I hear him say, 'Oh, Will! Will! Here he is right now! Here's the guy who wrote the song!' At ten years old I couldn't have dreamed that in the future this could happen to me, a kid from Cleveland!"

The third in this trilogy of albums was *Pardners*, consisting of cowboy and western songs, both classic and original. One tune, "The Song of the Screaming Cowboy," came from a vintage Donald Duck comic book story. "In the first panel, Donald comes rushing in and says, 'Kids! I've struck it rich! I just wrote a song!'" explained Ryan. "The first line comes right from the comic: 'Oh bury me thar / With my battered guitar / It is screamin' my heart out for you.'"

O

That Christmas, everyone involved in the big three recorded *Merry Christmas Carols*.

Ringwald contributed her last Disney solo, Groce and the kids sang the bulk of the songs, and Willio and Phillio took a break from comedy with Baron's touching ballad, "I Wish It Would Be Christmas All Year Long." Baron sang lead and Ryan provided backup. With the exception of 1958's "From All of Us to All of You," Mickey, Goofy, and friends had not previously sung Christmas songs on records. That changed with *Merry Christmas Carols*, which features them on several cuts. The album opens with Donald Duck and Chip 'n' Dale (Nash, Baron, and Ryan) doing their rendition of Ross Bagdasarian's "The Chipmunk Song" (an ironic twist considering that this song had bested Disney's Ludwig Mousensky and the All-Mouse Orchestra more than two decades earlier).

The following year, a Radio Shack exclusive LP called *The Disney Family Christmas Album* omitted the Groce singing tracks and replaced them with Disney characters singing for all the tunes. Radio Shack must have been pleased with the sales of this album; a year later the stores offered the *Mickey's Christ-*

Tony Pope (left) played Goofy to Clarence Nash's (right) Donald Duck on such 1980s LPs as *Goin' Quackers!* and *Pardners*. (Courtesy of Pat Lentz)

mas Carol LP, which combined portions of the 1974 *Dickens' Christmas Carol* record with soundtrack elements from the 1983 featurette. It marked the vinyl debut of Eddie Carroll in his new official capacity as Jiminy Cricket. It was also released in the picture disc series.

Picture discs, which date back to some of the earliest 78-rpm records, enjoyed a brief resurgence in the late 1970s and early 1980s. Disneyland/Vista was very successful in reissuing soundtracks such as *Snow White and the Seven Dwarfs* and *Mary Poppins* with full-color artwork pressed into the clear vinyl. They were so attractive that people also bought them as decorations. Even the soundtrack of the studio's most recent animated feature, *The Fox and the Hound*, was issued as a picture disc in addition to its Storyteller version.

O

The early 1980s were also the era of exercise albums and videos, led by Jane Fonda's immensely popular workout series. Disney muscled into this craze with *Mousercise*, a combination of efforts by tried-and-true Disneyland Records talent and up-and-coming

Left to right: Will Ryan, Hal Smith, Laurie Main, and Phil Baron were heard on numerous Disneyland records of the early 1980s. (Courtesy of Will Ryan)

newcomers. The title track weaved Disney tunes with a pounding beat (similar to *Hooked on Classics*, *Stars on 45*, and other such medleys). Al Capps, whose voice had been heard on albums of the mid-1960s, produced this rousing opener. The other cuts included exercise versions of "I Wan'na Be Like You" from *The Jungle Book* and "Step in Time" from *Mary Poppins*, with new lyrics by the Sherman brothers. Hal Smith demonstrated his versatility by impersonating the voices of Kaa the python, Colonel Hathi, and Baloo for the first of the two selections. Nash was back as Donald Duck in "Ducks Dance Too," another composition by Pat Patrick. Larry Groce had composed "Bug-a-Boo" for *Mickey Mouse Disco*, but the song was dropped from that album's final lineup and added to *Mousercise*.

Mousercise marked many firsts, including the involvement of Bambi Moé, who started her Disney career working for Tom Bocci, manager of music publishing. They worked closely with the A&R department to develop new projects and expand the catalog. Within six months, Bambi found herself doing A&R work for the record division, setting out to bring modern-day talent into the record output. She enlisted rhythm and blues luminary Edwin Starr to write and perform two songs for *Mousercise*—"Get the Money," which brought back Carl Barks's comic book villains the Beagle Boys, and "Tweedledee and Tweedledum," a rhythm-and-blues track very unusual for the label at the time (think Disney meets *Soul Train*). Also making their debut with *Mousercise* were Patty and Michael Silversher, a prolific songwriting duo who went on to create many songs for albums, CDs, and television shows. Their first song for Disney was "Pig Out," which faintly echoed the concept behind Groce's "Junk Food Junkie" hit.

Disneyland Records' penchant for having songwriters audition for a choice slot on an LP produced another cut on the *Mousercise*

Patty and Michael Silversher have created a great number of memorable songs for Disney records, TV shows, and films from the 1980s to the present. *Mousercise* contained their first Disney song, "Pig Out." (Courtesy of Patty Silversher; Disney characters © Disney Enterprises, Inc.)

On the *Mousercise* LP, composer Lois Blaisch was heard performing her new Sport Goofy theme song, "Keep on Tryin'." (Courtesy of Lois Blaisch)

The rock group Halyx, described by producer Bambi Moé as "a cross between *Star Wars* and the *Banana Splits*," was Buena Vista Records' aborted attempt to get into the true rock market. (© Disney Enterprises, Inc.)

Another voice heard for the first time on *Mousercise* belonged to Lora Mumford, whose arrival at Disneyland/Buena Vista Records began when the company decided to develop a rock band, given the name Halyx. "It was like *Star Wars* meets the *Banana Splits*," Bambi Moé said of the costumed band, which played at Disneyland Park and various Los Angeles venues. Moé recalled,

> They were fun. Lora's husband Tom was the keyboardist, and his keyboard was built into a golf cart he drove around on stage as the headlights flashed up into the audience. Roger Freeland, who was over six feet tall, wore a Wookie-like costume and wildly played bass. Tony Caputo, the percussionist, had a gymnastic rope so he could do somersaults and things. And Bruce Gowdy was the handsome leading man, sort of a space-age rock-and-roll guitarist to our Princess Leia type, who was Lora. The response of the Disneyland crowd was so phenomenal, it was causing the park a problem because they did not want people to get up and dance—it wasn't really allowed! Their sound was of the time, the sort of legitimate pop rock you would have heard on the radio, along the lines of Kim Carnes and Blondie.

Rather than recording their songs for the Buena Vista label, Halyx was signed by Electra Asylum Records. Before the first Halyx album could be released, however, Electra Asylum was absorbed into Warner Brothers Records, which reorganized and dropped some of their inherited talent, including Halyx.

Because Lora Mumford was already under contract, she was heard in many of the Disney records of the 1980s. The "Ducks Dance Too" cut on *Mousercise* was her Disneyland Records debut.

album. The word went out that Disney was looking for a theme song to go along with its new campaign promoting Goofy as a klutzy but enthusiastic sports star. Very specific instructions dictated just what would be covered in each verse of the song and how the whole thing would blend together, and one of the writers who tried her hand at it was Lois Blaisch, whose attempt at a new "Sport Goofy" theme, "Keep on Tryin'," ended up on *Mousercise*, with Blaisch performing.

Mousercise was a Platinum Award–winning best seller, inspiring tie-in merchandise. It was the first Disneyland record to be made into a daily children's series when the Disney Channel premiered in April 1983.

Left to right: Gary Krisel, Steven Spielberg, and Jymn Magon supervise young Drew Barrymore's narration for Disney's read-along adaptation of *E.T.: The Extra-Terrestrial* (Courtesy of Bambi Moé)

○

The Buena Vista Adventure seven-inch LP (or cassette) and book series, which began with the *Star Wars* releases, continued to gain momentum with the involvement of producer/director Steven Spielberg, who had already authorized the read-along version of *Raiders of the Lost Ark* (which costarred sales manager Eddy Medora's actress/wife Ann Marshall as Marion Ravenwood). He now took a personal interest in the Buena Vista version of his *E.T.: The Extra-Terrestrial*, narrated by Drew Barrymore, who was reprising her film role as Gertie. Jymn Magon recalled the recording session:

Drew, her mother, and I went over to the recording session, and Spielberg was there. He wanted to direct it! So he directed the whole thing, getting Drew to giggle and do all these extra things that he had added to the script. He laid out his leather jacket and tennis shoes down with his cap at the top, and it looked like E.T. lying there—he really was entertaining her. So I'm just sitting there, going "Wow! This is a lot of fun!" but I'm biting my nails because he's not follow-ing the script. This was a read-along, and the book was already in print! After he left, I got on the talk-back mike and said, "That was great! That was so much fun! You gave it so much energy! Now guess what? We're going to do the whole thing over again," and we re-recorded the whole thing. Sadly, I had to throw out everything that Steven had directed because it didn't match the book. . . . It was delightful of him to take the time to come out and do all that.

○

The success of *E.T.* and other read-alongs led to more lucrative associations in 1983 between Disneyland/Vista and major Hollywood heavy hitters, including Jim Henson (*The Dark Crystal*); Francis Ford Coppola (*The Black Stallion*), and the *Star Trek* movie producers. More *Star Wars* records followed: LP and read-along versions of *Return of the Jedi*, original read-along stories including *Planet of the Hoojibs* and *The Ewoks Join the Fight*, and even *Rebel Mission to Ord Mantell*, an original album-length drama written by National Public Radio's *Star Wars* radio series writer, Brian Daley.

Lora Mumford, seen here in a live Halyx perfomance, sang the Sport Goofy theme, "You Can Always Be Number One," appearing on the *Mickey Mouse Splashdance* LP in 1983. (Courtesy of Bambi Moé)

Back in the Disney character corral, the Disneyland/Vista brass were still looking for a Sport Goofy anthem. The next songwriter to make the attempt was Dale Gonyea, whose Victor Borge–style comedic music made him a popular concert artist as well as Disney Channel guest performer. "I was performing on a weeknight at the Ice House in Pasadena, a pretty well-known comedy/variety showcase that has been running for years," Gonyea recalled. "This particular night, there were so few people in the audience that we almost cancelled the show. I decided to go on anyway, and I'm glad I did because [Disney music publishing executive] Tom Bocci was in the audience." When Bocci asked if Gonyea would be interested in writing for Disney, "Of course I was *very* interested. We met that week at Tom's office in Burbank. I remember thinking it was really funny that Tom's secretary was named Winnie, another woman he worked closely with was named Bambi, and I learned that his wife was named Wendy. I thought I might have a better chance if I changed my name to Pinoc-

chio!" As Gonyea remembered the meeting, "At some point early in our discussions, [Bocci] mentioned that they were having a hard time coming up with the right song for the Sport Goofy theme. He asked me if I wanted to try coming up with a song, knowing that other songwriters were also submitting their songs for the same slot. I was happy to try. Not being an athletic kid, I felt that if anybody could write a Sport Goofy theme, it would be me. I always felt that when it comes to sports, our culture always overemphasizes the victory, whereas great rewards can be reaped simply by playing the game—hence, the song theme."

Gonyea's inspiring "You Can Always Be Number One," belted out by Lora Mumford at her most powerful, did indeed become the official Sport Goofy anthem, used in television specials and music videos for several years. It made its debut on vinyl on the 1983 Disneyland Records release *Mickey Mouse Splashdance*, an album with a unique history of its own.

○

While Michael Silversher was comanaging a music store in Palo Alto, California, he was also using Yamaha keyboards to create demos of songs he had written with his wife, Patty. The music so impressed the Yamaha representatives that they put him into their artist development program. "I went down to Yamaha with Michael," recalled Patty Silversher. "Someone said, 'I've never seen a composer evoke from a synthesizer such a real acoustical sound.' It turned out that he was the one who had designed it." "I started sending Disney some demos and Tom Bocci called to say my demos were sounding really interesting," Michael explained. "Gary Krisel was looking for songs for an album that was to be called *Mousetronics*."

Krisel gave Michael Silversher his first

crack at producing in tandem with Jymn Magon, so the couple moved to the Los Angeles area, where they wrote their first song for *Mousetronics*, "Gyro Gearloose," another salute to the days of Carl Barks's Disney comic books. Several Silversher songs were published but not recorded for the proposed album. One was called "I Don't Like This Push-Button World," to be sung by Grumpy. Another song, "Welcome to the World of Mousetronics," was years later rewritten as a theme park anthem for Mickey Mouse's sixtieth birthday and released on CD in Japan. After lots of work and waiting, Krisel approved a number of Silversher songs, including "One Little Android," "Digital Duck," "Hoedown at the Robot Farm," and "Chip 'n' Dale's Vacation." However, the Disneyland brass now felt that the idea of *Mousetronics* wasn't working out.

The success of the movie and music from *Flashdance* sent Disney officials down a different path. "They were thinking of changing the concept to *Splashdance*," said Michael. "We were concerned because none of these songs had anything to do with splashing. They told us we had to write some more." The songwriters came back with the title song for the newly christened *Splashdance* album. The album cover art literally came from Krisel's office wall, a painting of Mickey Mouse surfing.

With a few exceptions, all of *Splashdance* was written by the Silvershers and played by Michael on an innovative new Yamaha keyboard. "We produced it at Yamaha studios in Glendale," Magon recalled. "It wasn't really a studio; it was where they were developing new keyboards. They had come up with a breakthrough keyboard called the DX-7. At the time, it was state-of-the-art because you could put cartridges in it and prerecord things. Six cartridges could play in it simultaneously, and it had all these great sounds and everything. We got a great deal because they wanted somebody to use the DX-7. The music was almost all Michael."

Rounding out the album was "Minnie Mouse," a techno tune adapted for the album by Ronald and Russell Mael of the group Sparks. It was another new sound for Disneyland Records. For a more traditional style, "Mickey, She's Got a Crush on You" was performed by Gail Lopata. Jymn Magon helped write "Mousekemania," a musical tribute to the world of Disney character merchandise collecting. Ironically, out of the dozens of toys and products mentioned in the fast-paced lyrics, phonograph records were not among them! *Splashdance* also included a song that became a Disney theme park favorite. Gary Krisel was looking for something very special and guided the Silvershers through the creation of "Happy, Happy Birthday to You." Though the version on the LP is generic, special lyrics were written so the song could be used in Donald Duck's fiftieth birthday parades in California and Florida. The Silvershers watched in awe as the crowd reacted to their song at Disneyland.

"That was a great thrill, that whole thing," said Michael. "The 1984 Olympics were in Los Angeles, and the athletes were in the parade. We walked in and heard the usual 'Happy Birthday' and then the parade started with our song. Man, it was exciting because everybody in the world was sitting there, and they were really enjoying it. We could hear people singing the song afterwards. We were walking down Main Street to the ice cream store and there's a mother and her child and they were singing it to each other. Now that was a big thrill, something I will never forget."

13

It's a Gold Record, Charlie Brown!

The Charlie Brown brand of Buena Vista Records was going strong in the early 1980s. Five TV specials were adapted into story LPs, while ten specials and one feature film (*Snoopy, Come Home*) were adapted into seven-inch book and record sets. The only TV special that tied into a song album was 1984's *Flashbeagle*.

On November 29, 1983, in the midst of the same *Flashdance* fashion and music craze that had spawned Disney's *Splashdance*, Charles M. Schulz published a *Peanuts* strip in which Snoopy danced around in a torn tee shirt and headband. In the final panel, Snoopy remarks, "Flashbeagle!" Around the same time, *Peanuts* film and TV producer Lee Mendelson was looking for a new idea for a special and was also coproducing the Charlie Brown Records with Disneyland/Vista. "Somehow that all evolved into the *Flashbeagle* project," recalled lead vocalist/cocomposer Desirée Goyette. "We had a show in the works; there was a rough script that Schulz was creating. Because there was so much music involved, Lee approached Disney to do the album."

An arrangement was approved by which Disney would own 50 percent of the music publishing but Mendelson and company could use the songs for free on the TV show, *It's Flashbeagle, Charlie Brown*. The half-hour special would showcase only a handful of songs, so Goyette and composer Ed Bogas were encouraged to create additional material to fill out the LP. "Gary Krisel, Jymn Magon and Bambi Moé spurred us on to do more songs," Goyette recalled. "They kept holding *Mickey Mouse Splashdance* up as a model for what they wanted. It was the most team-oriented recording I've ever worked on. We would have meetings and discuss things as a committee then we would go off and write. Gary wanted every song to sound like an ABBA hit. We laughed because it seemed like funny juxtaposition, but it all worked out. Ed was an equal partner on all the writing, and Lee had a lot of creative ideas he would throw out to us."

Goyette sang the title song with Joey Scarbury, a Hollywood vocalist whose biggest hit had been the "Believe It or Not" theme from the TV series *The Greatest American Hero* and who was heard on a number of other Disney LPs of the period, frequently in tandem with Lora Mumford. "Vocally, my favorite song is the *Flashbeagle* theme because I really had to stretch myself," said Goyette. "I never really sang that hard core. I have a sweet voice, so I had to get nastier. It was a real challenge! I didn't know I could do that with my voice." The titular beagle has a solo called "Snoopy's Big Debut." Recalled Goyette, "I wrote that when I was doing a one-woman show in 1980. It used to say,

Singer/composer Desirée Goyette performs the *Flashbeagle* theme song during a personal appearance. (Courtesy of Bambi Moé)

'This is my big debut.' Lee really liked it and said 'Let's adapt it for Snoopy,' so I changed the words."

When the TV special was about to air on CBS, some publicity arose surrounding the fact that Marine Jehan, who had performed the dances for Jennifer Beals in the *Flashdance* film, would do the same for Snoopy. Jehan's movements were rotoscoped, a process that allows animators to adapt live-action footage to animation. Not publicized were the other *Peanuts* characters who were rotoscoped dancing by none other than Jymn Magon and Bambi Moé, along with Goyette and horn arranger Bill Meyers. "I'm actually in the show," said Magon. "They needed

dancers. They brought in Marine Jehan, and we watched her perform for Snoopy. Then they had this 'Pigpen Hoedown' number and we danced. I was Schroeder, if I'm not mistaken."

The project came full circle when Charles M. Schulz's original "Flashbeagle" comic strip was reprinted on the back cover of the record album.

O

Children's records based on cuter-than-cute licensed characters were all over the store shelves in the 1980s, from Smurfs and Pound Puppies to Pac Man and Care Bears. This was an era of "first-come, first-served" among licensees, long before media conglomerates began to control the soup-to-nuts handling of characters on their own recordings, films, and books.

Rainbow Brite was Hallmark Cards' answer to American Greetings' immensely popular Strawberry Shortcake character, targeted to little girls. Rainbow and her colorful group of friends were already a line of toys and the stars of their own animated TV series, produced by DIC Entertainment, when Disneyland/Vista acquired the recording rights to Rainbow Brite and set about to produce albums and read-alongs. But while Strawberry Shortcake received ultra-low-budget treatment on her licensed records, Rainbow Brite's vinyl adventures turned out to be something special. Part of the reason was that the Disneyland team didn't skimp on quality. "You might get away with something cheap a few times," said Eddy Medora, "but to get repeat business, you really need to keep the standards high."

"When we write a song, we get very emotional, especially with ballads," said Patty Silversher, who wrote several songs for the new endeavor with her husband, Michael. "We got just as emotional with Rainbow

Desirée Goyette:
Heavenly Voices

Bambi Moé (left) and Desirée Goyette (right) became close friends as well as Disney Records collaborators. (Courtesy of Bambi Moé)

Desirée Goyette could sing before she could speak. She actively pursued music as a child and planned to become a concert pianist. Early on, she was advised to write music as well as sing. It came naturally, as did performing. She began making a living teaching piano, singing, modeling, and doing voice-overs.

She thought she had arrived when she became a performer at Marriott's Great America theme park. "It was fabulous to me. Six shows a day, six days a week for $150 a week—I thought I was living high! It really taught me, hands on, the everyday experience of theater. By the late 1970s, I had an agent in San Francisco." When Great America made her the goodwill ambassador for the park, Goyette became comfortable with appearing on TV and radio on the road. She got back into live performing with a one-woman show at the San Jose Center for the Performing Arts before she landed a role on a TV series, *The New You Asked for It*. Hosted by impressionist Rich Little, the series premiered in 1980. Goyette explained, "I was one of the cohosts. Viewers would write and tell us what they wanted to see, and the show would fly me all over the world to do feature stories. In two and a half years, I did over one hundred episodes. It was a tremendous experience."

The executive producer of *The New You Asked for It* was Lee Mendelson, who had already made television history by producing all the *Peanuts* specials. He remembered Goyette's musical skills from his first interview with her and asked her to write music for *No Man's Valley*, an animated NBC special about endangered animals. She was subsequently paired with musician/composer Ed Bogas on the special *Here Comes Garfield*, for which she received her first Grammy nomination. More *Garfield* and *Peanuts* specials followed, along with voice work, including the lead voice in *The Romance of Betty Boop* (and she even played Betty on camera for the Macy's Thanksgiving Parade). After working together for seven years, she and Mendelson married, although they divorced eleven years later.

The *Flashbeagle* special and album represented her first collaboration with Disneyland/Vista Records. With Bogas, she wrote all the songs for the special and additional songs for the LP. One of the extra songs was "Someday, Charlie Brown," a memorable ballad she later sang at Carnegie Hall in a tribute to Charles Schulz and his landmark comic strip.

A friendship with Bambi Moé grew out of the *Peanuts* sessions, and Goyette was asked back to the Disney label to do vocals for the *Totally Minnie* album. Later, when Moé became a Disney music supervisor, she brought Goyette in to sing "Down to the Sea" in *The Little Mermaid II: Return to the Sea*.

Goyette's life took a different turn in the mid-1990s, when she lost both her mother and brother to cancer. She immersed herself in inspirational music and founded Lightchild Publishing, which publishes and provides recordings of such uplifting songs as "From Where He Stands." "I've sung in church from age fourteen," she said. "Members of the congregation have asked when I was going to write out all the songs that I sing for them so others can perform them. That's why I started Lightchild." Today, Goyette continues doing voices for animation and toys, vocals for films, composing, and several benefit concerts a year. She is also happily married to Ed Bogas and the mother of twins. The couple serves as musical directors at Unity Church in Marin County, California.

Goyette still gets feedback from fans about her work, including *Flashbeagle*: "I get e-mails from people looking for the album, and they often mention 'Someday, Charlie Brown.' It's very gratifying. I've always loved doing music for children."

Brite as any other project." After setting out to find a singing voice for Rainbow, producers at Disney and DIC thought to ask Bettina Bush, the voice of the animated character. "They didn't know I sang," said Bush. "They had been auditioning other girls to sing. I was in a recording session for the cartoon and was singing to myself, and they said, 'Do you sing?' I started rattling off my credits. I was about six or seven at the time. They started laughing, and I think they asked me to sing 'Happy Birthday.' I said, 'Do you want to hear some of the songs I *really* sing?' And I did 'Don't Cry for Me, Argentina.' It was really funny. Of course, I thought, why would you think of using somebody else?"

With Bush singing and speaking for Rainbow, Michael Silversher as Twink, Will Ryan as Lurky, and a children's chorus directed by Betty Joyce, the first album, *Paint a Rainbow in Your Heart*, was recorded in a Los Angeles studio. The result was a richly orchestrated, highly inspired production that is a fine listening experience even for those who couldn't care less about Rainbow Brite. One of the reasons it turned out a cut above other such albums was that the coproducer, Jim Andron, made his Disney debut with this album and definitely wanted to impress the mouse. "I was trying to get a foothold with Disney," said Andron, "so we took extra time and care." The LP went gold, and a Christmas album and five read-along book and record sets followed.

Andron clearly scored points with Disneyland/Vista. He was asked to create all-purpose background music for read-alongs, augmenting the music that Pat Patrick, Gary Powell, and others had created. Sometimes the music would be scored more or less to a story, and then the music would be put into a library for further use. Andron added, "Later on I created some music without a specific project when I was working with Ted Kryczko. He would need this kind of emotion or that, and I would write it."

○

Ted Kryczko was an accomplished theatrical actor/director who had earned his way into working for Magon in product development with his work on a new 20,000 *Leagues under the Sea* read-along recording, which had been left undone by the previous person in the position. "They couldn't decide who to hire and they were down to a couple of candidates," Kryczko recalled. "I asked them to let me try and do a project in which they felt I couldn't do harm, so I could demonstrate that I can do the job for them. They gave me the basic materials for 20,000 *Leagues* and told me to meet this guy at Prism Recording Studio. I went in for two or three days and put it together. They hired me before I completed it. The first thing I actually did on staff was an album-length *Peter Pan* story cassette."

Also in the early 1980s, when Gary Krisel received greater responsibility and could no longer oversee the record company in his usual hands-on style, he hired Shelley Miles to run the Disneyland/Vista operation, one of several people to hold that position over the next few years.

○

In 1984, Frank Wells and Michael Eisner took the helm of Walt Disney Productions, eventually renaming it the Walt Disney Company and making changes throughout the organization. One of Eisner's wishes was to make the company more of a player in cartoons for Saturday morning and daytime TV, his previous realms of expertise. Gary Krisel became head of the new Walt Disney television animation division, and Steve DeWynt became the new chief of Disneyland/Vista Records.

With thirty-five gold records and other

accomplishments under his belt, Jymn Magon had already been itching to find new challenges. "It was as high up in the record company as I could go creatively," Magon recalled. "I had done so many albums, and how many read-alongs can you do? It was the ceiling for me. The only way to move up in the record company was in the business end, and I was not a business major. I didn't make deals. So I found myself in Eisner's living room at a meeting when they were looking for people to do TV shows." Magon's old friends were sorry to see him leave. "Jymn was my hero," said Bambi Moé. "Whether he knew it or not, I studied him. I feel everything I learned creatively and on the producing side, I owe to Jymn. The principles I learned have stayed with me through my whole career."

○

Magon may have been a tough act to follow, but writer/producer Ron Kidd was up to the task. "I had spent much of my early career producing hundreds of filmstrips for schools that involved still pictures and audio soundtracks," said Kidd. "In the late 1970s, I got my first freelance assignment with Walt Disney Educational Media. I made over a hundred filmstrip and audio sets over five or six years." This connection led to his position as the new director of product development.

When Tom Bocci also departed, the search was on for someone to assume his duties in music publishing. Moé recalled the day Chris Montan arrived for an interview. "Nobody knew who he was. I told them he was a singer/songwriter. I said, 'He wrote a song for Laura Brannigan! This is great!'"

Lois Blaisch composed and performed the charming "Rainbow Land" song for the *Rainbow Brite: Paint a Rainbow in Your Heart* album. (Courtesy of Lois Blaisch)

Left to right: Producers Ron Kidd and Bambi Moé with composer Jim Andron during a recording session. (Courtesy of Bambi Moé)

And then there was Randy Thornton. "As far as hiring Randy, if I'd only done one thing in the whole time that I was there, that would have earned my money," Kidd said. "He was this Disney fan who was extremely bright and a little eccentric. I thought, 'There's something about this guy. I think he's gonna be great,' and sure enough he was." Thornton was originally brought aboard to support the staff, but his passion for the Disney legacy inspired him to take every project beyond expectations. "One of his responsibilities was the vault—keeping track of our tapes and things," Kidd recalled. "So many masters had been neglected for a long time, and he took it upon himself to see what was there, catalog it, reorganize it, and in the process discovered a bunch of things that we didn't even know we had." It wasn't long before Thornton was working on read-alongs and restoring soundtracks. "I had just begun to scratch the surface with soundtracks," said Kidd. "He worked with me on those and dug up a lot of the original material. He took it to a whole new level."

O

The Walt Disney Company began making inroads into television animation with the premieres of two series, which were also adapted into several read-alongs. *Wuzzles* cartoons and records benefited from having renowned humorist Stan Freberg as narrator. Since Jymn Magon was the story editor on *Adventures of the Gummi Bears*, he adapted those scripts for the records.

However, the company had been floundering in the theatrical movie department for some time. The two major releases of 1985, *Return to Oz* and *The Black Cauldron*, opened to lackluster receptions. Although both were made into read-alongs and a story LP of *Black Cauldron* was released, neither musical score was released on Disney records. Instead, Sonic Atmospheres released David Shire's *Oz* soundtrack and Varese Sarabande produced Elmer Bernstein's *Cauldron* score.

O

Ron Kidd's duties were primarily organization and operation. "I would oversee and help plan. We would do thirty book-and-tape projects a year and five to ten music albums. Being a writer, I would pitch in and write some things and do a little bit of the production, but the first album where I was listed as co-producer was *Children's Favorites*, volume 3." Kidd's involvement in this volume resulted in a richer, fuller sound than the earlier two. "I had been a musician all my life, so I asked for more full arrangements and full song treatments. When we brought the master back, Shelley was concerned that it was not 'kiddie' enough. Pat Patrick and I had thought all along that kids would still love it but that the parents would also enjoy listening to it."

Betty Joyce again handled the children's choral work, but she was unavailable for *Children's Favorites*, volume 4 and the *Rainbow Brite Christmas* album. The new choral director was Dawn Halloran, daughter of 1960s Disneyland vocal veteran Jack Halloran. She sang a bit on *Children's Favorites 4* as well.

O

The mid-1980s saw the rise of MTV and the pop stars it helped launch, particularly the edge-pushing Madonna. The Walt Disney Company responded to the trend by marketing Minnie Mouse in a hip, stylish way, and the result was a line of products under the umbrella "Totally Minnie." For the tie-in *Totally Minnie* record album, Montan and Moé called on both old friends and artists new to the label. Desirée Goyette, Lora Mumford, and even Ted Kryczko's wife, Debbie

Patty and Michael Silversher:
Two to Make Music

The songwriters behind more than two decades of memorable Disney songs met in a Palo Alto, California, theater company. They first collaborated and won first place in an international song contest and later created the South Bay Songwriters' Association, now called West Coast Songwriters, with a current membership of more than twelve hundred. "One of the women who volunteered in our organization had a brother who worked in Disney Music Publishing," recalled Michael Silversher. "He had asked her if she knew anybody who wrote songs. They were doing an album called *Mickey Mouse Rock*. Patty and I wrote a bunch of songs and wiped out our savings making demos of five songs. One was a 'Surfer Goofy' song; another was a Bob Dylan–style song for Donald Duck. But the album never happened, and they rejected the songs."

Patty and Michael met Bambi Moé at a BMI workshop, and she introduced them to Tom Bocci. He asked them to call if they were planning a Los Angeles trip. They did and scored their first success with the song "Pig Out" on the 1981 *Mousercise* album. The Silvershers then moved to Los Angeles to start submitting songs for a new album called *Techno Mickey*. Subsequently renamed *Mousetronics* and finally *Mickey Mouse Splashdance*, the LP represented Michael's first producing credit.

"The Disney people would say, 'We need a song called this,' or "We're looking for a song about that,'" said Michael. "We were always involved with these songwriter 'cattle calls,' always up against the usual suspects. It was amazing how many of our songs they picked. We have over one hundred songs that Disney either recorded or published." They wrote for *Totally Minnie*, *Rock around the Mouse*, the *Rainbow Brite* LPs, and for read-alongs including the Mercer Mayer *Little Critter* book-and-record series.

One of their favorite songs came about when they were first writing for Disney. "Some kids were doing a scavenger hunt in our neighborhood," Michael recalled. "Patty asked them, 'What would you wish for?' One of the kids said, 'I wish I was magic.' We thought that was the neatest thing we'd ever heard." When the team presented "I Wish I Was Magic" to Bocci, he loved it but said, "This song throws me for a loop because it doesn't fit with what we're doing right now. Let me think about it." The song sat unused for eight years until Ron Kidd found it in a drawer and made it the theme for the *Favorite Fairy Tales* cassette-and-book series narrated by cartoon veteran Marvin Kaplan.

In association with old friend Jymn Magon, the duo also wrote the TV themes to *Gummi Bears* and *TaleSpin* plus incidental songs that appeared on the shows. A collection of these themes and songs were collected on a CD called *The Disney Afternoon*, named for the daily Disney TV lineup. They went on to write songs for direct-to-video features, including *The*

Gates (as the voice of Minnie), were welcomed into the studios. Making their Disney vinyl debuts were Karla Bonoff and Brenda Russell. Jai Winding, who served as producer/keyboardist, had been Madonna's producer as well. Original songs, including some by the Silvershers, made up the bulk of the LP. A Sherman favorite, "Let's Get Together" from *The Parent Trap*, was included as a duet between Lora Mumford and Gail Lopata. The album even included a parody of Toni Basil's hit, "Mickey," sung in fervent cheerleader style by the ever-enthusiastic Goyette.

Clarence Nash had died in 1985, and Sam Kwasman assumed the role of Donald Duck. Like "Disco Mickey Mouse" composer Tom Worrall, Kwasman had spent many years with the *Disney on Parade* arena shows, doing the voice of Donald live when needed. For *Totally Minnie*, Kwasman had his biggest moments in the song "Dear Daisy," featuring Bonoff dispensing cryptic and frequently useless advice to the lovelorn. The Disney studio put lots of promotion behind the new franchise, even producing a TV special featuring Elton John and the "new" Minnie.

The big screen animated feature for 1986 was *The Great Mouse Detective*. It was somewhat of a success—certainly more so than *The Black Cauldron*—but Disney curiously put very little merchandising behind it. The record company chose to release a read-along but no soundtrack album, even though the music boasted Henry Mancini and Melissa Manchester. Years later, a CD of the score was released by Varese Sarabande.

Buena Vista Records did, however, create a soundtrack album and read-along cassette for *The Chipmunk Adventure*, a theatrical feature starring what had been Jimmy Johnson's competition decades earlier. Next up was *Solid Gold Chipmunks*, a thirtieth-anniversary collection of songs by Alvin, Simon, Theodore, and David Seville that had all been previously released on rival labels. The reemergence of the Chipmunks on the Disneyland/Vista labels represented yet another

Bambi Moé and writer Pat DeRemer, who wrote and performed many of the songs for 1986's *Totally Minnie* LP. (Courtesy of Bambi Moé)

Composer Ellie Baer performed as Daisy Duck on 1987's *Rock around the Mouse*. (Courtesy of Ellie Baer)

Sam Kwasman was heard as Donald Duck in *Disney on Parade* arena shows of the early 1970s. He quacked again for *Totally Minnie* in 1986. (Courtesy of Sam Kwasman)

irony for Johnson and Camarata's forgotten Ludwig Mousensky and the All-Mouse Orchestra.

O

Mousensky notwithstanding, Disney's prime characters were still a priority, and the Disneyland/Vista team, including visionary producer Shepard Stern, set about to find new ways to feature them. "*Totally Minnie* alienated some parents because of the Madonna thing," said Michael Silversher. "Shep said, 'Why don't we go back to the 1950s? Kids love fifties music.'" The result was 1987's *Rock around the Mouse*.

Stern, who had written and produced music for TV, theater, and advertising in New York for many years, was anxious to bring established artists to the Disneyland label.

"A lot of these fifties diners were starting up at the time," said Stern. "And Disney, no matter how hard they tried, were very fifties." "Shep had no fear about calling famous people," said Kidd. "In fact, he loved it. He would call Paul McCartney or somebody and say, 'I'm from Disney, and I'd like you to do this project.' He was really good at making connections with these high-profile people." One of these notables was rock-and-roll giant Little Richard, who agreed to sing the Silvershers' "Gawrsh Golly Goofy."

One of the Silvershers' favorites is the Elvis-style "Pinocchio's Boogie," sung by Rick Schulman. When it was being recorded in Nashville, Stern wondered if Elvis's backup singers might be interested in doing the album. "I thought, we're in Nashville," recalled Stern. "Aren't the Jordanaires around? Pat Patrick said 'Let's call them,' and they did it."

Not all the singers on the album were household names. "Paige Morehead was a receptionist who was a good singer," said Pat Patrick. "We were deciding what key the female vocal should be. I asked her to sing in this key, and she was so good I said, 'We've got a singer right here; we don't need to call anyone in.'" Morehead sang on "Mickey Motion" and "Here's to the Ears of Love." Patrick wrote "Love Struck Duck" and ended up singing it on the album. "He had done it on the demo and Shep kept saying it had this naive, sincere quality," said Kidd. "Pat wasn't sure if he wanted to do it for a couple of days, but finally he agreed to do it." Patrick later recalled playing in a show in Atlanta: "A guy asked me, 'What's your biggest hit?' I said 'Love Struck Duck'! I loved it. It was great fun."

"Shep would get a wild idea about an approach," Kidd recalled. "The unusual opening of 'Mickey and Minnie on a Moonlit Night' was his idea. A guy in Chicago had sent him this audition cassette with some very good singers. It sounded like a group of kids on a playground, doing an a cappella version of the song. So he had this cassette with him when we got to Nashville and he suggested putting this on the beginning of the actual song, then segueing into this beautiful studio recording. To me, that is really a great moment." Also remarkable about this song is the fact that only two singers, overdubbed many times over, create its smooth, lush chorus.

Ellie Baer had composed several songs for the LP and was cast as the voice of Daisy Duck singing "Quackety Quack" and "Everything Is Ducky with Donald." The new official voice of Donald, animator Tony

Anselmo, assumed the squawk of the foul-tempered fowl.

The resulting album was a source of pride for all involved. "We tried hard," said Stern. "It was a labor of love. The bar was raised after that, and it led to other projects."

O

One of those projects was *Silly Songs*, the last vinyl album starring Mickey and the gang and the last on the Disneyland label. Though it lacked the star power of *Rock around the Mouse*, it was a solid success that still exists in various forms today. One amusing note about the album is that it had solos by engineer George Charouhas, who sang for Clarabelle Cow. "You can hear me sing 'What's Your Name?'" he said. "Fortunately, I don't get credit, but the kids love it when I sing that way. I'm channeling Julia Child."

By the time Walt Disney Pictures released the animated feature *Oliver and Company* (1988), the advent of the compact disc was bringing the era of the vinyl record to a close. The pop soundtrack for this film, featuring Billy Joel, Bette Midler, Ruth Pointer, and Huey Lewis, was the only vinyl album issued on the new Walt Disney Records label. The same year, the groundbreaking live-action/animated film *Who Framed Roger Rabbit?* inspired a cassette read-along and a story album for Buena Vista Records plus a soundtrack album on the Touchstone label. There would no longer be such a label as Disneyland Records.

The second golden age of Disney vinyl records was gone but not forgotten. "Those of us who were there knew that we were part of something really special, unique and wonderful," said Bambi Moé. "I look back and think to myself, regardless of where I might go and what I might do, I was part of this really incredible legacy."

14

You Can Always Be Number One

In the years that followed the passing of vinyl records, and as Disneyland Records became Walt Disney Records, the company explored the compact disc format gradually. These products evolved just as records had done.

The first CD in the catalog was *Snow White and the Seven Dwarfs*, a reissue of the 1980 Storyteller narrated by Hal Smith, with bonus features including the deleted soundtrack song, "Music in Your Soup" and interviews with Walt Disney and Ward Kimball. A full-color book was bound into the long, narrow package. Though well received, there were some rumblings among fans that a music soundtrack of *Snow White* was more appropriate, making use of the clearer digital capabilities of CDs. (In an odd move, RCA Victor issued soundtrack CD's of *Snow White* and *Pinocchio* from their early 78-rpm masters, with less than crystalline results.)

It made sense that Irwin Kostal's 1982 performance of *Fantasia* was the first complete Disney music soundtrack on CD since the music had been digitally recorded for the film. Next came *The Disney Collection*, two volumes of greatest hits material that were among Randy Thornton's first archival assignments. "Ron [Kidd] and Ted [Kryczko] had me sit down and listen to all the music and take notes about flaws, artifacts, and things like that," said Thornton. "I came back with a huge stack of notes, and Ron said,

'We're going to have to watch you, aren't we?'"

O

Like many other studios, in the late 1980s Disney marketed its characters as infants, in this case, the Disney Babies. A series of albums was produced to tie in, the most remarkable of which was *Disney Babies Lullaby*. "They wanted to simply reissue existing lullaby songs from earlier records," Shepard Stern recalled. "I said we should re-record it. Nothing really had been done like this yet and it was exciting to do."

What made the album unique was that it was recorded as if it were live, without editing and sweetening to artificially enhance the sound and cover up any imperfections. "The album is a live direct digital in a complete take," Stern added. "You can even hear the sound of the harpist's feet on the pedals. It was a magical project; the next album, *Wake Up*, was also a lot of fun."

"I've always loved that album," Ron Kidd said of *Lullaby*. "It had a wonderful performance kind of quality. And Bob Sherman told me that Karen Taylor's version of 'Stay Awake' was his favorite other than the one in the movie [*Mary Poppins*]." Other songs were performed by *Rock around the Mouse* and *Silly Songs* alumni Rick ("Yo, Mickey Mouse!") Schulman and the always-youthful Paige Morehead.

○

The first story album recorded for compact disc was *Bambi*, narrated by Tony-winning stage and screen actor Richard Kiley, who also narrated the animated sequence in *Jurassic Park* (1993). "I always loved the *Bambi* Storyteller," said Kryczko, who produced the CD. "Richard Kiley was probably the greatest narrator I ever worked with, bar none. He did most of it in one take. I did not have access to the separated sound elements of the film [dialogue, music, effects], so everything had to be written to fit into preexisting holes, and he had to read the script to fit. I'd say, 'Richard, we've got 4.6 seconds,' and he'd read it in 4.55! He was amazing." Continued Kryczko, "We found an interview with Walt in the archives and recorded a new interview with Henry Mancini and added them as bonus features, much as we do on DVDs today. We also interviewed [master animators] Ollie Johnston and Frank Thomas at Ollie's house. It was special to be working on something from that early history of Disney. You feel as if you're touching one of the golden films, something you saw as a kid. I feel very passionate about that particular work." (The interview portions of this disc were reissued on the 2005 *Bambi* soundtrack CD, released in tandem with the film's premiere on DVD.)

○

Ron Kidd and Randy Thornton are especially pleased to have been involved with the first digitally remastered CD reissue of *Mary Poppins*. To assure the highest-quality sound, they returned to the original film tracks rather than simply redoing the vinyl album. "That may have been my favorite project at Disney," said Kidd. "We worked with Bruce Botnick and Sean Murphy doing the engineering, with Irwin Kostal and the Shermans in the studio with us. Ted and I went to the Sherman house in Beverly Hills and recorded

an interview in which they told us about how Walt used to ask them to come to his office and play 'Feed the Birds' for him on Friday afternoons. It was a privilege to work with them."

"My high school band director was a major influence on me, and *Mary Poppins* was one of his favorites," said Thornton. "I figured if I could get the soundtrack done on CD, I could give it to him as sort of a thank you. But I was a clerk back then so I had no aspirations that I could actually produce it. Ron came to the vault one day and said that in order to do *Mary Poppins*, we needed something really impressive to pull it over with our administration. I said, "Do they know that this is here?' It was the Shermans' original *Poppins* demo tape from 1962. Ron's jaw dropped. Even the Shermans thought the tape was lost. When it was played for the bosses, they approved the project."

○

Thornton's first read-along project was based on *ALF*, an NBC sitcom about a furry alien who lived with a suburban family. After Kidd asked Thornton to write an outline for a book and cassette, he came up with three: one based on the series pilot and two original stories.

Disney recordings based on outside licensees were dwindling by the late 1980s as the studio began to generate more of its own properties. One of the few remaining licensed characters to make his way to Buena Vista Records was the stop-motion animated character Gumby. While the Gumby read-alongs were aimed at children, company executives decided that the character's appeal to baby boomers warranted a more unusual approach. The result was *Gumby: The Green Album*, an eclectic mix of songs inspired by the animated icon featuring a myriad of performers including Dweezil Zappa, Brave Combo, Flo and Eddie, and Frank Sinatra Jr. Produced by Shepard Stern, the alternative nature of the Gumby album earned it notice as one of the best albums of the year by *Rolling Stone* magazine.

○

When *The Little Mermaid* made a big splash in theaters, it easily had the greatest impact on the record company up to that time. *Mermaid* combined Disney storytelling at its best with a fully integrated, Broadway-style score by Howard Ashman and Alan Menken, who were best known at the time for the musical version of *Little Shop of Horrors*.

To the studio's surprise, the film became as much a hit with adults as it was with children. The same thing was happening with its songs, which became the most widely marketed since those of *Mary Poppins*. One of the film's supporting characters, a Caribbean crab named Sebastian, was featured on his own albums, tied in with concerts and TV specials featuring the multitalented Samuel E. Wright, who provided the voice.

○

While *The Little Mermaid* CD was swimming off store shelves, plans had also been mounted to create CD versions of classic soundtracks starting with *The Jungle Book*. Before this project was finished, the record division was split into two halves: Walt Disney Records under Mark Jaffe, and Disney Audio Entertainment under Judith Cross. Disney Audio Entertainment handled book and cassette read-alongs, while Walt Disney Records continued with original albums and soundtracks, including a remastered issue of *Pinocchio*. The two halves eventually reunited, enabling Thornton to produce the music soundtrack for *Snow White*, a six-month task utilizing seven different sound sources and more than a thousand edits.

○

In the early 1990s, children's concert entertainers such as Raffi and Sharon, Lois, and Bram were enjoying success in live performances, on videos, and on CDs. Walt Disney Records began to release albums by such children's favorites as Norman Foote, Parachute Express, and Craig 'n Company. Craig's success with the label led to his performance at the grand opening of Mickey's Toontown at Disneyland.

In the wake of such multiartist events as "We Are the World" and Live Aid, Stern had begun to look for an opportunity to gather even more celebrated performers to the label for a good cause. That project came along when Elisabeth Glaser, who had lost her daughter, Ariel, to AIDS, started a nonprofit organization dedicated to the special needs of children with the disease.

"She came to Disney hoping that they could do something," said Stern, who had to work under a very limited budget. "One of her friends had a connection with Bob Dylan, who had recorded 'This Old Man' in his bedroom with his son, Jacob. Once we had this recording, it was easier to enlist other great artists. Donations of tracks started pouring in from all over the world." With its front cover adorned with artwork by Ariel Glaser, *For Our Children* featured Carole King, Paul McCartney, Elton John, Bruce Springsteen, Barbra Streisand, Meryl Streep, and Brian Wilson, among other celebrated performers. It raised millions for the Pediatric AIDS Foundation and inspired a follow-up CD and live concert. "It was hailed as one of the greatest children's records of all time," Stern said. "People hold it up in comparison to later, similar projects. That was the crowning achievement of my career."

○

The first recording produced for compact disc to star the full cast of Disney's main stable of characters, *The Twelve Days of Christmas*, is also one of the finest. Produced by Robin Frederick, it's an eclectic mix of holiday favorites and original songs that marked the CD debut of official voices Wayne Allwine as Mickey Mouse, Russi Taylor as Minnie and Donald's nephews, Tony Anselmo as Donald Duck, Bill Farmer as Goofy, and Alan Young as Scrooge McDuck. The performers remember the recording as a particularly fun project, and it also brought back one of the Silvershers' best songs, "A Gift of Love," originally written for *Rainbow Brite Christmas*.

The biggest Disney event of 1991 was the premiere of *Beauty and the Beast*, the only animated feature nominated for a Best Picture Academy Award. Ashman and Menken even more masterfully blended Broadway sensibilities into a Disney fairy tale to create a work of greater depth and scope than *The Little Mermaid*. And unlike *Mermaid*, this film featured a pop version of its title song over the end credits that gave record producers a hit single to market. This version, by Peabo Bryson and Celine Deon, was a chart-topping hit (though the single version was not released on the Disney label). The following year, *Aladdin* also struck gold at the box office and on the pop charts as Alan Menken and Tim Rice's "A Whole New World" received the same treatment, this time sung by Bryson and Regina Belle.

In 1993, Walt Disney Records returned to its first chart-maker, Annette Funicello, with a two-disc boxed set called *Annette: A Musical Reunion with America's Girl Next Door*. Disney historian Stacia Martin helped select the songs that best encompassed Annette's singing career and teamed with Bruce Botnick to make the songs sound better than they had when they were first released. Tutti Cama-

rata and the Sherman brothers were also on hand for the reengineering process.

"We had a meeting with Annette at her house," recalled Thornton. "We played some stuff for her, and she was just absolutely lovely, everything that you would imagine Annette Funicello would be. She was just tickled that someone was paying attention to her singing career. We made a tape for her. She was still going down to the [Disneyland] park every weekend. She said later she would listen to this tape on those trips and all these memories would come flooding back. They wanted a tribute for the end of the set, so I took Jimmie Dodd's 'Annette' song and reedited it to have a instrumental bridge between each verse, with her friends each saying something to her—Frankie Avalon, Tommy Sands, Shelley Fabares, and Paul Anka."

Read-along book and cassette sets remained a mainstay of Walt Disney Records in the 1990s, but a number of advances had occurred under the supervision of Kryczko, Thornton, and engineer Jeff Sheridan. "We would cut the music specifically for the action (as opposed to having a music bed playing in the background) and added more sound effects," said Thornton. "We treated our work as if it were postproduction on a film. One of the things that helped us do that was digital technology."

In addition to books, several read-alongs were expanded and packaged with pop-up books and play sets. Some of read-alongs based on classic stories, including *Snow White* and *Pinocchio*, were completely reorchestrated. The new music was created in Austin, Texas, by songwriter/producer Gary Powell, who has worked on more than eighty Disney recordings to date, including the Karaoke series. "It was a major challenge," said Powell. "It's not really orchestrating; it's really a restoration process." Locating what limited original music existed in the Disney vaults, Powell pieced together the scores for full orchestra, individual musicians, and vocals, sometimes transcribing by ear. Powell also provided new scores for read-along film sequels such as *Ariel and the Mysterious World Above* (based on *The Little Mermaid*) and *Iago Returns* (based on *Aladdin*), modeling them on the style of the original composers. Said Powell, "I generally get a feel for what the team did in terms of instrumentation and orchestral voicing. It's mostly about keeping the texture and feel the same."

○

In 1994, *The Lion King* became Disney's highest-grossing animated feature. Its soundtrack album, with songs by Elton John and Tim Rice, was the first soundtrack from an animated film to hit Number 1 on the *Billboard* charts. The Record Industry Association of America had just instituted its Diamond Award for albums selling ten million copies, and *The Lion King* was the first recipient.

The Lion King helped make Disney music product hotter than ever, and under the new management of Carolyn Mayer Beug, more product was needed to meet the demand. "They began to see the value of the classic soundtracks, so I was assigned *Bambi*, *Cinderella*, and *Sleeping Beauty*," Thornton said. In the years to follow, he would also produce world-premiere soundtracks for *Alice in Wonderland*, *Lady and the Tramp*, and *101 Dalmatians*, all of which had never been released as full-length soundtrack albums.

In addition to reawakening classic soundtracks, Beug decided to give new life to beloved Disney tunes with fresh interpretations by contemporary artists. Among the impressive efforts in this initiative were *The Music of Cinderella*, featuring Linda Ronstadt, Bobby McFerrin, and David Sanborn, and *Music from the Park*, a collection saluting the Walt Disney World twenty-fifth anniversary with performances by Patti Austin, Barenaked Ladies, the Rembrandts, and Brian McKnight (singing the celebration's anthem, "Remember the Magic").

Producers Michael J. Becker, Harold Kleiner, and Marco Marinangeli received a Grammy nomination for one of the most acclaimed albums in the series, *Take My Hand: Songs from the 100 Acre Wood*, a delightfully eclectic set of Winnie the Pooh–inspired songs performed by the Chieftains, Maureen McGovern, and Tyler Collins. Another Pooh collection, *Friends Forever*, followed: it too featured the voices of Pooh and pals. Pop versions of Disney favorites continue to be released through the highly successful DisneyMania series, produced by the accomplished Jay Landers, who was Barbra Streisand's A&R executive for nearly two decades and who has worked as a producer for Frank Sinatra, Neil Diamond, and Josh Groban.

○

Throughout the 1990s, Walt Disney Records continued to benefit from strong theatrical releases with great songs, including *Toy Story*, *Hercules*, *A Bug's Life*, *Toy Story 2*, and *Tarzan* (which earned Walt Disney Records its first Grammy for Best Soundtrack Album). The songs from the 1990s features were also now placed alongside earlier Disney hits in a number of compilations, culminating in a multidisc set celebrating the studio's seventy-fifth anniversary.

A book-and-recording series called "Sing-Alongs" emerged, combining music from recent hit films with original songs. One of these original tunes, "The Claw" from *Toy Story Sing-Along*, presented Powell with an unusual challenge. No amount of studio technology would make the singers sound like the little green aliens from the movie. "Frustrated with the results, I remembered floating birthday balloons as a kid and how much fun it was to talk with lungs full of helium," he recalled. "I had a five-foot-tall tank delivered to the studio and made a bouquet of balloons for each of the four singers. It took some practice for them to all breathe in the helium at the same time before each line and maintain the right load. I don't think we've ever laughed harder in a session!"

O

With Disney vinyl records already a thing of the past, cassettes were becoming less prominent. "In 1997–98, we were still making 85 percent cassettes, but by 1999–2000, it had fallen to 50 percent," said Ted Kryczko. "Then the whole thing switched rapidly to where we do 95 percent CDs now. Even when we do cassettes, they're usually in combination packs where you'll find three or four read-alongs with a cassette and CD, just in case Mom and Dad have cassette decks in the car or old boom boxes. Cassettes have even gone away for three- to five-year-olds."

O

As the recording formats changed, so did the lives of the past and present players at Disneyland/Buena Vista/Walt Disney Records. Jymn Magon spent several years at Walt Disney Television Animation, wrote the story and cowrote the screenplay for *A Goofy Movie*, and is now a sought-after screenwriter, working on numerous film and TV projects for DIC, Sony, MGM, and other studios. He returned to the Disney fold to write the read-along for *Home on the Range*.

After his experiences recording Disney albums in Nashville, Ron Kidd and his wife fell in love with the city and moved there permanently. Author of dozens of children's books, plays, and novels, Kidd is senior editor at United Methodist Publishing.

Also in Nashville, Pat Patrick continued recording all kinds of music in what became three recording studios. In addition to touring with his own Pat Patrick Band, he started a music publishing company that has signed such hit makers as Kent Blazy, Rob Crosby, and Billy Dean.

Tom Bocci has enjoyed being a music supervisor for movies and TV shows for more than a decade. Also a thriving Hollywood music supervisor is Bambi Moé, who had moved up in the Disney ranks to vice president of TV animation music. Shepard Stern produced music for a number of companies and clients and has written some Disney songs. Chris Montan stayed at Disney and is now president of music for the entire studio.

George Charouhas and Dawn Halloran married in 1991 and now are raising a family. George co-owns a postproduction studio in Hollywood's Universal building, where he mixes movie trailers, TV spots, DVDs, and promos, but he hardly ever sings in the voice of Clarabelle Cow.

Not long after leaving Walt Disney Records, Carolyn Mayer Beug had taken her twin daughters to school in Boston and was flying back home with her mother on September 11, 2001, when terrorists crashed the plane into the World Trade Center. The tragedy not only shook the world but proved personally devastating to the family and friends Beug left behind. "It affected a lot of people," remembered Thornton. "I was actually about to have lunch with her. I just loved her. She was great. She could be stern, but always fair and you can't ask for more than that. She was always taking the company places—outings, barbecues, things like that. She made sure we had jackets, hats, and other things with the company logo. She really made us feel as if were part of something."

○

Visionaries such as Beug led Walt Disney Records to a level of success that couldn't have been dreamed of in the company's early days. Since 1989, the company has been responsible for anywhere from 40 to 80 percent of the market. It's not only the Number 1 children's label but also the Number 1 soundtrack label, with a current catalog that embraces the best of classic Disney and the newest innovations in music.

"We've had gross sales of over $100 million in the last few years," said Ted Kryczko. "And we're expanding our age categories where we could go beyond the eight- to nine-year-olds and appeal to twelve- to fourteen-year-olds. It's been a huge growth in the business."

The teen queen who led Walt Disney Records to unprecedented pop music success was Hilary Duff, whose rise somewhat mirrored that of her long-ago predecessor Annette Funicello. When Duff was appearing in the Disney Channel series *Lizzie McGuire*, she embarked on a music career as the star of the show and later as a solo singer. Her Buena Vista/Hollywood Records album, *Metamorphosis*, topped the *Billboard* charts. Within weeks, it was the Number 1 album with the Number 1 single and Number 1 music video, going triple platinum. Albums such as *The Princess Diaries* and the *Disneymania* series included Duff and other popular young artists, including Jesse McCartney, Jump 5, Raven-Symoné, and Christy Carlson Romano.

○

The recording division is now called Buena Vista Music Group and is headed by Bob Cavallo. It encompasses Walt Disney Records (with Robert Marick at the helm of domestic business and David Agnew leading Walt Disney Records worldwide), Hollywood Records (offering mainstream pop music and soundtracks), and Lyric Street Records (featuring country stars), all involving some of today's most outstanding artists.

Families remain at the core of Walt Disney Records. New soundtracks and classic compilations continue to collect gold and platinum records. "We don't think of ourselves as a children's label so much as a family label," Ted Kryczko explained. "We appeal to everyone from kids to parents and grandparents, so the entire family can share it together. We have our catalog of Disney titles, we have recordings from the theme parks, which tend to appeal especially to adults, and we have a lot of archive material that we've been putting out."

Randy Thornton's most ambitious archival project is *Fiftieth Anniversary: A Musical History of Disneyland*, a comprehensive, six-disc, seven-hour boxed set that takes listeners through the park's attractions of today and yesterday. A special edition of the set, sold at Disneyland and Walt Disney World, includes a vinyl reproduction of the first in-house LP produced and released, *Walt Disney Takes You to Disneyland*, bringing the record company back to its roots.

Another of Thornton's archival projects involves CD kiosks that allow Disney theme park guests to choose and create their own made-to-order discs. The selections include current Disney albums, of course, as well as a substantial number of digitally remastered vintage Disneyland Records recordings, from Camarata's *Alice in Wonderland* and *Tin-panorama* to *Babes in Toyland* and *Professor Ludwig Von Drake*, to name a few. In a reverent nod to the early years, Thornton named the system Wonderland Music Company, after Jimmy Johnson's original Main Street, U.S.A. shop.

"David Agnew and I were having lunch with Tutti not long ago, and I brought his *Alice* on CD and a couple of others," recalled Thornton. "He said, 'You've really done a great job with the soundtracks.' So I was thinking, 'Okay, stick a fork in me, I'm done!' When *the* guy who did it originally himself and was passionate about it tells you that you're doing a good job, that's all you need."

○

On October 16, 2003, Camarata was honored at the Disney Legends ceremony at the Walt Disney Studio, a yearly tribute to select individuals who have made substantial contributions to the Disney legacy. Camarata accepted the award with his wife by his side and his friends Richard Sherman, Thurl Ravenscroft (both previous recipients), and Robie Lester in attendance. A plaque commemorating Camarata's status as a Disney Legend is now permanently installed in the Legends Plaza on the studio lot. He remained active with music and writing projects until his death on April 13, 2005, at the age of ninety-one.

With new technology coming every day, such as downloadable Disney music and stories on iTunes, Walt Disney Records has come a long way since the days when Camarata and Jimmy Johnson (who died in 1976) pioneered the studio's first in-house record label. But many of the great recordings of the past still live on alongside popular new hit albums.

"I'm particularly proud that we've been able to maintain a level of creativity in our products over such a long span of time," said Ted Kryczko, who has achieved the greatest longevity of anyone at Walt Disney Records. "They hold up against anything anyone else has done. It's an amazing body of work created by a lot of great people. People tell me that they used to listen to our records as a kid. Now they have kids of their own, and they're looking for the same records to share with their kids. I've heard it time and time again: 'When we go to buy music for our kids, if it's Disney, we know it's going to meet a certain standard.' They recognize the difference. That's something to be proud of."

Appendix:
Grammy Nominations and Awards

* Award winner

1959
Best Soundtrack Album or Recording of Original Cast from a Motion Picture or Television
Sleeping Beauty

1961
Best Soundtrack Album or Recording of Original Cast from a Motion Picture or Television
Babes in Toyland, Tutti Camarata
Best Soundtrack Album or Recording of Original Cast from a Motion Picture or Television
The Parent Trap, Tutti Camarata

1960
Best Recording for Children
Mother Goose Nursery Rhymes, Sterling Holloway
Best Recording for Children
101 Dalmatians, Tutti Camarata, producer

1963
Best Recording for Children
Addition and Subtraction, Rica Owen Moore

1964
Best Original Score Written for a Motion Picture or Television Show (composer award)
* *Mary Poppins*, Richard M. Sherman and Robert B. Sherman

Best Recording for Children
* *Mary Poppins*, Julie Andrews, Dick Van Dyke, David Tomlinson, Glynis Johns, Ed Wynn, Buena Vista
Best Recording for Children
Chim Chim Cheree and Other Children's Choices, Burl Ives

1965
Best Recording for Children
Winnie the Pooh and the Honey Tree, Sterling Holloway, Sebastian Cabot

1967
Best Recording for Children
Carnival of the Animals, Tutti Camarata, Symphonie-Orchester Graunke
Best Recording for Children
A Happy Birthday Party with Winnie the Pooh, Sterling Holloway
Best Recording for Children
The Jungle Book, motion picture cast

1970
Best Recording for Children
The AristoCats, Tutti Camarata, musical producer, (Tutti Camarata, Sterling Holloway, Phil Harris, Robie Lester, Mike Sammes Singers)

1973
Best Recording for Children
Songs from the Electric Company TV Show

1974
Best Recording for Children
* *Winnie the Pooh and Tigger Too*, Sebastian
    Cabot, Sterling Holloway, Paul Winchell
Best Recording for Children
America Sings, Burl Ives and others
Best Recording for Children
Robin Hood, various artists, narrated by Roger
    Miller

1976
Best Recording for Children
Dickens' Christmas Carol, Mickey Mouse and
    Scrooge McDuck
Best Recording for Children
Snow White and the Seven Dwarfs, [complete]
    original soundtrack
Best Recording for Children
Winnie the Pooh for President, Sterling
    Holloway, Larry Groce

1977
Best Recording for Children
A Charlie Brown Christmas, various artists
    (written by Charles M. Schulz)

1978
Best Recording for Children
Charlie Brown's All-Stars (television special)
Best Recording for Children
The Hobbit (soundtrack), Orson Bean, John
    Huston, Hans Conried
Best Recording for Children
Charlie Brown's All-Stars (television special)

1979
Best Recording for Children
You're in Love, Charlie Brown

1981
Best Recording for Children
The Fox and the Hound (soundtrack)

1984
Best Recording for Children
Flashbeagle

1988
Best Album of Original Instrumental Back-
    ground Score Written for a Motion Picture or
    Television
Who Framed Roger Rabbit? Alan Silvestri

1989
Best Recording for Children
Oliver and Company (story and songs from the
    motion picture), various artists

1990
Best Album of Original Instrumental Back-
    ground Score Written for a Motion Picture or
    Television
*The Little Mermaid—Original Motion Picture
    Soundtrack* (instrumental score), Alan
    Menken (various artists)
Best Song Written Specifically for a Motion Pic-
    ture or Television
* "Under the Sea" (from *The Little Mermaid—
    Original Motion Picture Soundtrack*), Alan
    Menken, Howard Ashman
Best Song Written Specifically for a Motion Pic-
    ture or Television
"Kiss the Girl" (from *The Little Mermaid—
    Original Motion Picture Soundtrack*, Alan
    Menken, Howard Ashman
Best Recording for Children
* *The Little Mermaid—Selections from the
    Film Soundtrack*, Alan Menken, Howard
    Ashman
*The Little Mermaid—Selections from the Film
    Original Soundtrack*, Roy Dotrice, narrator
    [released by Dove Books on Tape, later reis-
    sued on Walt Disney Records]

1992
Album of the Year
Beauty and the Beast (soundtrack)
Song of the Year (songwriter's award)
"Beauty and the Beast," Alan Menken, Howard
  Ashman
Best Performance by a Duo or Group with
  Vocal
• Celine Dion, Peabo Bryson, "Beauty and the
  Beast"
Best Instrumental Composition Written for a
  Motion Picture or Television
• "Theme from Beauty and the Beast," Alan
  Menken
Best Song Written Specifically for a Motion Pic-
  ture or Television
• "Beauty and the Beast," Alan Menken,
  Howard Ashman
Best Album for Children
• *Beauty and the Beast* (film soundtrack), Alan
  Menken, Howard Ashman
Best Historical Album
The Music of Disney—A Legend in Song, vari-
  ous artists

1993
Song of the Year (songwriter's award)
• "A Whole New World (Aladdin's Theme),"
  Alan Menken, Tim Rice
Best Performance by a Duo or Group with
  Vocal
• Peabo Bryson, Regina Belle, "A Whole New
  World (Aladdin's Theme)"
Best Instrumental Composition Written for a
  Motion Picture or Television
• "Aladdin," Alan Menken
Best Song Written Specifically for a Motion Pic-
  ture or Television
• "A Whole New World (Aladdin's Theme),"
  Alan Menken, Tim Rice
"Friend Like Me" (from *Aladdin*), Alan
  Menken, Howard Ashman
Best Musical Album for Children

• *Aladdin* (soundtrack), various artists
Tim Burton's The Nightmare before Christmas
  (soundtrack), various artists
Best Spoken Word Album for Children
Aladdin Sound and Story Theater, various
  artists

1994
Song of the Year (songwriter's award)
"Can You Feel the Love Tonight?" Elton John,
  Tim Rice
"Circle of Life," Elton John, Tim Rice
Best Pop Vocal Performance, Male
• Elton John, "Can You Feel the Love Tonight?"
Best Instrumental Composition Written for a
  Motion Picture or Television
The Lion King, Hans Zimmer
Best Song Written Specifically for a Motion Pic-
  ture or Television
"Can You Feel the Love Tonight?" Elton John,
  Tim Rice
"Circle of Life," Elton John, Tim Rice
Best Instrumental Arrangement Accompanying
  Vocals
• Andrae Crouch, Lebo Morake, Hans Zimmer,
  "Circle of Life" (from *The Lion King*) (Car-
  men Twillie)
Best Musical Album for Children
• *The Lion King* (Soundtrack), Mark Mancina,
  Jay Rifkin, Chris Thomas, Hans Zimmer
Best Spoken Word Album for Children
• *The Lion King Read-Along*, Robert
  Guillaume, Ted Kryczko, Randy Thornton

1995
Best Pop Vocal Performance, Female
Vanessa Williams, "Colors of the Wind"
Best Song Written Specifically for a Motion Pic-
  ture or Television
• "Colors of the Wind," Alan Menken, Stephen
  Schwartz
Best Instrumental Arrangement Accompanying
  Vocals

Bobby McFerrin, "Bibbidi-Bobbidi-Boo" (from *Cinderella*)
Best Musical Album for Children
Pocahontas Sing-Along, Alan Menken, Stephen Schwartz
Winnie the Pooh's Take My Hand, Michael L. Becker, Harold J. Kleiner, Marco Marinangeli (The Chieftains, Kathie Lee Gifford, various artists)

1997
Best Spoken Word Album for Children
The Original Story of Winnie the Pooh, Long John Baldry (A. A. Milne)

1998
Best Spoken Word Album for Children
The Lion King II: Simba's Pride
Best Musical Show Album
* *The Lion King: Original Broadway Cast Recording*

1999
Best Soundtrack Album
* *Tarzan*, Phil Collins
Best Instrumental Composition Written for a Motion Picture, Television, or Other Visual Media
* *A Bug's Life*, Randy Newman

2000
Best Musical Album for Children
* *Woody's Roundup Featuring Riders in the Sky*
Best Musical Show Album
* *Elton John and Tim Rice's Aida*
Best Spoken Word Album for Children
Dr. Seuss' How the Grinch Stole Christmas

2002
Best Musical Album for Children
* *Monsters, Inc.: Scream Factory Favorites*, Riders in the Sky
Best Spoken Word Album for Children
Monsters, Inc. DVD Read-Along

Bibliography

"Annette Makes a Record." *Walt Disney's Magazine*, February 1959.

Ansen, David. "When You Wish upon a TRON." *Newsweek*, July 5, 1982.

Ault, Donald, ed. *Carl Barks: Conversations*. Jackson: University Press of Mississippi, 2003.

Baranick, Alana. "Tony Pope" (obituary). *Cleveland Plain Dealer*, February 23, 2004.

Bowles, Jerry. *Forever Hold Your Banner High!* Garden City, N.Y.: Doubleday, 1976.

Brady, James. "In Step with Roy E. Disney." *Parade Magazine*, October 14, 2001.

Braun, William R. "The Two Lives of Marni Nixon." *Opera News*, October 2004.

Bright, Randy. *Disneyland: Inside Story*. New York: Abrams, 1987.

Bryant, Anita. *A New Day*. Nashville: Broadman, 1992.

Brooks, Ben. "Sunset Sound—The First 25 Years." *Billboard*, November 28, 1987.

Buck, Jerry. "Winchell Brings Tigger to Life." Associated Press story, October 20, 1988.

Canemaker, John. *The Art and Flair of Mary Blair*. New York: Disney Editions, 2003.

Clark, Jim. "In Celebration of a Good Life: Hal Smith." *The Bullet*, March 12, 1994.

Cotter, Bill. *The Wonderful World of Disney Television*. New York: Hyperion, 1997.

Craddock, Van. "Survivors of Original Mickey Mouse Outfit Doing Well." *Longview (Tex.) Daily News*, November 28, 1980.

DeLong, Thomas A. *Radio Stars: An Illustrated Biographical Dictionary*. Jefferson, N.C.: McFarland, 1996.

"Disney Rerecords *Fantasia*." Associated Press story, March 11, 1982.

Edwards, Cliff (obituary). United Press International story, July 1971.

Einstein, David. "Paul Frees, His Voice Sounds Familiar." Associated Press story, June 29, 1980.

Finch, Christopher. *Winnie the Pooh: A Celebration of the Silly Old Bear*. New York: Disney Editions, 2000.

"For Annette, It's Spooky." United Press International story, July 1, 1976.

Funicello, Annette, and Patricia Romanowski. *A Dream Is a Wish Your Heart Makes: My Story*. New York: Hyperion, 1994.

Gill, Suzanne. "Scripts! Microphones! Action!" TVData Features Syndicate, July 9, 1999.

Goldmark, Daniel, and Yuval Taylor, eds. *The Cartoon Music Book*. Chicago: A Cappella, 2002.

Heide, Robert, and John Gilman. *Disneyana: Classic Collectibles 1928–1958*. New York: Hyperion, 1994.

Holloway, Sterling (obituary). Associated Press story, November 24, 1992.

Hubler, Craig. "Bruce Botnick—The Start of a New Era." *Billboard*, November 28, 1987.

———."Donn Landee—The Silence Is Broken." *Billboard*, November 28, 1987.

———."Jim Messina—Looking Back."*Billboard*, November 28, 1987.

———. "Tutti's Turn to Trumpet." *Billboard*, November 28, 1987.

[Huemer, Dick.] "A Christmas Adventure in Disneyland." *Family Circle*, December 1958.

Johnson, Jimmy. "Inside the Whimsy Works." Unpublished manuscript, 1975.

Johnson, John. "Fess Parker Is King of the Wine Frontier." *Los Angeles Times*, August 29, 2002.

Keller, Keith. *The Mickey Mouse Club Scrapbook*. New York: Grosset and Dunlap, 1975.

Kernan, Michael. "Macdonald Drummed Up a Job as a Sound Effects Man." *Dallas Times Herald*, June 2, 1982.

Kerns, William D. "Trouble in Disneyland." *Southwest Airlines Magazine*, July 1981.

Koenig, David. *More Mouse Tales*. Irvine, Calif.: Bonaventure, 1999.

———. *Mouse Tales*. Irvine, Calif.: Bonaventure, 1995.

———. *Mouse under Glass*. Irvine, Calif.: Bonaventure, 2001.

Kurtti, Jeff. *Since the World Began: Walt Disney World, the First Twenty-five Years*. New York: Hyperion, 1996.

Lawson, Tim, and Alisa Persons. *The Magic behind the Voices*. Jackson: University Press of Mississippi, 2004.

Maltin, Leonard. *The Disney Films*. 4th ed. New York: Disney Editions, 2000.

"Mickey Is on Comeback Trail." Associated Press story, October 17, 1982.

Mills, Bart. "Disney Looks for a Happy Ending to Its Grim Fairy Tale." *American Film*, July–August 1982.

Mintz, Aaron. "Woman of 1000 Voices [Gloria Wood]." N.d., unidentified clipping in possession of Jay Deane.

Murray, R. Michael. *The Golden Age of Walt Disney Records, 1933–1988*. Dubuque, Iowa: Antique Trader, 1997.

Nash, Bruce, and Allan Zullo. *The Wacky Top 40*. Holbrook, Mass.: Adams, 1993.

Ohmart, Ben. *Welcome, Foolish Mortals: The Life and Voices of Paul Frees*. Boalsburg, Penn.: BearManor Media, 2004.

Ohmart, Ben, and Joe Bevilacqua. *Daws Butler: Characters Actor*. Boalsburg, Penn.: BearManor Media, 2005.

Oliver, Myrna. "Buddy Baker" (obituary). *Los Angeles Times*, July 31, 2002.

"Oz Books, Films, Merchandise Produce Millions." Associated Press story, July 21, 1985.

Peterson, Monique. *The Little Big Book of Disney*. New York: Disney Editions, 2001.

———. *The Little Big Book of Pooh*. New York: Disney Editions, 2002.

Prima, Louis (obituary). United Press International story, August 25, 1978.

Rothel, David. *Those Great Cowboy Sidekicks*. Waynesville, N.C.: WOY, 1984.

Rovin, Jeff. *Of Mice and Mickey*. New York: Manor, 1975.

Santoli, Lorraine. *The Official Mickey Mouse Club Book*. New York: Hyperion, 1995.

Scott, Vernon. "Disney Deflowered?" United Press International story, July 13, 1978.

Sherman, Robert B., and Richard M. Sherman. *Walt's Time: From before to Beyond*. Santa Clarita, Calif.: Camphor Tree, 1998.

Sibley, Brian. *Three Cheers for Pooh*. New York: Dutton Children's Books, 2001.

Smith, Dave. *Disney A to Z*. New York: Hyperion, 1998.

Surrell, Jason. *The Haunted Mansion: From the Magic Kingdom to the Movies*. New York: Disney Editions, 2003.

Tieman, Robert. *The Disney Treasures*. New York: Disney Editions, 2003.

Tietyen, David. *The Musical World of Walt Disney*. Milwaukee: Leonard, 1990.

"Walt Disney: Father Goose." *Time*, December 27, 1954.

Williams, Pat, and Jim Denney. *How to Be Like Walt*. Deerfield Beach, Fla.: Health Communications, 2004.

Index

References to illustrations appear in **boldface**.

A&M Records, 95
ABBA, 170
"Abba Dabba Honeymoon," 108
Abbate, Nancy, 13
Abbott and Costello, 15
ABC-Paramount, 13, 20
ABC-TV, 10, 13, 20, 29, 34, 74, 95
Acting Out the ABC's, 60, 66, 116
Adair, Tom, 121, 123
Adamson High School, 159
Addition and Subtraction, 66, 72
Adelquist, Hal, 17
Adventures in Music: Melody, 43
Adventures in Odyssey, 96, 120, 143, 147, 153, 163
Adventures of Gulliver, The, 58
Adventures of Jonny Quest, The, 123
Adventures of Ozzie and Harriet, The, 48, 153
Adventures of Sonny and Buddy, The, 122
Adventures of the Gummi Bears, 176, 177, 178
Afterbeats, The, 46
Agnew, David, 187, 188
Airmen of Note, The, 135
Aladdin, 112, 115, 184, 185
Alan Young Show, The, 142
Albert, Eddie, 141
ALF, 182
Alice in Wonderland (film), 8–9, 40, 45, 63, 107
Alice in Wonderland (record), 20, 23, 25, 27, 28, 32, 55, 92, **128**, 150, 185, 187, 188

"Alice in Wonderland Meets the White Rabbit," 67, 69
Alien Nation, 111
Alien Worlds, 147, 150
All about Dragons, 40, 94, **128**
All American College Orchestra, 138, 139
All Ashore, 65
"All in the Golden Afternoon," 9
All the King's Saxes, 37
All the Songs from Winnie the Pooh, 87
Alldis, John, 104
Allen, Ella, 60
Allen, Rex, 47, 140
All-New Mickey Mouse Club, The, 149, 151, 155
Allwine, Wayne, 119, 142, 184
Aloni, Amindav, 83
Alpert, Herb, 115
Altadena, Calif., 81
Alvin and the Chipmunks, 41, 145, 178–79
"Amapola," 20
America Sings, 140
American Academy of Dramatic Arts, 30, 65
American Adventure, The, 32
American Bandstand, 11, 46
American Greetings, 171
American Legion Hall, 38
American Madness, 30
American Society of Composers, Artists and Publishers (ASCAP), 9
American Tail, An, 89
American-International Pictures, 50, 132

Am-Par Records, 13, 20
Amsberry, Bob, 13
Anaheim, Calif., 9
Andersen, Hans Christian, 118
Andrews, Julie, 55, 81, 83, 108, 111
Andrews Sisters, 7, 78, 108
Andron, Jim, 174, **175**
Andy Griffith Show, The, 118, 122, 153
"Animal Imitation Song," 66
Animal Jam, 178
Animal Stories of Aesop, 61
Anka, Paul, 52, 184
Annette, 29, 48, 184
Annette: A Musical Reunion, 184
Annette on Campus, 75
Annette Sings Anka, 52
Anselmo, Tony, 180, 184
"Anything Can Happen," 141
Apple Dumpling Gang, The, 36
Archer, Frances, 18–19, 20, 25, 38, 54
Archie Show, The, 32
Archimedes the owl, 70
"Are We Dancing?," 101
Ariel and the Mysterious World Above, 185
AristoCats, The (film), 96, 120, 125, 127, 128
AristoCats, The (record), 96, 125, **128**
AristoCats and Other Cat Songs, The, 125
Armstrong, Louis, 22, 112
Armstrong Evans-Black carpets, 124
Army Air Corps, 20
Ashman, Howard, 183, 184
Atencio, Xavier, 98, 99, 118, 121
Atlantis: The Lost Empire, 147
Audley, Eleanor, 8, 118
Austin, Patti, 185
Austin, Tex., 184
Autumn, 37
Avalon, Frankie, 51, 184
Avengers, The, 102

Babes in Toyland (film), 42, 62
Babes in Toyland (record), 60, 62, 187
Back to the Beach, 51

Baer, Ellie, **179**, 180
Bagdasarian, Ross, 41, 164
Bagheera, 31, 105, 116, 130
Bahlor, Tom, 140
Bailey, Pearl, 135
Bain, Valerie, 102
Bainbridge Records, 36
Baird, Sharon, 13, 17
Baja Marimba Band, 114
Baker, B. J., 89
Baker, Buddy, 87, 99, 121, 123, 131, 140
Ball, Lucille, 46, 58
"Ballad of Davy Crockett, The," 10, 11, 12, 28, 75, 117
Baloo the bear, 89–90, 116, 165
"Baloo's Blues," 116
Bambi, 44, 54, 94
Bambi (film), 7, 9, 61, 67, 94, 122
Bambi (record), **21**, 22, 29, 32, 38, 47, 55, 94, **128**, 182, 185
Banana Splits, The, 166
"Bare Necessities, The," 74, 108
Barefoot Mailman, The, 35
Barenaked Ladies, 185
Barks, Carl, 53, 54, 165, 169
Barnet, Charlie, 20
Barney Bear, 63
Baron, Phil, 161, 162–63, 164
Barrie, Sir James, 9
Barry, John, 160
Barrymore, Drew, 167
Basil, Toni, 178
Baskett, James, 32
Bassey, Shirley, 103
Batman, 45
Baum, L. Frank, 121, 123–24
BBC, 103, 113, 128
"Be a Clown," 35
Beach Boys, The, **93**, 114
Beagle Boys, 54, 69, 165
Beals, Dick, 53, 69, 86, 99
Beals, Jennifer, 171
Bean, Orson, 147

Beanblossom, Billie Jean, 13
Beauty and the Beast, 112, 115, 184
Becker, Michael J., 185
Bedknobs and Broomsticks (film), 78, 129–30, 152
Bedknobs and Broomsticks (record), 102, 129–30
"Bein' Green," 126
Belew, Gypsy, 127
"Believe It or Not," 170
"Bella Notte," 68
Belle, Regina, 184
Belmont University, 132
Bend of the River, 31
Bennett, Tony, 102
Benny Hill Show, The, 102
Berlin, Irving, 6, 7
Bernstein, Bob, 7
Bernstein, Elmer, 176
Bernstein, Leonard, 81
Best Loved Fairy Tales, 66–67
Best Stories of Aesop, **59**, 61
Bestor, Don, 6
Betty Boop, 173
Beug, Carolyn Mayer, 185, 186–87
Beverly Hills, Calif., 18, 182
Beverly Hills Women's Club, 18
Big Bad Wolf, 67, 123
Big Band Alumni Orchestra, 68
Big Fisherman, The, 47
Big Thunder Mountain Railroad, 32
Billboard, 8, 115
Birmingham, Ala., 107
Black Beauty, 88, 97, **128**
Black Cauldron, The, 176, 178
Black Hole, The, 160
Black Stallion, The, 167
Blackbeard's Ghost, 117
Blackburn, Tom, 10
Blair, Mary, 79–80
Blaisch, Lois, **165**, 166, **175**
Blakely, Larry, 105, 115, 118
Blazy, Kent, 186

Bletcher, Billy, 67
Bleyer, Archie, 12
Bliss, Lucille, 8, **67**, 69, 146, **149**
Blondie, 166
Blue Hawaii, 46
Bluebird Records, 6
Boatniks, The, 124–25
Bob McGrath Sings, 140
Bocci, Tom, 165, 168, 175, 177, 186
Bogas, Ed, 170, 173
Bolger, Ray, 62, 121
Bond's Clothing, 61
Bonoff, Karla, 178
Boone, Pat, 134
Boone, Randy, 48
Borge, Victor, 168
Born Free, 133, 139
Boston, Mass., 12, 186
Botnick, Bruce, 114–15, 182, 184
Bourne, Bonnie, 6
Bourne, Saul, 6, 7
Bourne Music Company, 6, 7
Bouvier, Jacqueline, 65
Boy Called Nuthin', A, 118
Bozo the Clown, 69, 91
Bradbury, Ray, 5
Brannigan, Laura, 175
Brave Combo, 182
Brer Rabbit, 32
Brer Rabbit and the Tar Baby, 128
Brewer, Teresa, 48
Bricusse, Leslie, 136
Brigadoon, 35
Briggs, Katie, 126
British Decca, 20
"British Grenadier, The," 40
Broadcast Music Inc. (BMI), 9, 177
Broccoli, Albert, 78
Brophy, Edward, 32
Brown, Jerry, 132
Brunner, Bob, 131, 134
Brunner, Francis and Barbara, 134
Bruns, George, 10, 23, 62, 117

Brussels World's Fair, 34
Bryant, Anita, 126–27, 129
Bryson, Peabo, 184
Buck Privates Come Home, 15
Buena Vista Adventure series, 167
Buena Vista Music Group, 187
Buena Vista Pictures, 47
Buena Vista Records, 36, 47, 48, 50, 52, 58, 62,
    70, 77, 80, 83, 93, 100, 102, 104, 105, 108,
    110, 113, 114, 133, 141, 144, 147, 155, 156,
    160, 170, 178, 180, 182
"Bug-A-Boo," 165
Bugs Bunny, 91
Bug's Life, A, 185
Burgess, Bobby, 13, 121
Burgess, Jack, 7
Burnett, Carol, 111, 135
"Burning Bridges," 132
Burns, George, 154
Burnside, Dennis, 156
Burr, Lonnie, 13, 16–17, 121
Burton, Corey, 146, 147–48, 149, 150, 154
Burton, Tim, 44
Burtt, Ben, 155
Bush, Bettina, 174
Busker Alley, 78
Butera, Sam, 83
Butler, Daws, 146, 147, 149, 154
Buttram, Pat, 88, 125

Cabot, Sebastian, 87, 105, 140, 145
Cadence Records, 12
California Adventure, 70
California Community Foundation, 51
California Institute of the Arts, 82
Callpari, Joe, 153
Calvin, Henry, 34, 35
Camarata, Tutti, 20–22, 23, 25, 27, 33–34,
    36–38, 39, 43, 47, 49, 50–51, 54, 55, 56, 58,
    60, 62, 65, 66–67, 69–70, 77, 79, 82, 83, 84,
    87, 91, **93**, 94, 95, 96, 97, 101, 102–3, 104,
    105, 109, 110, 112–13, 114–15, 116, 127,
    130, 131, 139, 140, 148, 179, 184, 187, 188

Camelot, 111
Campbell, Collin, 121
"Cancion de Amor," 95
Candido, Candy, 121, 125
"Candle on the Water," 132
Candoli, Pete, 36, 46
"Candy Man," 132, 133
Candy Man and Other Sweet Songs, 136, 139
Cantor, Eddie, 45
Capitol Records, 10, 12, 17, 26, 36, 46, 68, 69,
    91, 119, 132, 152
Capps, Al, 97, 108, 165
Capra, Frank, 30
Captain Hook, 146, 147
Captain Midnight, 122
Caputo, Tony, 166
Caravelles, The, 128
Care Bears, 171
Carne, Judy, 130
Carnegie Hall, 173
Carnes, Kim, 166
Carney, Art, 45
Carnival of the Animals, 104
Carousel, 34, 45
Carpenter, Carleton, 108
Carpenter, Mary Chapin, 160
Carrell, Ruth, 15, 16
Carroll, Diahann, 107
Carroll, Eddie, 164
Carroll, Lewis, 8
"Carrot Stew," 160
Carson, Johnny, 52
Carter, Gaylord, 118
Casals, Pablo, 138
Cascade Records, 12
"Casey Jones," 69
Casper the Friendly Ghost, 58
Cavallo, Bob, 187
CBS, 12, 23, 75, 83, 111, 171
Cedartown, Ga., 30
"C'est Chiffon," 44
"C'est Si Bon," 44
Champaign-Urbana, Ill., 74

Chappell, 84, 103
Charles, Ray, 102
Charlie Brown Christmas, A, 155
Charlie Brown Records, 155, 170
Charlie Brown's All-Stars, 155
Charlotte's Web, 78
Charouhas, George, 147, 148–49, 156, 158, 180, 186
Chef Ahmalette's Health Diet, 147
Chef Tony, 154
Cheshire Cat, 30
Chevalier, Maurice, 70, 93
Chicago, Ill., 36, 63, 88, 161, 162, 180
Chicago Symphony Orchestra, 65
Chieftans, The, 185
Child, Julia, 180
Children's Favorites, 158, 159–60, 176
Children's Riddles and Game Songs, 80, 86, 91
Chilling, Thrilling Sounds of the Haunted House, 72, 73, 76, 99, 127, 134, 136
Child's Garden of Verses, A, 18, 20, 54
"Chim Chim Cheree," 155, 156
"Ching, Ching," 46
Chip 'n' Dale, 53, 95, 162, 164
Chip 'n' Dale Chipmunk Fun, 69
"Chip 'n' Dale's Vacation," 169
Chipmunk Adventure, The, 178
"Chipmunk Song, The," 41, 162, 164
Chitty Chitty Bang Bang (film), 78
Chitty Chitty Bang Bang (record), 102
Choldenko, Gennifer. *See* Johnson, Gennifer
Christensen, James, 131
"Christmas Adventure in Disneyland, A" (poem), 43
Christmas Adventure in Disneyland, A (record), 43–44, 46, 86, 91
Christmas Trees of Disneyland, 43
Churchill, Frank, 76, 96
Churchman, Ysanne, 113
Cincinnati, Ohio, 15
Cincinnatus, 31
Cinderella (film), 7, 8, 39, 69, 91, 118
Cinderella (record), **21**, 22, 32, 38, 55, 92, 148, 151, 185

Cinderella II: Dreams Come True, 91
Cinnamon Bear, The, 76
Cisco Kid, The, 122
"Civilization," 108
Clarabelle Cow, 180, 186
Clark, Dick, 46
"Claw, The," 185
Clayton, Jan, 34
"Clementine," 54
Clemmons, Larry, 116
Cleveland, Ohio, 154, 161, 162, 163
Clokey, Art, 31
Clooney, Rosemary, 9, 40
Coconut Grove, 74
Cole, Bill, 88–89, 111, 131, 140
Cole, Nat King, 68
Cole, Tommy, 13
College of Santa Fe, 19
Collins, Tyler, 185
Columbia College, 36
Columbia Pictures, 24, 35, 36, 63, 65, 122
Columbia Records, 8, 12, 38, 52, 83, 138
Colvig, Pinto, 69, 80, 91
Combat, 119
"Come to Me, Bend to Me," 35
Conger, Gwen, 20
Conklin, Donna, 74
Conlon, Jud, 45, 107
Connery, Sean, 47
Conniff, Ray, 83
Conrad, William, 147
Conried, Hans, 147
Continentals, The, 74
"Cooking with Minnie Mouse," 16
Coppola, Francis Ford, 167
Coral Room, 55
Corcoran, Kevin, 35
Corky and White Shadow, 28
Coronets, The, 102
Corpus Christi, Tex., 18
Corrigan, Lloyd, 28
Cosby, Bill, 62
Costa, Mary, **52**

Country Bear Jamboree (attraction), 32, 86, 89, 120, 161
Country Bear Jamboree (record), 131
Country Cousin, The, 91
Courtland, Jerome, 34, 35–36
Courtland, Mary, 35
Coward, Noel, 33
Cowardly Lion of Oz, The, 123–24
Craig, Scott, 156
Craig 'n' Co., 183
Crawford, Johnny, 13
Crazy Over Daisy, 27
Creakin' Leather, 36
Cricket Records, 23
Crockett, Davy, 10, 11, 20, 31, 35, 155
Crosby, Bing, 6, 22, 45, 47, 77, 88, 124
Crosby, Mary Frances, 124
Crosby, Rob, 186
Cross, Judith, 183
Crusader Rabbit, 69
Crystal Cathedral, 41
Cummings, Bob, 35
Cummings, Jim, 30
Curb, Mike, 132, 133, 141
Curb Records, 132, 133, 159

Daisy Duck, 178, 179, 180
"Dakota," 110, 112
Daley, Brian, 167
Dallas, 124
Dallas, Tex., 135, 159
"Dalmatian Plantation," 56
Dance Annette, 50
Dancing in Peacock Alley, 37
Daniel, Florence, 134
Daniel Boone, 11, 12, 31
Darby, Ken, 111
Darby O'Gill and the Little People, 47
Dark Crystal, The, 167
Darlene of the Teens, 27
Date Nite at Disneyland, 47
Davey and Goliath, 58
Davidson, John, 120

Davis, Bette, 83
Davis, Maxwell, 112
Davis, Nancy, 48
Davis, Sammy, Jr., 75, 102, 132, 133
Dawson, Todd, 74
Day, Dennis, 7, 13
Day, Doris, 9, 60
Day at Disneyland, A, 23, 29
Days of Our Lives, 73
De la Fuente, Charles, 49
De Shannon, Jackie, 115
Dean, Billie, 186
Dean, Merrill, 141, 144, 152
"Dear Daisy," 178
Dearborn, Mich., 145
DeBeck, Billy, 15
Decca, 23, 33, 34, 43, 48, 67, 86
Dees, Rick, 155
Dempster, Al, 46
Deon, Celine, 184
DePatie-Freleng, 124
DeRemer, Pat, **179**
Des Moines, Iowa, 85
"Detroit," 101
Detroit, Mich., 95
DeWynt, Steve, 174
Diamond, Neil, 185
DIC Entertainment, 171, 174, 186
Dick Tracy, 151
Dickens' Christmas Carol, 142, 143–44, 164
"Digital Duck," 169
Digital Magnetics, 115
Dinehart, Alan, 143
"Disco Duck," 155
"Disco Mickey Mouse," 156, 178
"Disco Mouse," 156
"Discovery Day," 155–56
Disney, Edna, **9**
Disney, Lillian, 34
Disney, Roy Edward, 6, 29, 32
Disney, Roy O., 5–6, 7, 9–10, 20, 26, 27, 29, 41, 44, 47, 56, 83, 99, 100, 126
Disney Afternoon, The, 177

Disney Audio Entertainment, 183
Disney Babies, 181
Disney Babies Lullaby, 181
Disney Channel, The, 49, 162, 163, 166, 168, 187
Disney Collection, The, 181
Disney Family Christmas Album, The, 164
Disney on Parade, 156, 178, 179
Disney Players, The, 120
Disney Songs the Satchmo Way, 112–13
Disneyland (park), 9–10, 20, 23, 29, 32, 43–44, 48, 57, 58, 64, 72, 76, 86, 97–98, 107, 112, 118, 126, 131, 133, 140, 145, 159, 166, 169, 183, 184, 187
Disneyland (TV series), 10, 11, 16, 25, 29, 34, 44, 121
"Disneyland after Dark," 112
Disneyland Boys' Choir, 79
Disneyland Hotel, 74
Disneyland Monorail Game, 42
Disneymania, 185, 187
Disney-MGM Studios, 178
Disneyrama records, 70
"Do What the Good Book Says," 44
Dobie Gillis, 45
Dobkin, Lawrence, 131
Doctor Dolittle (film), 32, 58, 104
Doctor Dolittle (record), 104
Dodd, Dickie, 13
Dodd, Jimmie, 13, 15–16, 17, 27, 32, 44, 184
Dodge City, Kans., 115
Don Juans, 45
Donald Duck, 54, 69, 76, 99, 140, 156–57, 161, 163, 164, 165, 169, 177, 178, 179, 180, 184
Donald Duck and His Friends, 53–54
Donald Duck and Uncle Scrooge's Money Rocket, 54
Donohue, Michael, 76, 121
"Don't Cry for Me, Argentina," 174
Doors, The, 114
Do-Re-Mi Children's Chorus, 83
Dorsey, Jimmy, 20
"Down to the Sea," 173

Dr. Seuss' How the Grinch Stole Christmas, 40, 147–48
Dragnet, 122
Drake, Tom, 86
Draper, Lois, 111
Dream Is a Wish Your Heart Makes, A, 47
"Drummin', Drummin', Drummin'," 110
"Ducks Dance Too," 165, 166
DuckTales, 143, 144
Duff, Hilary, 187
Dumbo (film), 7, 30, 43
Dumbo (record), 7, **21**, 22, 32, 47, 70
Dumbo's Circus, 163
Dunnich, Brenda, 113
Dylan, Bob, 177, 183

Eberle, Bob, 20
Ebsen, Buddy, 11–12, 28
Echoes of Disneyland, **37**
Ed Sullivan Show, The, 11
Eddy, Nelson, 7
Edmiston, Walker, 143
Edwards, Beverly, 123
Edwards, Cliff, 17, 20, 23, 24–25, 26, 32, 44, 53, 66, 105
Edwards, Sam, 61, **108**, 109, 122–23, 124, 125, 127, 130, 140, **144**, 146
Eeyore, 40, 97
Einstein, Albert, 93
Eisner, Michael, 174, 175
Electra Asylum Records, 166
Electric Company, The, 135, 140
Electric Prunes, The, 126
Ellenshaw, Peter, 22
Ellington, Duke, 83
Elmo Aardvark, 163
Emig, Alan, 114
Emil and the Detectives, 117
Empire Strikes Back, The, 151
Enchanted Tiki Room, 110
"E-N-C-Y-C-L-O-P-E-D-I-A," 20
Epcot, 32, 78, 138
Escape, 122

Escape to Witch Mountain (film), 36
Escape to Witch Mountain (record), 141
Espinosa, Mary, 13
E.T.: The Extra-Terrestrial, 167
Evans, Monica, 125
"Evening with Mary Martin and Friends," 34
"Everything Is Ducky with Donald," 180
Ewoks Join the Fight, 167

Fabares, Shelley, 184
Facts of Life, The, 161
Fahey, Brian, 102–3, 104, 124
Fain, Sammy, 8
Falcon Crest, 36
Family Band, The, 110
Family Circle, 43
Famous Adventures of Mr. Magoo, The, 95
Fantasia (film), 7, 27, 38, 42, 104, 112
Fantasia (record), 38–39, 41, 181
Fantasmic!, 151
FantaSound records, 104
Faraday, Michael, 93
"Farewell to the Mountains," 11
Farmer, Bill, 153, 184
Father Goose, 86
Father Knows Best, 48
Fawcett, Farrah, 36
FedEx, 136
"Feed the Birds," 79, 182
Ferdin, Pamelyn, 110
Fess Parker Yarns and Songs, 11, 27, **37**
"Fiddle Dee Dee," 54
Fiddler on the Roof, 102
Fiedler, John, 145
Field, Sally, 35
Fiftieth Anniversary: A Musical History of Disneyland, 187
Filmation Associates, 32, 123, 150
Finch, Peter, 135, 139
Finian's Rainbow, 102
Fireside Theater, 48–49
First Nighter, The, 73
First Willio and Phillio Album, The, 162

Fischer, Clare, 141
Fisherman Bear, 130
Fitzgerald, Ella, 115
Flashbeagle, 170–71, 173
Flashdance, 169, 170, 171
Fleischer Studios, 43
Flint, Shelby, 152
Flintstones, The, 83, 143
Flipper, 107
Flo and Eddie, 182–83
Florida Citrus Growers' Association, 126
Flower the skunk, 61
Flying Nun, The, 35–36
Flying Tigers, 15
Folk Heroes, 75
Folk Songs from the Far Corners, **37**, 38
Fonte, Alison, 156
Foote, Norman, 183
For Our Children, 183
Foray, June, 140, 147
Ford, Tennessee Ernie, 12
Fort Smith, Ark., 60
Fort Worth, Tex., 11
Foster, Stephen, 159
Four Freshmen, 74
"Fourth Anniversary Show," 121
Fox and Crow, 63
Fox and the Hound, The, 164
Fraidy Cat, 76
Franchi, Sergio, 111
Franklin, Ben, 32, 93
Freberg, Stan, 91, 119, 146, 176
Fred Flintstone, 83
Frederick, Robin, 184
Freeland, Roger, 166
Frees, Paul, 12, 44, 63–64, 66, 98, 107, 118, 147
French Chef, The, 162
"Frere Jacques," 54
Friends Forever, 185
Frierson, Eddie, 156
Frito-Lay, 131
"Frog Went A-Courtin'," 54
"From All of Us to All of You," 44, 164

"From Where He Stands," 173
Frontiersmen, The, 10
Frosted Flakes, 40
"Frosty the Snow Man," 69, 152
Frosty's Winter Wonderland, 152
Fun and Fancy Free, 17, 69
Fun and Sounds of Christmas, 136
Fun with Music, 71, 141
Funicello, Annette, 13, 27, 28, 29, 32, 46, 47, 48, 49–52, 54, 55, 62, 75, 76, 77, 93, 121, 132, 184, 187
Funicello, Joe and Virginia, 50
Furby, 154
Furman, Steve, 156
Further Adventures of Cinderella's Mice, 90–91
Further Adventures of Jiminy Cricket, 104, 105
Futuresonic, 135
"Futuristic Tree," 44

Gable, Clark, 107
Gabor, Eva, 96, 125, 152
Galileo, 93
Garber, Jan, 68
Garden Grove, Calif., 41
Garland, Judy, 64, 75, 121
Garrick's Gaieties, 30
Garson, Greer, 104
Gary, Linda, 146, 150–51
Gates, Debbie, 176, 178
"Gawrsh Golly Goofy," 179
Gay, Marion, 102
Gay Purr-ee, 64
General Hospital, 120
George, Hazel, 17, 44
George and the Happiest Millionaire, 101, 104
George Gobel Show, The, 11
Gershwin, George, 82
Gerson, Betty Lou, 56
"Get the Money," 165
"Ghost Riders in the Sky," 22
Giberto, Astrid, 75
"Gift of Love, A," 184
Gilbert, Billy, 69

Gile, Beverly, 18–19, 20, 25, 38, 54
Gilkyson, Terry, 74, 127
Gillespie, Darlene, 13, 25, 27, 28, 32, 34, 35, 121
Gilligan's Island, 75, 89, 111–12, 143
Gilmour, Ross, 102
Gingerbread Man, The, **128**
"Girl from Ipanema, The," 75
Glaser, Ariel, 183
Glaser, Elizabeth, 183
Glendale, Calif., 169
Gloria Wood Choir, 34, 45
Glor-Vir-Don Girls, 45
Gnome Mobile, The, 115
Goin' Quackers!, 161, 162, 163
Goff, Norris, **15**
Golden Horseshoe Review, **29**
Golden Records, 7, 8, 13, 18, 20, 23, 34, 91, 107
Goldilocks, 124
Goldman Hotel, 60
Gone with the Wind, 24
Gonyea, Dale, 168
"Goodbye to Toyland," 62
Goodman, Benny, 7, 37
Goodyear, 108
Goofy, 44, 53, 69, 80, 86, 153, 154, 164, 166, 184
"Goofy about Health," 151
Goofy Movie, A, 186
Goofy's TV Spectacular, 80, 91
Gowdy, Bruce, 166
Goyette, Desirée, 170–71, 172–73, 176, 178
Gozzo, Conrad, 36
Grabeau, Bob, 62, 67, 68
Grammys, 11, 41, 52, 55, 66, 97, 104, 111, 112, 125, 138, 140, 148, 173, 185, 189–92
Grand Canyon, 43
Grand Canyon Suite, 43
"Grandpa Bunny," 67
Grant, Cary, 86
Grant, Joe, 43
Grasshopper and the Ants (film), 6
Grasshopper and the Ants (record), 58, 61

Great Composers, The, 83
Great Moments with Mr. Lincoln, 76
Great Mouse Detective, The, 178
Great Operatic Composers, 76, 82
Greatest American Hero, The, 170
"Greatest Band, The," 156
Greeley, George, 61
"Green, Green Grass of Home," 102
Green Acres, 125
"Green Eyes," 20
"Green Grow the Lilacs," 11
Green Llama, The, 63
Green Nurd Theater, 145
Green Pastures Are before Me, 159
Griffin, Merv, 22
"Grim Grinning Ghosts," 121
Groban, Josh, 185
Groce, Larry, 145, 146, 158, 159–60, 161, 164, 165
Grofe, Ferde, 43
Grosset and Dunlap, 67
Grubby, 163
"Guantanamera," 95
Gulf Oil Company, 108
Gumby, 31, 182–83
Gumby: The Green Album, 182–83
Gunsmoke, 12, 122
Guthrie, Woody, 160
"Gyro Gearloose," 169

H. R. Pufnstuf, 143
Hackett, Buddy, 117
Hall of Presidents, The, 131
"Hallelujah," 11
Hallmark Cards, 171
Halloran, Dawn, 176, 186
Halloran, Jack, 69, 88–89, 97, 107, 109, 135, 176
Halyx, 166, **168**
Hamill, Mark, 147
Hanna-Barbera, 78, 83, 86, 143, 146, 150, 155
Hannibal, Mo., 24
Hans Brinker, 71

Hansel and Gretel, 76, 82, 121
Hansen, Charlie, 20, 26, 83–84
"Hap-Hap-Happy Snowman, The," 44
Happiest Millionaire, The (film), 78, 100–1, 120
Happiest Millionaire, The (record), 100–1, 104, 110
"Happy, Happy Birthday to You," 169
Happy Birthday, 71, **129**
Happy Birthday Party with Winnie the Pooh, A, 97, 115
"Happy Glow," 121
"Happy Mouse," 17
Happy Tunes Records, 155
Happy Wanderer in Europe, The, 46
Harriet, Judy, 13, 52
Harris, Phil, 89–90, 108, 113, 116, 125, 134
Harrison, Rex, 32, 58
Haunted Mansion, The (attraction), 40, 64, 72, 76, 107, 118, 121, 161
Haunted Mansion, The (record), 40, 118, 120, 121, 127, 140
Hawaiiannette, 50
Hayes, Bill, 12, 22
Heaven's Gift, 96
"Heffalumps and Woozles," 109
Heidi, 113, **129**, 131
Heidt, Horace, 45
Hemet, Calif., 19
Henson, Jim, 126, 167, 178
Hepburn, Audrey, 81
Herbert, Victor, 62
Hercules, 185
Here Comes Garfield, 173
"Here He Comes," 134
"Here We Go Round the Mulberry Bush," 54
"Here's to the Ears of Love," 180
"He's a Tramp," 31, 60
Heston, Charlton, 73
"Hey, Bellboy," 46
Hey There, It's Yogi Bear, 86
Hibler, Winston, 29, 79
Hicklin, Ron, 97, 108
"High Hopes," 158

Highland Avenue, 38
Hi-Ho, 33–34
Hill Street Blues, 61
Hilliard, Bob, 8
Hills Brothers coffee, 95
"Hip Hip Pooh Ray," 109
"Hippety Hop," 94
HMV Records, 6
Hobbit, The, 152, 155
"Hoedown at the Robot Farm," 169
Hoff, Gerry, 117, 125
Holiday, Billie, 115
Holidays with the Mouseketeers, 27, 46, 71
Holloway, Sterling, 27, 30, 54, 58, **59**, 61, **87**, 89, 91, 97, 109, 125, 145
Hollywood High School, 60
Hollywood Records, 187
Hollywood Revue of 1929, 24, 26
Holt, Bob, 146, 149
Holt, Tim, 24
Home on the Range, 186
"Home Sweet Home," 134
Honeymooners, The, 45
Honolulu, Hawaii, 16
Hooked on Classics, 165
Hooven, Marilyn, 67
Hope, Bob, 15
Hopper, Hedda, 74
Horse in the Gray Flannel Suit, The, 120
Horsemasters, The, 76, 78
"House Is Not a Home, A," 112
How to Be Like Walt, 58
"How Will I Know My Love?," 29
Howard, Ron, 118, 124, 127
Howdy Doody, 13
Howerton, Charles, 150–51
Huckleberry Finn, 78
Huckleberry Hound, 146
Huemer, Dick, 43
Huey, Dewey, and Louie, 99, 184
Humperdinck, Engelbert, 82, 102
Hunt for Red October, The, 136
Hurd, Enid, 102

Huston, John, 147
Hutton, Lauren, 150

"I Can't Do the Sum," 62
"I Cried for You," 26
"I Don't Like This Push-Button World," 169
I Love Lucy, 122
"I Love to Laugh," 82–83
"I Loved You Once in Silence," 111
I Married Joan, 153
"I Wanna Be Like You," 165
I Wanna Be Loved by You, 161
"I Wish I Was Magic," 177
"I Wish It Would Be Christmas All Year Long," 164
Iago Returns, 185
Ice House, The, 166
"I'd Like to Teach the World to Sing," 139
"If Ever I Would Leave You," 111
"If You Can't Say Something Nice," 94
"If You Want to See Some Strange Behavior," 116
"I'll Fly the Skyway," 127
"I'm Late," 9, 34
"I'm No Fool," 20, 24
"I'm Popeye the Sailor Man," 57
"In the Good Old Summertime," 138
"In a Silly Symphony," 6
Inside the Whimsy Works, 7
International Children's Festival, 139
International Horizons, 156
Iron Glove, The, 65
Irving Berlin Music, 6
Island at the Top of the World, The, 141
"It Won't Be Long 'Til Christmas," 104
Italiannette, 50
"It's a Kick," 116
It's a Small World (attraction), 49, 76, 79, 80
It's a Small World (record), 49, 76, 79–80, 116, 132, 133
It's Flashbeagle, Charlie Brown, 170–71
"It's Really Love," 52
"It's Tough to Be a Bug," 147

"I've Been Workin' on the Railroad," 54, 69
"I've Got Two," 126
Ives, Burl, 70, 108, 140

"Ja Da," 24
Jack Benny Program, The, 13, 40, 58
Jackson, Jack, 156
Jackson, Michael, 111
Jacksonville, Ore., 80
Jaffe, Mark, 183
Jaglom, Henry, 36
Jane Fonda's Workout, 164
Jani, Bob, 133
Jarrard, Rick, 74–75
Jarre, Maurice, 141
Jefferds, Vince, 127
Jehan, Marine, 171
Jenkins, Gordon, 86
Jerry Whitman Sings Songs from the Mister Rogers TV Show, 135, 136
Jetsons, The, 143, 146
Jillian, Ann, 62, 76
Jiminy Cricket, 17, 20, 23, 24, 26, 29, 44, 53, 54, 66, 72, 105, 164
Jimmie Dodd Sings His Favorite Hymns, 44
"Jingle Bones," 44
Joel, Billy, 180
Johann, John Lee, 13
John, Elton, 178, 183, 185
John Tracy Clinic, 120
Johnson, Gennifer, 110
Johnson, Glenys, **59**, 61
Johnson, Grey, **59**, 61, 66
Johnson, Jimmy, 7–8, 9–10, 16, 20, 22, 23, 25, 26, 27, 29, 31, 32, 34, 36, 38–39, 41, 44, 46, 50, 52, 54, 55, **56**, 62, 70, 72, 76, 77, 78, 79, 81, 83–84, 89–90, 92, 93, 94, 97, 99, 100, 104, 105, 108, 109, 110, 112–13, 116, 117, 124, 127, 130, 134, 140, 141, 178, 179, 187, 188
Johnson, Kirby, 74–75
Johnston, Ollie, 182
"Jolly Holiday," 57, 82, 86

Jones, Chuck, 40
Jones, Dean, 55, 117, 120
Jones, Spike, 57, 63, 107
Jones, Stan, 11, 22, 34, 36
Jones, Tom, 102, 135
Jordanaires, The, 74, 180
Journey Back to Oz, 123
Joyce, Betty, 158, 174, 176
Joyce, Jimmy, 140, 158
Jukebox Saturday Night, 74
Julliard School of Music, 20
Jump 5, 187
"June Night," 26
Jungle Book, The (film), 31, 89–90, 105, 116, 165
Jungle Book, The (record), 31, 105, 107, 108, 115, 130, 134, 152, 183
Jungle Book II, 116
Jungle Cruise, 110
"Jungle Fever," 116
"Jungle Tree," 44, 86
Jungle VIP's, 105, 108
"Junk Food Junkie," 145, 158, 159, 165
Jurassic Park, 182
"Just a Whisper Away," 62, 68

Kanady, Bill, 88, 89, 97, 101
Kanady, Jean, 101
"Kanine Krunchies Kommercial," 56, 60, 69
Kaplan, Marvin, 177
Kapp Records, 74, 83
Karloff, Boris, 63
Kartoon DisKo, 155
Kaye, Danny, 108, 111, 135
Keel, Howard, 47
Keep, Ted, 114
"Keep on Tryin'," 165–66
Keith, Brian, 120
Kellogg's, 40
Kelly, Gene, 26
Kermit the Frog, 126
Kern, Bonni Lou, 13
Kern, Jerome, 82

Kerr, Anita, 112
Kerr, Deborah, 81
Kerr, John, 86, 111
KFPW, 60
KGO, 68
KHJ, 159
Kidd, Ron, 175–76, 177, 179, 181, 182, 186
Kids of the Kingdom, 112
Kiley, Richard, 182
Kimball, Stella, 113
Kimball, Ward, 181
King, Carole, 183
King and I, The, 81
King Creole, 46
King Family, The, 74
King Kong, 155
King Louie, 90, 116
King of the Hill, 136
"King's Dilemma," 136
Kingsway Symphony Orchestra, 20
Kipling, Rudyard, 73
Kitt, Eartha, 20
Klein, Mannie, 36
Kleiner, Harold, 185
Knightsbridge Singers, The, 102
Knott's Berry Farm, 48
KOMO-TV, 57
Kostal, Irwin, 112, 181, 182
Krauss, Allison, 160
"Kris Kringle," 26
Krisel, Gary, 141, 143, 144, 145–46, 148–49,
   151, 155, 156, 157, 159, **167**, 168–69, 170,
   174
Krofft, Sid and Marty, 143
Kryczko, Ted, 174, 176, 181, 182, 184, 186, 187,
   188
KTSA, 122
KTTV-TV, 61
Kwasman, Sam, 178, **179**
Kyser, Kay, 45

La Padula, Johnny, 37
"Ladies in the Sky," 35

Lady and the Tramp (film), 31, 40, 67, 73, 134
Lady and the Tramp (record), 60, 67, 92, **128**,
   185
Laine, Frankie, 8
Land Before Time, The, 151
Landers, Jay, 185
Lane, Lois, **127**, 128, **133**, 139, 140, 146
Lansbury, Angela, 130
Lantz, Walter, 31, 63
Lassie, 34
"Last Waltz, The," 102
Latauska, Al, 26, 41
Laugh-In, 130
Laurie, Audrey, 103
Laurita, Dana, 134
Lear, Norman, 61
Learning Channel, The, 178
Learning to Tell Time Is Fun, 72
Lee, Bill, 16, **17**, 27, 62, **80**, 82, 85–86, 88, 94,
   97, 101, 110, 111, 121, 124, 131, 135, 139,
   140
Lee, Diana, 135, 139, 140
Lee, Peggy, 31, 67
Legend of Sleepy Hollow, The, 67
Leighton, Bernie, 37
Lentz, Pat, 154
Leslie, Joan, 107
Lester, Robie, 12, 53, 66, 67, 69, **80**, 91–92,
   94–97, 98, 99, 100, 104, 105, 110, 116, 117,
   118, 121, 123, 124, 125, 126, 127–28, 130,
   146, 148, 152, 154, 188
"Let There Be Peace on Earth," 48, 53
"Let's Get Together," 55, 178
Leven, Mel, 69
Lewis, Huey, 180
Lewis, Jerry, 111
Lewis, Shari, 75
Liberty Records, 41, 95, 114
Light Records, 41
Light Up the Sky, 120
Lightchild Publishing, 173
Lincolns, The, 74
Lindsey, George, 125

Lion King, The, 115, 185
Lion King: The Brightest Star, The, 151
"Litterbug Song, The," 69
Little, Rich, 173
"Little Black Rain Cloud," 87, 89
Little Critter, 177
Little Drummer Boy, The, 64, 88
Little Engine Who Could, The, 72
Little Gems, 54, 87, 129, 131
Little Gems from Big Shows, 34, 35, 46, 139
Little Golden Books, 67, 69, 91, 92, 144,
    145–46, 147, 148, 154, 159
Little House on the Prairie, 123
Little Lame Lamb, The, 33
Little Mermaid, The, 89, 112, 118, 183, 184,
    185
Little Mermaid II, The, 173, 178
Little Red Riding Hood, **129**
Little Richard, 179
Little Shop of Horrors, 183
Little Toot, 69, 99
Live Aid, 183
Living Free, 133, 139
Livingston, Alan, 91
Lizzie McGuire, 187
Lloyd, Anne, 8
"Loch Ness Monster, The," 94
Lofting, Hugh, 104
"Lollipops and Roses," 139
Lombard, Carol, 97, 101, 106, 107, 108, 124
"London Bridge," 54
London Records, 20, 37
"Lonely," 11
Lonesome Ghosts, 76, 99
"Long and Winding Road, The," 102
Lopata, Gail, 169, 178
Lorimer, Carole, 113
Lorre, Peter, 63
Los Angeles, Calif., 5, 13, 18, 37, 61, 88, 111,
    130, 140, 150, 157, 158, 159, 162, 166, 169,
    174, 177
Los Angeles Symphony, 11
Lost Horizon, 135

Love Boat, The, 36
Love Bug, The, 117, 120, 124
"Love Is a Many Splendored Thing," 68
"Love Me Tender," 27
"Love Struck Duck," 180
Lovett, Lyle, 132, 160
Luboff, Norman, 81
Lucas, Clyde, 45
Lucasfilm, Ltd., 155
Lucifer the cat, 91
Lucky Puppy, The, 92
Luddy, Barbara, 73, 109
Ludwig Mousensky, 39, 44, 91, 164, 179
Ludwig von Drake, 64, 66, 70, 147
Lugosi, Bela, 63
Lullaby Land, 6
Lum and Abner, 15
Luther, Frank, 6, 23
Lux Radio Theatre, The, 122
Lynde, Paul, 73
Lyric Street Records, 187

MacArthur, James, 119
Macdonald, Jimmy, 8, 17, 35, 39, 44, 53, 69, 91,
    97, 119, 120, 133
"Macho Duck," 156–57
"Macho Man," 156
MacMurray, Fred, 44, 55, 61, 104, 146
Macon, Ga., 122
Macy's Thanksgiving Day Parade, 173
Mad Madam Mim, 70, 76
Madonna, 176, 178, 179
Mael, Ronald and Russell, 169
Magic Kingdom, 162
Magical Music of Walt Disney, The, 133, 152
Magilla Gorilla, 145
Magon, Jymn, 120, 144, 145–46, 148–49, 152,
    154, 155, 156, 157, 159, 161, 162, 167, 169,
    170, 171
Main, Laurie, 145, **164**, 174, 175, 176, 177, 186
Make Mine Music, 7, 27
Malden, Karl, 55
Mame, 46

Man of La Mancha, 104
Man Who Came to Dinner, The, 120
"Managua, Nicaragua," 45
Manchester, Melissa, 159, 178
Mancini, Henry, 68, 95, 111, 135–36, 178, 182
Mandel, Johnny, 141
"Manhattan," 30
Manhattan School of Music, 138
Mann, Johnny, 40, 81
Mantovani, 115
Marek, George, 83
Marick, Robert, 187
Marinangeli, Marco, 185
Marinaro, Ed, 61
Marriott's Great America, 172
Marshall, Ann, 167
Martin, Dean, 88, 111, 135
Martin, Mary, 22, 32–34, 83, 93, 108
Martin, Stacia, 184
Marvel Productions, 150, 151
Marvelous Land of Oz, The, 121
Mary, Mary, 120
Mary Poppins (film), 31, 50, 57, 78–79, 81,
    83–84, 86, 100, 104, 120, 129, 152, 165, 181,
    183
Mary Poppins (record), 81–84, 86, 92, 121, 164,
    182
Matrix, The, 107, 112, 151
Matthews, Junius, 70, 94, 97
Maverick, 48
Mayer, Louis B., 81
Mayer, Mercer, 177
McCartney, Jesse, 187
McCartney, Paul, 179, 183
McCune, Ida Sue, 140
McFerrin, Bobby, 185
McGovern, Maureen, 185
McGrath, Bob, 138–39
McGraw, Tim, 132
McIntire, John, 86
McKennon, Dallas, 31–32, 53, 58, 63, 67, 69,
    84, 94, 98, 105, 116, 117, 121, 123, 124–25,
    130, 131, 146

McKnight, Brian, 185
McKuen, Rod, 112
McLaughlin, Sarah, 160
Meader, Vaughn, 62
Medford, Mass., 45
Medora, Eddy, 155, 157, 167, 171
Meet Corliss Archer, 122, 144
Meet Me Down on Main Street, 27, **29**
Megargel, Tex., 95
MelloMen, The, 16, **17**, 27, 40–41, 85–86,
    88–89, 95, 99, 111, 131, 134, 141, 161
Melodies for Midnight, 37
Mendelson, Lee, 155, 170, 173
Menken, Alan, 183, 184
Mercer, Johnny, 68
Meremblum, Peter, 81
"Merlin Jones," 75
Merlin the magician, 70, 142, 143
Merlino, Gene, 110, 111–12, 140
Merry Christmas Carols, 120, 162, 163–64
Messick, Don, 155
Messina, Jimmy, 114
Metamorphosis, 187
Meyers, Bill, 171
MGM, 24, 32, 63, 86, 108, 121, 123, 132, 186
"Mickey," 178
"Mickey, She's Got a Crush on You," 169
"Mickey and Minnie on a Moonlit Night," 180
Mickey and the Beanstalk, 69, 128
"Mickey Motion," 180
Mickey Mouse, 5, 6, 17, 44, 53, 54, 69, 76, 113,
    119, 120, 133, 141, 142, 143, 155, 164, 180,
    184
Mickey Mouse: This Is My Life, 131, 133
Mickey Mouse and His Friends, 113, 133
"Mickey Mouse and Minnie's in Town," 6
Mickey Mouse Club, The, 11, 13–17, 18, 20, 22,
    24, 27, 28, 29, 48, 49, 57, 69, 71, 93, 121,
    141, 142, 150, 163
*Mickey Mouse Club: Mousekedances and
    Other Favorites*, 141, 157
Mickey Mouse Club Magazine, 108

Mickey Mouse Club Records, 13–14, 16–17, 20, 22, 24, 27, 29, 34, 40, 44, 53, 71, 113, 141
Mickey Mouse Club Song Hits, 141
Mickey Mouse Disco, 156–57, 158, 161, 165
"Mickey Mouse March, The," 16, 132, 141
Mickey Mouse Revue, 131, 133
Mickey Mouse Rock, 177
Mickey Mouse Splashdance, 168–69, 170, 177
Mickey Mouse the Brave Little Tailor, 116
Mickey Mouse's Birthday Party, 91
Mickey Mouse's Christmas Surprises, 44
Mickey's Christmas Carol, 142, 144, 153, 163, 164
"Mickey's Fortieth Birthday," 113
Mickey's Grand Opera, 6
Mickey's Philharmagic, 112
Mickey's Toontown, 183
Mickey's Twice Upon a Christmas, 143
Midler, Bette, 111, 180
Mighty Hercules, The, 42
Mile-Long Bar, 131
Miles, Shelley, 174, 176
Miller, Doris, 74
Miller, Glenn, 68, 135
Miller, Jill, **53**
Miller, Julius Sumner, 93
Miller, Mitch, 8, 13, 138
Miller, Roger, 134
Miller, Ron, 163
Miller, Sy, 48, **53**
$1,000,000 Duck, 120
Mills, Hayley, 46, 55, 70, 78
Milne, A. A., 30, 87, 97, 109
Minnelli, Liza, 132
Minnie Mouse, 5, 169, 176, 178, 184
"Minnie's Yoo Hoo," 113, 133
"Minstrel Boy, The," 74
Miracle of the White Stallions, 74
Misadventures of Merlin Jones, The, 31
Mister Ed, 53, 142
Mister Magoo's Christmas Carol, 73
Misty the Mischievous Mermaid, 118
Miyazaki, Hayao, 120

Moé, Bambi, 165, 166, 170, 171, **172**, 173, 175, 176, 177, **179**, 180, 186
Monkees, The, 115
Monkey's Uncle, The, 93
Monroe, Bill, 160
Monroe, Marilyn, 46
Montalban, Ricardo, 61
Montan, Chris, 175, 176, 186
Moore, Clement C., 26
Moore, Rica, 65–66, 72
More Jungle Book, 116
More Mother Goose, 66, **129**
Morehead, Paige, 180, 181
Morey, Larry, 96
Morse, Robert, 125
Mother Goose, 54, 57
Mother Goose Nursery Rhymes, 54, 61, 70, 94, 154
Motion Picture and Television Hospital, 68
Mountain Stage, 160
Mouse Factory, The, 51, 113, 120, 133
Mouse Factory Presents Mickey and His Friends, The, 133
"Mouse Square Dance," 91
"Mousekemania," 169
Mousercise, 164–66, 177
"Mousetrap," 156
Mousetronics, 168–69, 177
Mr. Duck Steps Out, 157
Mr. Funny Buttons, 31
Mr. Toad, 43
MTV, 176
"Mule Train," 8
Multiplication and Division, 66
Mumford, Lora, 166, 168, 170, 176, 178
Munro, Janet, 47
Muppets, 126, 139
Murphy, Sean, 182
Murray, Anne, 132
Music Academy of the West, 82
Music from the Park, 185
"Music in Your Soup," 96–97, 181
Music of Cinderella, The, 185

Musical Kaleidoscope, A, 47
Musical Love Story, A, 34
Musical Tour of Disneyland, A, 23
Musical Tour of France, A, 93
Musicland Publishing, 12
Mussi, Rose, **56**, **84**
Muth, Marcia, 18
My Fair Lady, 81, 84
My Favorite Blonde, 15
"My Little Girl," 34
My Little Margie, 11
"My Old Flame," 63
My Port of Call, 86
"My Way's the Highway," 127
"My World Is Beginning Today," 96

Nash, Clarence, 53, 69, 99, 156–57, 163, 164, 165, 178
Nashville, Tenn., 132, 155, 156, 158, 159, 179, 186
National Public Radio, 167
"Nature Boy," 68
Nature Guide about Birds, Bees, Beavers, and Bears, A, 99
Nausicaa of the Valley of the Winds, 120
NBC, 11, 23, 31, 49, 124, 130, 152, 173, 182
Neal, Patricia, 73
Nelson, Doug, 49
Nelson, Ricky, 48, 115
Nelson, Steve, 69
Nero, Franco, 111
New Adventures of Spin and Marty, The, 44
New Iberia, La., 119
New Mickey Mouse Club, The, 51, 156, 159
New Orleans Square, 76
New York, N.Y., 8, 9, 30, 42, 64, 107, 140, 150, 152, 159, 162, 179
New York World's Fair, 76
New You Asked for It, The, 173
New Zoo Revue, The, 139
Newhart, Bob, 62
Newton, Ernie, 86, 110
Newton, Isaac, 93

Night before Christmas, The, 26
Nightmare before Christmas, The, 44
Nine, 82
Nixon, Marni, 81–83
Nixon, Richard, 131
No Man's Valley, 173
Nolan, Jeanette, 86
Norfolk, Neb., 40
Norman, Arthur, 13
Norman, Loulie Jean, 63, 106, 107, 110, 121, 131
Norris, Lee, 140
Northwestern University, 73, 88
Norvo, Red, 20
Novack, Gregory and Susan, 125

"O Susanna," 159
O'Brien, Cubby, 13, 34
O'Brien, Margaret, 81, 91
Ocko, Daniel, 8
O'Connell, Helen, 20
O'Connor, Donald, 74, 75
Odyssey Productions, 156
Official Album of Disneyland/Walt Disney World, 161
O'Hara, Maureen, 55
"Old Fashioned Girl," 48
Old Navy, 147
Old Yeller (record), 27, 35
Olive Oyl, 57
Oliver!, 102
Oliver and Company, 180
Olsher, Laura, 72, 73, 76
O'Malley, J. Pat, 47, 56
Omnibus, 18
"On a Slow Boat to China," 45
"On the Ice," 94
"On Top of Old Smokey," 74
One and Only, Genuine, Original Family Band, The (film), 78, 110, 120
One and Only, Genuine, Original Family Band, The (record), 110, 112, 115
101 Dalmatians (film), 31, 69

101 Dalmatians (record), 56, 60, 67, 70, 92, 185
"One Little Android," 169
Ontario, Canada, 95
Operation Pacific, 122
Orange Bird, The, 96, 123, 126–27, 129, 131
"Orange Tree," 127, 129
Orbison, Roy, 132
Orphans' Benefit, The, 6, 17
Osmond, Donny and Marie, 111, 132, 133
Ottawa, Ill., 138
Ovation Records, 133, 152
Over Here, 78
"Over the Rainbow," 121
"Oz-Phabet, The," 123

Pac-Man, 171
Page, Patti, 8
Paint a Rainbow in Your Heart, 174, 175
Pal, George, 31–32, 64
Palm Springs, Calif., 18, 20
Palm Springs Desert Museum, 34
Palo Alto, Calif., 168, 177
Parachute Express, 183
Pardners, 120, 162, 163
Parent Trap, The (film), 55, 78, 178
Parent Trap, The (record), 55
Paris, Tony, 47
Parisian Life, 37
Parker, Fess, 10, 11–12, 22, 27, 31
Parker Brothers, 89
Parris, Pat, 146
Parsons, Kelly, 156
Partridge Family, The, 36, 140
Pasadena, Calif., 168
Pat Patrick Band, 186
Patrick, Pat, 156, 158, 165, 174, 176, 180, 186
Patterson, George, 74–75
Paul Frees and the Poster People, 63
PBS, 126
Peanuts, 155, 170–71, 173
Peary, Harold, 91
Pease, Paul, 44
Peck, Gregory, 122

Pecos Bill, 127
Peed, George, 42
Peet, Bill, 41, 42
Peg Leg Pete, 67
"Pencil Song, The," 16
Pendleton, Karen, 13, 34
"People in Your Neighborhood," 138
Pepsi-Cola, 131
Perkins, Les, 146
Perri, 29
Peter, Paul and Mary, 94
Peter and the Wolf (record), 27, 92, 148
Peter Cottontail, 67, 69, 94, 146
Peter Pan (film), 9, 45, 99, 107
Peter Pan (record), 29, 55, 70, 151, 174
Peter Pan and Wendy, 92
Peter Pan Records, 23, 42, 155
Petersen, Paul, 13
Pete's Dragon (film), 36, 132, 152
Pete's Dragon (record), 152
Petoskey, Mich., 153
Phil Harris and Alice Faye Show, The, 23
Philadelphia Orchestra, 38
Phish, 160
Pickwick Records, 136
Picture discs, 164
Pied Piper, The, 6
"Pig Out," 165, 177
Piglet, 89, 97, 109, 145, 163
Piglet's Big Movie, 109
"Pigpen Hoedown," 171
Pillsbury Doughboy, 64
"Pineapple Princess," 50
Pink Panther, The, 124
Pinky Lee Show, The, 13, 48
Pinocchio (film), 7, 17, 24, 42, 124
Pinocchio (record), 7, **21**, 22, 32, 47, 70, 94, **129**, 181, 183, 184
"Pinocchio's Boogie," 179–80
Pirates of the Caribbean (attraction), 97–99, 161
Pirates of the Caribbean (record), 40, 98–99
Planet of the Hoojibs, 167
Playhouse 90, 150

Plummer, Christopher, 86
Pluto, 28, 54, 76
PM Magazine, 162
Pogo Possum, 145
Pointer, Ruth, 180
Poky Little Puppy, The, 144
Polka Parade, 60
Pollyanna, 55
"Pooh for President," 145, 159
"Popcorn Sack," 63
Pope, Tony, 30, 146, 147, 154, 157, **164**
Porgy and Bess, 52, 107
Portland, Ore., 13, 31
Pound Puppies, 171
Powell, Gary, 174, 184–85
Power and the Glory, The, 115
Presley, Elvis, 27, 46, 74, 111, 179–80
"Pretending," 77
"Pretty Irish Girl," 47
Prima, Louis, 83, 89–90, 97, **98**, 116
Prince and the Pauper, The, 71
Prince Planet, 107
Princess Diaries, The, 187
Principia College, 145, 159
Prism Recording Studio, 174
Private Snuffy Smith, 15
Professor Ludwig von Drake, 64, 66, 187
Pryor, Joseph, 101
"Puff, the Magic Dragon," 94
Puppetoon Movie, The, 64
"Pup-Pup-Puppet Polka, The," 123
"Pussy Cat Polka, The," 16
"Put Your Head on My Shoulder," 52
Putnam, George, 61

"Quackety Quack," 180
Quinn, Gino, 10

Radio City Music Hall, 130
Radio Shack, 164
Raffi, 183
Raiders of the Lost Ark, 167
"Rain, Rain, Rain, The," 109

Rainbow Brite, 171, 174, 177
Rainbow Brite Christmas, 174, 176, 184
"Rainbow Connection, The," 138
"Rainbow Land," 175
Rainbow Road to Oz, The, 121, 123
Ramones, The, 147
Random Act of Kindness, 96
Ranger J. Audubon Woodlore, 69, 99
"Ranger's Guide to Nature, The," 99
Rankin/Bass, 64, 96, 150, 152, 155
Raphael, Fred, 8, 9
Raposo, Joe, 126
Rasey, Uan, 36
"Rather Blustery Day, A," 109
Raven-Symoné, 187
Ravenscroft, Thurl, 16, **17**, 27, 40–41, 62, 69,
    85, 86, 93, 94, 97, 98, 99, 110, 111, 118, 121,
    126, 131, 140–41, 146, 188
Rawhide, 111
Rawls, Lou, 133
RCA, 6, 7, 8, 12, 23, 43, 83, 100, 159, 181
Read-Along series, 91–92, 94, 95, 100, 116, 126,
    127–29, 133, 140, 144, 145–46, 147, 150,
    154, 155, 159, 162, 167, 174, 176, 177, 178,
    182, 183, 184–85
Reagan, Ronald, 48–49
Rebel Mission to Ord Mantell, 167
Record Industry Association of America, 105,
    157, 185
Red Ryder, 122
Red Skelton Show, The, 111, 158
Reddy, Helen, 132, 152
Redgrave, Vanessa, 111
Redway, Mike, 102
Reluctant Dragon, The, 94
REM, 160
Rembrandts, The, 185
"Remember the Magic," 185
Renaday, Pete, 118, 119–20, 131, 134, 161
Renoudet, Pete. *See* Renaday, Pete
Republic Pictures, 15
"Rescue Aid Society," 96, 152
Rescuers, The (film), 96, 152

Rescuers, The (record), 152
Return of Jafar, The, 91, 178
Return of the Jedi, 167
Return to Oz, 151, 176
Rey, Alvino, 74
Reynolds, Debbie, 108
Rhapsody in Blue, 107
Rice, Tim, 184, 185
Rice-A-Roni, 45
Riddle, Sam, 74
Riha, Bobby, 110
Rimes, LeAnn, 132
Ringwald, Molly, 161, 163–64
Rip Van Winkle, 67
River of No Return, 46
RKO Radio Pictures, 24, 155
Road Runner, The, 111
Road to Hong Kong, 102
Robin Hood (film), 120, 133–34
Robin Hood (record), 133–34
Robinson, Edward G., 23
"Rock and Roll Waltz, The," 50
Rock around the Mouse, 177, 179–80, 181
"Rockabye Baby," 54
Rocky and Bullwinkle, 64, 147, 148
Rod Rocket, 123
Rodgers and Hammerstein, 34
Rodgers and Hammerstein's Cinderella, 86, 88
Rodgers and Hart, 30
Roger Wagner Chorale, 11
Rogers, Ginger, 23
Rogers, Roy, 7
Rolling Stone, 183
Rollins, Jack, 69
Romance of Betty Boop, The, 173
Romance Returns, 61
Romano, Christy Carlson, 187
Ronstadt, Linda, 185
Rooney, Mickey, 65, 96
Rooney, Mickey, Jr., 13
Rooney, Tim, 13
Rootin' Tootin' Hootenanny, A, 71
Ross-Myring, Brian, 83, 114

Rothel, David, 25
Royal Air Force, 102
"Rubber Duckie," 126
Rubber Duckie and Other Songs from Sesame Street, 126
Rudolph the Red-Nosed Reindeer, 152
Ruggles, The, 153
"Rumbly in My Tumbly," 89
Russell, Andy, 7
Russell, Brenda, 178
Ryan, Will, 161, 162–63, 164, 174

Saga of Andy Burnett, The, 29, 34, 35
Saggy Baggy Elephant, The, 144
Salamunovich, Paul, 79
Salt Lake City, Utah, 49
Sammes, Mike, 101, 102–3, 104, 109, 113, 123, 124, 125, 130
San Antonio, Tex., 122
San Fernando Valley Youth Foundation, 34
San Francisco, Calif., 64, 68, 111, 172
San Gabriel, Calif., 48
San Jose Center for Performing Arts, 173
Sanborn, David, 185
Sandpipers, The, 8, 13, 95
Sands, Tommy, 55, 62, 184
"Santa, How Come Your Eyes Are Green When Last Year They Were Blue?," 97
Santa Barbara, Calif., 82
Santa Claus, 5
Santa Claus Is Comin' to Town, 64, 96, 152
Santa Fe, N.Mex., 18–19
Sarabande, Varese, 176, 178
Sarnoff, David, 23
Sarson, Christopher, 162
Sartori, Mary, 13
Saturday Night Fever, 155
Savage Sam, 74
Savannah, Ga., 132
Say One for Me, 47, 48
Scarbury, Joey, 170
Scarecrow of Oz, The, 31, 76, 83, 121, 123
Scarsdale, N.Y., 61

Scharf, Walter, 136
Schlitz Playhouse of Stars, 150
Schreiber, Avery, 124
Schuller, Robert, 41
Schulman, Rick, 179, 181
Schulz, Charles M., 78, 155, 170, 171, 173
Schumann, Walter, 81
Schwartz, Sherwood, 75
Scott, Bill, 147
Scott, Bronson, 13
Scotti, Bill, 6
Scrooge, 136
Scrooge McDuck, 31, 53–54, 142, 143–44, 184
Scrooge McDuck and Money, 53
Sea, The, 112
Sears, Roebuck & Co., 87, 145
Seattle, Wash., 57, 58
Secret Garden, The, 81
"Señor Santa Claus," 97, 98
Sesame Street, 125–26, 138, 139, 140
Sesame Street Fever, 155
Seven Dreams, 86
Seven Dwarfs and Their Diamond Mine, The, 94, 96–97
77 Sunset Strip, 45
Seville, David, 41, 178
"Shadow of Your Smile, The," 68
Shaggy Dog, The, 48, 50, 63
"Shaggy Dog Shag," 44
Shannon, Pamela, 82, 121
Sharon, Lois and Bram, 183
Shaul, Dave, 74
Shaw, Robert, 81
"She Never Felt Alone," 96
Shelley, Carole, 125
Shelton, Anne, 104
Shepard, Ernest, 89, 97
Shepherd, Bill, 102
Sheridan, Jeff, 184
Sherman, Al, 77
Sherman, Allan, 62
Sherman, Richard M., 49, 50, 55, 60, 64, 70, 76–79, 82, 84, 87, 93–94, 95, 96, 100, 101, 109–10, 124, 127, 130, 165, 178, 182, 184, 188
Sherman, Robert B., 50, 55, 60, 64, 70, 76–79, 84, 87, 93–94, 95, 100, 109–10, 124, 127, 130, 165, 178, 181, 182, 184
Sherock, Shorty, 36
Shertzer, Hymie, 37
Shields, Arthur, 47
Shimkin, Arthur, 7
Shindig, 74
Shire, David, 176
"Sho Jo Ji," 20
Shore, Dinah, 7, 107, 111
Shore, Roberta, 44, 47, 48–49, 120
"Shrimp Boats," 8
"Siamese Cat Song," 67
Sigmund and the Sea Monsters, 143
Silly Songs, 180, 181
Silly Symphonies, 5, 58, 76, 139
Silver-Burdett, 160
Silvers, Phil, 125
Silversher, Michael, 165, 168–69, 171, 174, 177–78, 184
Silversher, Patty, 165, 168–69, 171, 177–78, 184
Simeone, Harry, 88
Simon and Schuster, 7
Simpson, Billy, 145
Sinatra, Frank, 77, 111, 115, 158, 185
Sinatra, Frank, Jr., 183
"Sing," 138
Sing-Along series, 185
"Singin' in the Rain," 24, 26
Singing Sergeants, The, 135
Skelton, Red, 45
Sklar, Marty, 79
Skylarks, The, 107
Sleeping Beauty (film), 25, 31, 43, 118
Sleeping Beauty (record), 25, 34, 52, 92, 148, 185
"Sleepy Time Gal," 24, 26
Slezak, Walter, 117
Slipper and the Rose, The, 78
Smith, Hal, 30, 146, 149, 153, **164**, 165, 181

Smith, Max, 16, 17

Smith, Michael, 13

Smith, Paul, 44

Smoke, 118

Smurfs, 69, 171

Snoopy, 145, 170–71

Snoopy Come Home, 78, 170

"Snoopy's Big Debut," 170–71

Snow White and the Seven Dwarfs (film), 5, 7, 30, 87, 97, 121

Snow White and the Seven Dwarfs (record), 7, **21**, 22, 32, 43, 55, 94, 164, 181, 183, 184

Snow White's Scary Adventures, 57

Snyder, Tom, 28

So This Is Washington, 15

Solid Gold Chipmunks, 178

"Soliloquy, C'est Moi," 111

"Someday, Charlie Brown," 173

"Someone's Waiting for You," 152

Something Borrowed, Something Blue, 51

Sommerville, Jerry, 74

Son of Flubber, 31

"Song of the Screaming Cowboy, The," 163

Song of the South (film), 7, 22, 32

Song of the South (record), **21**, 22

Songs from "Annette," 27, 46

Songs from the Jungle Book, 105, 107, **129**

Songs from Sesame Street 2, 135

Songs of the National Parks, 40

Songs of the Shaggy Dog, 44, 48, 63, 94

Sonic Atmospheres, 176

Sonny and Cher, 111, 135

Sorcerer's Apprentice, The (film), 8

Sorcerer's Apprentice, The (record), 27

Soul Train, 165

Sound of Music, The (film), 86, 93, 104, 158

Sound of Music, The (record), 93, 100

Sounds of Christmas, The, 134, 136

Soupy Sales Show, The, 11

South Pacific, 33, 86

Space Ghost, 58

Sparks, 169

Spector, Phil, 102

Spectreman, 151

Speedy Alka-Seltzer, 53

Spider-Man, 150, 151

Spielberg, Steven, 89, 167

Spike Jones' Spooktacular, 63, 107

Spin and Marty, 16, 22, 31

Spirited Away, 120

"Spoonful of Sugar, A," 83

Sport Goofy, 165–66, 168

Sportsmen Quartet, 40

Spring, 37

Springfield, Buffalo, 115

Springsteen, Bruce, 183

Spyri, Johanna, 113

St. Charles Borromeo Church, 79

St. Louis, Mo., 24, 159

Stack, Robert, 65

Stafford, Jo, 8

Stalling, Carl, 113

Stand Up and Cheer, 40

Star Trek, 107, 167

Star Wars, 60, 147, 155, 160, 166, 167

"Stardust," 36

Starita, Rudy, 103

Starr, Edwin, 165

Starrett, Charles, 24, 25

Stars on 45, 165

"Stay Awake," 83, 181

Steamboat Willie, 6

Steinbeck, John, 20

Steele, Bob, 15

Steele, Tommy, 55

Steiner, Ronnie, 13

"Step in the Right Direction, A," 130

"Step in Time," 165

Stern, Shepard, 179–80, 181, 183, 186

Stevens, Bob, 16

Stevens, Sally, 106–7, 109, 124

Stevenson, Robert Louis, 20

Stewart, Jimmy, 31

Stokowski, Leopold, 38, 81

"Stop, Look and Listen," 17, 20

Stories from the Mouse Factory, 133

Stories of Uncle Remus, 31, 32
Storm, Billy, 70
Storm, Gale, 11
Story of the Absent-Minded Professor, The, **59**, 61
"Story of Thumper, The," 67
"Storybook Land Christmas Tree," 43–44
Stravinsky, Igor, 81, 138
Strawberry Shortcake, 171
Streep, Meryl, 183
Street of Dreams, The, 68
Streisand, Barbra, 102, 111, 183, 185
"Strummin' Song, The," 76, 78
Stuart, Jeromy, 126
Studio 54, 155
Submarine Streetcar, The, 72
"Substitutiary Locomotion," 130
Summer, 37
Summer, Donna, 156
Summer Magic, 70
Sun Rays, The, 155
Sunset Sound Recorders, 56, 58, 62, 69, 79, 105, 108, 109, 114–15, 118
Sunshine Tree Terrace, 127
"Supercalifragilisticexpialidocious," 79
Susie, the Little Blue Coupe, 127
Sutherland, Mark, 13
"Sweet Gingerbread Man," 139
Sweetland, Lee, 107
Sweetland, Sally, 94, 106, 107
Sweier, Victor, 125
Swenson, Karl, 70
Swing Era, 68
Sword in the Stone, The, 57, 70, 76, 94, 143
Sylte Sisters, **71**
Symphonie Orchester Graunke, 43, 104
Symposium on Popular Songs, A, 70, 84

Tadevic, Jim, 156–57
Take My Hand, 185
"Talent Roundup," 141
TaleSpin, 177
Talking Mickey Mouse, 120

"Tall Paul," 50, 52, 77, 78
Tandem Productions, 61
Tarzan, 185
Taylor, Betty, 140
Taylor, Deems, 38
Taylor, Karen, 181
Taylor, Russi, 184
Tea and Sympathy, 111
Tebow, Bob, 88, 89, 109
Teddy Ruxpin, 120, 163
Teen Street, 71
Teenage Mutant Ninja Turtles, 120
Ten Songs from Mary Poppins, 82
Terribly Sophisticated Songs, 95
Terry-Thomas, 134
Tex Williams Show, The, 48
That Darn Cat, 161
"There's a Harbor of Dreamboats," 77
"This Old House," 40
"This Old Man," 183
This Was the West, 36
Thomas, Frank, 182
"Thomasina," 75, 125
Thompson, Bill, 53, 99
Thompson, Ruth Plumly, 123
Thompson Cafeterias, 65
Thornton, Randy, 176, 181, 182, 183, 184, 186–88
Three Little Pigs (film), 6, 91
Three Little Pigs (record), 92, 123, 150
Three Little Wolves, 6
Three Lives of Thomasina, The, 95, 125
Three Mesqueteers, The, 15
Thru the Mirror, 157
"Thumper Song, The," 94
Thumper the rabbit, 61, 94, 122
Thumper's Great Race, 94, 128
Thunder Alley, 132
Thunderbirds, 102
Tibbett, Lawrence, 35
Tigger, 89, 97, 109, 146, 163
Tigger Movie, The, 78
Time Machine, The, 142

Time-Life Records, 36, 68
Timothy Mouse, 32
Tin Woodman of Oz, The, 107, 124
Tinker Bell, 44, 92
Tinpanorama, 46, 84, 187
Toby Tortoise, 94
Today, 18
"Today Is Tuesday," 141
Todd, Mel, 102
Together with Music, 33
Tokyo Disneyland, 131
Tolkien, J. R. R., 152
Tom and Jerry, 63, 76
Tom Sawyer, 78
tom thumb, 32, 142
Tomorrow, 28
Tonight Show, The, 18, 52
Tony the Tiger, 40, 41, 126
"Toot Toot Tootsie," 24
Top Cat, 143
Top Tunes of the 50s, 27
Totally Minnie, 173, 176, 177, 178, 179
Toucan Sam, 64
Touchstone Records, 180
Toy Story, 185
Toy Story Sing-Along, 185–86
Toy Story 2, 185
"Toyland," 62
Tracey, Doreen, 13, 121
Tracy, Spencer, 120
Transformers, The, 147
Travers, Pamela, 129
Travolta, John, 78
Trick or Treat (film), 76, 140
Trick or Treat (record), 140
"Triple R Song," 22, 31
Triscari, Joe, 36
Trouble with Girls, The, 111
True Value Hardware, 108
"Trumpeter's Prayer," 36
Tubby the Tuba, 93
Tufeld, Dick, 141
Tune, Tommy, 78

Turtles, The, 115
Tutti's Trumpets, 36–37
TV Guide, 28
TV Land, 89, 142
"Twas Brillig," 20
'Twas the Night Before Christmas, 152
"Tweedledee and Tweedledum," 165
Twelve Days of Christmas, The, 184
Twelve O'Clock High, 122
20,000 Leagues Under the Sea, 174
20th Century Fox, 32, 155
Two Weeks with Love, 108
Tyler, Ginny, 32, 55–56, 57–58, 61, 62, 66, 67,
    98, 113, 116, 123, 124, 140, 146
Tyler, Tom, 15

UCLA, 36, 95
"Ugly Bug Ball," 70
Ugly Dachshund, The, 93–94
Ugly Duckling, The, **129**
Ukulele Ike Sings Again, 25
Ullmann, Liv, 135, 139
"Unbirthday Song, The," 9
Underhill, Don, 13
United Methodist Publishing, 186
United Recorders, 74
United States Air Corps, 95
University of California at Northridge, 150
University of Illinois, 74
University of Michigan, 138
University of Texas, 150
"Up, Down and Touch the Ground," 89
UPA Studios, 64
Ustinov, Peter, 55, 117, 134
Utica, N.Y., 50

Vallee, Rudy, 101
Valley Beth Shalom, 163
Van Dyke, Dick, 55
Van Helsing, 112
Van Horne, Randy, 81
Van Nuys, Laura Bower, 110
Vanderbilt University, 132

Vera-Ellen, 46
Verne, Jules, 141
"Very Good Advice," 9
Victor Records, 6, 7
Village People, The, 156
Virgil Convalescent Hospital, 25
Virginian, The, 48, 49
Voice of America, 160
"Volare," 88
Von Ever, Renee, 62
Von Ever, Sheila, 62
Von Ever, Sonya, 62
Vonnair Sisters, The, 62
"Vulture Song, The," 108

Wade, Ed, 74–75
Wagner, Roger, 81
Wagon Train, 48
Wait Till Your Father Gets Home, 143
Waiting for the Sun, 114
Wake Up, 181
Waldo, Janet, 122, 143, **144**
Wallace, Oliver, 23, 27
Walmsley, Jonathan, 109
Walsh, Bill, 20, 59, 61
Walt Disney Educational Media, 147, 175
Walt Disney Imagineering, 79
Walt Disney Music Company, 8, 9, 20, 30, 134,
    141
Walt Disney Song Fest, A, 27
Walt Disney Takes You to Disneyland, 23, 110,
    187
Walt Disney Television Animation, 186
Walt Disney World, 32, 50, 57, 64, 86, 100, 112,
    126–27, 131, 133, 138, 185, 187
Walt Disney World Band, The, 131
Walt Disney's Christmas Concert, 39, 41, 91
Walt Disney's Happiest Songs, 108
Walt Disney's Magazine, 108
Walt Disney's Merriest Songs, 108
Walter, Bruno, 38
Waltons, The, 109
Ward, Jay, 64, 69, 146, 147

Ward Gospel Singers, 114
Waring, Fred, 12
Warner Brothers, 61, 62, 112, 132, 140, 151, 166
Warren, Lesley Ann, 120
"Watch Out for Goofy," 156, 157
Wayne, John, 15, 122
Wayne, Redd, 102
We Are the World, 183
Weaver, Dennis, 12
Webb, Jack, 122
WED Enterprises, 79
Welcome to Pooh Corner, 162
"Welcome to Rio," 156
"Welcome to the World of Mousetronics," 169
Welles, Mel, 150
Wellingtons, The, 74–75, 125
Wells, Frank, 174
Wentworth, Martha, 57, 70, 76, 121
Wenzel, Paul, 72, 108
We're the Mouseketeers, 29
West, Mae, 76
West Coast Songwriters, 177
West Side Story, 55, 81, 82
West Virginia Endowment for the Arts, 160
West Wing, The, 151
Western Printing and Lithographing, 144, 152
Western Songs for Children, 71
Westward Ho! The Wagons (film), 11, 22
Westward Ho! The Wagons (record), 22
"Whale of a Tale, A," 75
What a Wonderful Thing Is Me, 135, 140
"What? No Mickey Mouse?," 113
"Whatcha Gonna Do," 108
"What's Your Name?," 180
Wheat Lies Low, The, 159
Whelchel, Lisa, 156, 161
"When You Wish Upon a Star," 7, 112, 161
"Where Will the Dimple Be?," 40
Whimsey Works, 58
Whistler, The, 122
White Christmas, 46, 134
Whitehead, Paul, 155, 156
Whiteman, Paul, 20

Whitfield, Jordan, 53
Whitman, Jerry, 135–36, 139, 140
Who Framed Roger Rabbit?, 120, 180
Who Killed Cock Robin?, 6, 76
Whole Darn Shooting Match, The, 120
"Whole New World, A," 184
"Who's Afraid of the Big Bad Wolf?," 6
Wible, Nancy, **71**
Wilder, Virginia, 143
Wilder Brothers Studio, 143
Wilkinson, Lois. *See* Lane, Lois
Williams, Andy, 102, 132
Williams, John, 60, 155
Williams, Pat, 58
Williams, Roger, 74
Williams, Roy, 13, 17
Willie and the Yank, 119
Willie the Giant, 69, 143–44, 163
Willio and Phillio, 161, 162–63, 164
Willy Wonka and the Chocolate Factory, 136,
    139
Wilson, Brian, 183
Wilson, Ken, 44
Winchell, Paul, 109, 124, 140
Winchell, Walter, 61
Winding, Jai, 178
Winnie the Pooh and a Day for Eeyore, 162
Winnie the Pooh and the Blustery Day (film),
    109
Winnie the Pooh and the Blustery Day (record),
    109
Winnie the Pooh and the Heffalumps, 109
Winnie the Pooh and the Honey Tree (film), 87,
    93, 109
Winnie the Pooh and the Honey Tree (record),
    83, 87, 89, 100, 140
*Winnie the Pooh and the North Pole
    Expotition*, 109
Winnie the Pooh and Tigger, 109
Winnie the Pooh and Tigger Too (film), 109,
    140, 141
Winnie the Pooh and Tigger Too (record), 140,
    146

Winnie the Pooh for President, 30, 145
Winnie-the-Pooh, 30, 40, 88, 108–9, 116, 145,
    178, 185
Winter, 37
Witch Hazel, 140
Witch's Tale, The, 76
"With a Flair," 130
Witty, John, 113
Wizard of Oz, The (film), 36, 107, 121, 123
Wizard of Oz, The (record), 121, 123, 124, **129**
Wonder, Stevie, 75
"Wonderful Thing about Tiggers, The," 108,
    109, 140
Wonderful World of Color, 64, 75, 99, 112
Wonderful World of Disney (magazine), 108
Wonderful World of Disney (TV series), 108
Wonderland Music Company, 9, 10, 12, 187
Wonderland Music Store, 70
Wonders of Life Pavilion, 151
Wong, Curtis, 156
Wood, Donna, 45
Wood, Gloria, 16, 39, 44, 45–46, 99, 121
Wood, Natalie, 81
Woods, Ilene, 8
Woody Woodpecker, 91
"Woody Woodpecker Song, The," 45
Words and Music, 86
World Is a Circle, The, 135, 139
World War II, 20, 42, 61, 63, 85, 102, 134
Wormser, Jack, 73
Worrall, Tom, 156, 178
"Would I Love You," 8
Wright, Samuel E., 183
Wrigley's gum, 88
"Wringle Wrangle," 11, 22, 26
Wuzzles, The, 176
Wynn, Ed, 123, 147
Wynonna, 132

Yamaha keyboards, 168, 169
Yankee Doodle Dandy, 107
Yankee Doodle Mickey, 120, 161
"Yo Ho," 99

Yogi Bear, 86, 145, 146
York, Gil, 61, 66
York, Kelly, 61, 66
York, Teri, 56, 60–61, 62, 66, 67, 68
York, Tracy, 61
You and Me, Kid, 163
"You Are a Human Animal," 24
"You Can Always Be Number One," 168
"You Gotta Be a Football Hero," 77
Young, Alan, 45, 53, 142–43, 144, 184
Your Hit Parade, 35
"You're a Mean One, Mr. Grinch," 40
"You're Never Too Old to Be Young," 96–97
"You're Sixteen," 78
"Yours," 20
Yours Truly Johnny Dollar, 122

Zappa, Dweezil, 182
"Zip-A-Dee-Doo-Dah," 155, 156
Zoom, 162
Zorro, 29, 34, 161